The Republic of Love

*Chicago Studies in Ethnomusicology*
*A series edited by* Philip V. Bohlman, Bruno Nettl, *and* Ronald Radano

*Editorial Board*  Margaret J. Kartomi
Anthony Seeger
Kay Kaufman Shelemay
Martin H. Stokes
Bonnie C. Wade

# The Republic of Love
## Cultural Intimacy in Turkish Popular Music

Martin Stokes

The University of Chicago Press
Chicago and London

Martin Stokes is University Lecturer in Ethnomusicology at Oxford University and a fellow of St. John's College, Oxford. He is the author or editor of several books, including *The Arabesk Debate: Music and Musicians in Modern Turkey*.

The University of Chicago Press, Chicago 60637
The University of Chicago Press, Ltd., London
© 2010 by The University of Chicago
All rights reserved. Published 2010
Printed in the United States of America

19 18 17 16 15 14 13 12 11 10     1 2 3 4 5

ISBN-13: 978-0-226-77505-0 (cloth)
ISBN-13: 978-0-226-77506-7 (paper)
ISBN-10: 0-226-77505-4 (cloth)
ISBN-10: 0-226-77506-2 (paper)

Library of Congress Cataloging-in-Publication Data
Stokes, Martin.
  The republic of love : cultural intimacy in Turkish popular music / Martin Stokes.
    p. cm.
  Includes bibliographical references and index.
  ISBN-13: 978-0-226-77505-0 (cloth : alk. paper)
  ISBN-13: 978-0-226-77506-7 (pbk. : alk. paper)
  ISBN-10: 0-226-77505-4 (cloth : alk. paper)
  ISBN-10: 0-226-77506-2 (pbk. : alk. paper)   1. Popular music—Turkey—20th century—History and criticism. 2. Songs, Turkish—20th century—History and criticism. 3. Müren, Zeki, 1931–1996. 4. Gencebay, Orhan. 5. Aksu, Sezen. 6. Singers—Turkey. 7. Yahya Kemal, 1884–1958. Aziz Istanbul. 8. Yahya Kemal, 1884–1958—Musical settings—History and criticism. I. Title.
  ML3502.T9S76 2010
  781.6309561'09045—dc22
                                                    2010007675

∞ The paper used in this publication meets the minimum requirements of the American National Standard for Information Sciences—Permanence of Paper for Printed Library Materials, ANSI Z39.48-1992.

# Contents

*Acknowledgments*  vii
*Note on Orthography, Notational Conventions, and Names*  xiii
*List of Illustrations*  xvii

| | | |
|---|---|---|
| 1 | Introduction | 1 |
| 2 | Zeki Müren: Sun of Art, Ideal Citizen | 35 |
| 3 | The Affectionate Modernism of Orhan Gencebay | 73 |
| 4 | Why Cry? Sezen Aksu's Diva Citizenship | 107 |
| 5 | Three Versions of "Beloved Istanbul" | 147 |
| 6 | Conclusion | 189 |

*Sources*  195
*Index*  213

# Acknowledgments

My move to Chicago in 1997 meant, among many other things, an interruption of regular fieldwork visits to Istanbul dating back to 1981. But it did permit an extended moment of reflection. I had written and published a number of articles and book chapters on Turkish music, and was on the point of writing more. These were "Shedding Light on the Balkans: Sezen Aksu's Anatolian Pop," in *Balkan Popular Culture and the Ottoman Ecumeme*, edited by Donna Buchanan (Lanham, MD: Scarecrow, 2007); "The Tearful Public Sphere: Turkey's Sun of Art, Zeki Müren," in *Music and Gender: Perspectives from the Mediterranean*, edited by Tullia Magrini (Chicago: University of Chicago Press, 2004); "Beloved Istanbul: Realism and the Transnational Imaginary in Turkish Popular Culture," in *Mass Mediations: New Approaches to Popular Culture in the Middle East and Beyond*, edited by Walter Armbrust (Berkeley: University of California Press, 2000) and "East, West, Arabesk," in *Western Music and its Others: Difference, Representation, and Appropriation in Music*, edited by Georgina Born and David Hesmondhalgh (Berkeley: University of California Press, 2000). My sense of the connection between these independently conceived essays grew, and the idea of completely rewriting and rethinking each element in the light of an overarching theme—cultural intimacy—took hold.

I went back to Istanbul to teach a summer semester at Boğaziçi

University in 2006. At that point, the project of this book began to take definite shape. This was a summer of nearly constant conversation with musicians, music journalists, and scholars, along with concert attendance and archival work. Istanbul had changed greatly since my previous visit. Publishing on Turkish music was more buoyant than ever. Academic writing on Turkish popular culture was no longer treated as a strange eccentricity. Recordings by Kalan, an industrious record label devoted to archival and hitherto lost or repressed repertories, had completely changed the musical landscape. It seemed easier than ever to meet and talk to people, move about, and find things. YouTube was quickly becoming an invaluable archival resource for film clips and old television broadcasts, as well as a vital means of communication between people interested in music. I felt I learned more that summer than I had in the previous twenty years.

I finished reading Orhan Pamuk's recent novel, *Masumiyet müzesi* (The museum of innocence; İletişim 2008), just as this book was going to press. My sense of the timeliness of the topic of cultural intimacy has grown considerably over the last few months, and I wish I had been able to refer more to Pamuk's novel while writing this book. The novel explores the political traumas of the late 1970s and 1980s through an allegorical love story saturated with popular cultural references. Pamuk's bourgeois narrator falls in love with a distant cousin, breaking off a relationship with his Westernized fiancée and scandalizing his wealthy friends and family in the process. He encounters the world of his genteel but impoverished relatives as a stranger, discovering, in his efforts to get close to his beloved, parts of the city and ways of life that have been either marginalized or devalued in his country's Westernizing drive. Time stands still as Pamuk's narrator loses himself in rapt contemplation of what is for him a highly mysterious world. In Pamuk's novel, to adapt Adorno's well-known phrase, the two torn halves of Turkish culture always fail to add up to an integral freedom. The story's ending is inevitably tragic. The museum referred to in the book's title is a monument to the dead lover, constructed out of scraps of her everyday life in the run-down area of Istanbul. I have recently heard that the Beyoğlu Municipality is to open a real museum on this site in 2010, under Pamuk's direction, as part of the European City of Culture celebrations. The museum is to document the fabric of everyday Turkish life from 1950 to 2000 through photographs, films, art, and bric-a-brac.

At one point in Pamuk's novel, the narrator likens himself disparagingly to a foreign anthropologist. I can sense more than a bit of myself in that characterization, but I do not share his pessimism about the nature of the affectionate gaze. The music that I admire so much lives its own cheerful and energetic life, and requires no introductions, justifications, or museum-izing from me. My efforts to find out about it have involved me in life-affirming conversations stretching back decades, so the list of thank-yous in a long one. In Istanbul I would like to start by thanking İbrahim and Gülşen Can, who have always given me my first and warmest welcome after periods of absence. İbrahim's irreverent and sardonic commentary on Turkish politics, society, and culture has been constant fun and an education in itself. Friends at the Istanbul State Conservatory—Ersin Baykal, Şehvar Beşiroğlu, Metin Eke, Songül Karahasanoğlu, Nermin Kaygusuz, and Süleyman Şenel—and at Boğaziçi University—Ayfer Bartu, Faruk Birtek, Cem Behar, Çağlar Keyder, Nükhet Sirman, Zafer Yenal—have been a source of constant support and welcome critique. Esra Özyürek, whom I first met at Boğaziçi, sent me a copy of her book while mine was in medias res. Readers will note its swift and significant impact. I would like to thank Ayşe Öncü and Meral Özbek, who responded to some specific questions, but whose work has also been an inspiration at a more general level. I am grateful to Kenan Çayır, Adnan Çoban, Naim Dilmener, Tunçay Gülersoy, Mehmet Güntekin, Muzaffer Özpınar, Sacit Suhabey, Orhan Tekelioğlu, and Şanar Yurdatapan for sharing their knowledge and expertise with me. Sezen Aksu, Orhan Gencebay, and Timur Selçuk were more than generous with their time, and more than gracious with my stumbling questions. I regret that it has taken such a long time to have something to show them. Anne Ellingsen, who shares my love of Turkish popular culture, led me on a whirlwind tour of the popular musical establishment in 1996. I reflect on many of our jointly conducted interviews—notably with Sacit Suhabey, Muzaffer Özpınar, Sezen Aksu, and Cem Karaca—throughout this book. They wouldn't have happened without her tireless pursuit of contacts, intermediaries, and phone numbers. Necati Sönmez accompanied us during our interview with Sezen Aksu, and I am grateful to him for allowing me to use a photograph he took on that occasion. I would also like to record the support of S. Süheyla Şentürk and her staff at the Beyazit Devlet Kütüphanesi throughout the summer of 2006.

The first draft of this book was written while I was still at the University of Chicago. The social scene in the Fazlur Rahman common room at the Center for Middle Eastern Studies was a constant distraction, but one I could not have managed without. Apart from anything else, I had instant recourse to the very considerable expertise of Kağan Arık, Melissa Bilal, Bob Dankoff, Cornell Fleischer, Cihangir Gündoğdu, Franklin Lewis, Kaya Şahin, Hakan Özoğlu, Metin Yüksel, and others. I am grateful to Rusty

Rook for presiding over this significant institution. Specific chapters of this book were read and critiqued in detail in workshops and conferences at the University of Chicago by Orit Bashkin, Holly Shissler, Shayna Silverstein, and Kabir Tambir. I am indebted to conversations on topics close to the heart of this book with Martha Feldman, Berthold Hoeckner, Travis Jackson, and Larry Zbikowski in the music department, and with Ayhan Akman, Robert Bird, Jim Chandler, Jim Fernandez, Kelda Jamison, David Levin, William Mazzarella, Michael Raine, Lisa Wedeen, and Jeremy Walton in the university community at large. My closest colleague at Chicago, Phil Bohlman, was a constant inspiration. The conversation initiated by the cultural intimacy seminar of spring 2001 seems to keep going, in virtual fashion, years after the event. For this and many other things, I'm grateful to Aileen Dillane, Byron Dueck, Jeffers Englehardt, and Josh Pilzer. Other people in Chicago I would like to thank are Issa Boulos, Ayşe Draz, Rita Koryan, and Öykü Potuoğlu-Cook. For their hospitality and conversation during this period after talks based on my early drafts of these chapters, I am grateful to Çiğdem Balım, Tom Bauman, Steve Blum, Donna Buchanan, Jane Goodman, Suncem Koçer, Inna Naroditskaya, Jonathan Shannon, and Tom Turino.

This book was completed at Oxford. I read most of an early draft at various seminars and public lectures around the United Kingdom early in 2008. For comments and discussions following these readings I thank Walter Armbrust, Bojan Bujic, Georgina Born, Terence Cave, Eric Clarke, Serkan Delice, Reidar Due, Larry Dreyfus, Laudan Nooshin, John O'Connell, Kerem Öktem, Goffredo Plastino, and Gökhan Yücel. I would also like to thank Deniz Kandiyoti and Meliz Serman for their comments on chapters 2 and 6, respectively. Support from St. John's College enabled a couple of brief fact-checking trips late in the day. Michael Gilsenan was my supervisor here at Oxford in the 1980s, and this book owes a great deal to his continued encouragement. Richard English and Harvey Whitehouse have helped me keep things in perspective over pints.

Two anonymous readers at the University of Chicago Press provided crucial insights and criticisms, which guided a major redrafting. Mena Hanna provided a keen eye and technical assistance with the music examples, and Catriona Stokes helped with the map. Elizabeth Branch Dyson patiently saw this book through from beginning to end, expertly steering me off the rocks on countless occasions. I am very grateful to her and to all of the University of Chicago Press's editorial team, particularly Renaldo Migaldi.

Finally, I dedicate this book, with love and affection, to Lucy Baxandall. She will appreciate the irony of my dedicating a book on intimacy to her, since it has so systematically kept us apart, and for so long. Sometimes I have been doing research in Istanbul. At other times I have just been sitting here in Oxford at this very computer, though I might as well have been a continent away. Without her, for so many reasons, this book never would have happened.

# Note on Orthography, Notational Conventions, and Names

Modern Turkish has officially used Roman script since 1928. A great deal of orthographic ambiguity still hovers, however, over words of non-Turkish derivation. I have tended to use the simplest recognizable versions. Where the choice of orthography involves important representational issues (for instance between the French-derived *müzik* and the Arabic-derived *musıki*), I have tried to explain, if only in footnotes, what is at stake as I go along. I have rendered plurals using the English *-s* rather than the Turkish plural suffix, which would involve considerations of vowel harmony and other grammatical constructions that potentially could be confusing for non-Turkish readers: so, *makam*-s rather than *makamlar*.

As a very rough rule of thumb for the non-native speaker, Turkish words are best pronounced avoiding stress. All vowels should be pronounced as open vowel sounds, avoiding dipthongs if none are indicated by the spelling. Umlauts work roughly as in German. Turkish *c* is pronounced like the English *j* as in *jam*. *J* is pronounced like the final "ge" of the French *rouge*. *Ç* is pronounced like "ch" as in *church*. *Ş* is "sh" as in *sugar*. *İ* (with a dot) and *ı* (without a dot) are distinguished, roughly, as "ee" and "uh." The *ğ* is not pronounced in Istanbul Turkish but it lengthens the preceding vowel, or functions as a kind of slide if it is placed between two vowels.

|   | Sharps | Flats |
|---|--------|-------|
| 1 | 𝄲 | 𝄳 |
| 4 | ♯ | ♭ |
| 5 | 𝄰 | 𝄭 |
| 8 | ♯ | ♭ |
| 9 | × | ♭♭ |

**Table 1.** Ezgi-Arel system sharps (*diyez*) and flats (*bemol*), arranged according to comma (*koma*) intervals.

Music notational practices differ greatly in their representation of those non-diatonic intervals that Western-trained musicians sometimes refer to as "quarter tones." Rival systems still circulate in the Turkish art music world. I use the Ezgi-Arel method as opposed to the Töre method to represent the system most commonly used, which divides the tone into nine equal commas (see table 1). I sometimes refer to modal constructions in this way (e.g., "A–B four commas flat–C four commas sharp–D," as opposed to the equally tempered "A–B flat– C sharp–D"). In folk-music notational practice, the "quarter-flattened" interval is usually represented by a numeral 2 (or 3) above the sharp or flat in question, indicating two (or three) commas up or down. In this book, notes after the musical examples will serve to further remind readers of the meaning of such signs. One should bear in mind that in musical performance, the intonations given to these pitches differ subtly but significantly depending on social context (for instance, nightclub versus concert hall) and their position in a piece of music or improvisation. These discussions may be hard going for people who do not read much music, but I hope that the surrounding text will in most cases make the general argument clear.

Readers should consult the discography to find all of the music discussed in this book, but *Zeki Müren Saadettin Kaynak şarkıları* (Kalan 2005), Orhan Gencebay's *Batsın bu dünya* (Kervan 1975), Sezen Aksu's *Işık doğudan yükselir / Ex oriente lux* (Seyhan 1995) and Münir Nurettin Selçuk's *Kalamış* (Coşkun 1989) are easy to locate and buy; they contain the songs transcribed and discussed in chapters 2 through 5. Various versions of the songs can of course be found free online, but readers should be aware that they are not necessarily the versions being discussed or transcribed here.

The surname law in 1936 obliged all Turks to take a single chosen last name, which I generally use (e.g., Müren, Gencebay, Aksu). This is not always appropriate for people born before the law was passed. So I generally refer, as many Turks do, to Yahya Kemal Beyatlı as "Yahya Kemal" and Münir Nurettin Selçuk as "Münir Nurettin," rather than as "Beyatlı" and "Selçuk" respectively. When it is important to include last names for academic reference purposes, I usually follow the Turkish convention whereby the newly adopted last name is included in parentheses: Yusuf Ziya Bey (Demirci), Zekaizade Ahmet (Irsoy) Efendi.

Place names follow modern Turkish conventions unless they are very common in English. So, for instance, I use the spellings Istanbul and Izmir rather than İstanbul and İzmir, unless the words are embedded in Turkish quotations or titles. For Istanbul neighborhoods and place names in the text, particularly in chapter 5, please consult the map below.

**Map 1.** Neighborhoods in Istanbul

# Illustrations

**Map**

Map 1. Neighborhoods in Istanbul  *xv*

**Figures**

Figure 2a. Illustration from Zeki Müren cassette box (*Dilek çeşmesi*)  *46*
Figure 2b. At the Zeki Müren Museum, Bodrum  *62*
Figure 3a. Cover of Orhan Gencebay cassette box (*Beni biraz anlasaydın*)  *79*
Figure 4a. Sezen Aksu  *130*
Figure 5a. Book-benches at the Aşiyan Museum, Istanbul  *148*
Figure 5b. Municipality anti-alcohol campaign, 1995  *153*
Figure 5c. Enjoying the view from Çamlıca  *183*

**Table**

Table 1. Ezgi-Arel system sharps (*diyez*) and flats (*bemol*), arranged according to comma (*koma*) intervals  *xiv*

**Music Examples**

2a. "Menekşelendi sular," opening instrumental section  *50*
2b. "Menekşelendi sular," opening vocal section  *50*
2c. "Menekşelendi sular," chorus (*semai*)  *50*

2d. Notated version of "Menekşelendi sular," middle section  *52*
2e. *Nihavent makamı*  *52*
2f. Zeki Müren's recording of "Menekşelendi sular," middle section  *56*
3a. Orhan Gencebay's "Batsın bu dünya," instrumental introduction  *85*
3b. Orhan Gencebay's "Batsın bu dünya," "opening" section  *86*
3c. *Muhayyerkürdi makamı*  *87*
3d. Tonal procedures in *muhayyerkürdi makamı*  *89*
3e. Orhan Gencebay's "Batsın bu dünya," "*zemin*" and "*meyan*" sections  *89*
3f. Orhan Gencebay's "Batsın bu dünya," chorus section  *90*
3g. Seher's anxious glance  *91*
3h. Orhan walking  *91*
4a. Sezen Aksu's recording of Aşık Daimi's "Ne ağlarsın," first verse  *108*
5a. "Aziz İstanbul," opening. From Aksüt 1994  *164*
5b. "Aziz İstanbul," "lullaby" figure  *165*
5c. "Aziz İstanbul," "call to prayer" figure  *166*
5d. "Aziz İstanbul," female chorus  *166*
5e. "Aziz İstanbul," instrumental rendition of first vocal line  *170*

# 1

# Introduction

"*Güleyim mi, ağlayayım* [I don't know whether to laugh or cry] . . ."

These were last public words spoken by the Turkish "Sun of Art" (*Sanat Güneşi*), Zeki Müren. Moments later, he collapsed. It was 24 September 1996. Turkish Radio and Television was making a documentary about his life in their studios in Izmir, Turkey's principal Aegean city. One of the guests had just presented him with a microphone—apparently the very microphone that on 1 January 1951 had launched his career as Turkey's preeminent vocalist in the popular art music tradition.[1] Journalist Mehmet Altan described the moment in an obituary in *Sabah* two days later.

> With a tense, but definitely excited smile, he asked, "'That's really it?"
> 
> Yes, that really was it. . . . The first microphone that made him a star, insinuating his way into a society with his unbelievable voice, a number 12 microphone from the Ankara Radio studio.
> 
> He held the microphone with some difficulty, and a few words came struggling from his mouth. "I don't know whether

---

1. Pictures of microphone, television show, and funeral can be found at http://www.sanatgunesi.com/0resimler.htm (accessed 5 January 2009).

to laugh or cry . . ." Death was at hand. He would meet his end with that same microphone in his hand, the number 12 microphone with which that crystal-clear voice began its life.[2]

He died, then, as he had lived: in the public eye, on a characteristic note of emotional ambivalence, clutching the very piece of technology that had made him and his voice a national institution. A circle had been neatly closed. A state funeral—an unusual honor for a queer sentimentalist—seemed to set the seal, claiming the meaning of his life for the nation.

Zeki Müren's death in 1996 represented not so much the passing of an era in Turkish popular culture as a moment of transformation. It was, in part, a moment of musical transformation in Turkey—a moment of nostalgic backward glances, shifting cultural hierarchies, new technologies, and anxieties about national heritage. Broadly similar situations have been noted elsewhere in the region, posing comparable ethnographic questions: in Syria (Shannon 2006), Bulgaria (Buchanan 2006; Rice 1996), Greece (Tragaki 2007), and Israel (Regev and Seroussi 2004).[3] It was also a moment of social, political, and cultural transformation—one I will try to understand throughout this book in terms of various lines of academic inquiry, some long-standing, others more recent: postcolonial and global cities (Mitchell 1988; Sassen 1998, 2006), the public sphere in late liberalism (Sennet 1976; Berlant 1997; Warner 2002), and cultural intimacy (Herzfeld 1997; Berlant

---

2. Müren's momentary hesitation may have been due to the fact that his 1951 broadcast was most likely to have come from Istanbul's radio station, not Ankara's. The concert was described in an early interview with *Radyo Dünyası*'s Edip Akın (Akın 1951, pp. 5–9), who reported that Müren was in Ankara until New Year's Eve, at which point he returned to Istanbul, having arranged a meeting with him at 8:40 p.m. at the Beler Hotel in Beyoğlu, Istanbul. Müren's friend Faruk telephoned to say that the singer had been called away to sing a radio concert in Suzan Güven's place—presumably in Istanbul. Müren and Akın met up afterwards, and the concert Müren had just given was the topic of conversation. The Istanbul Radio listings for that New Year's Eve were typical in their range of offerings. Following afternoon news, listeners would have heard programs devoted to orchestral overtures; dance band music; Turkish folk and classical songs; Ellen Miller, Victor Silvester, and the Vincent Lopez Orchestra; and jazz. The 7:00 p.m. news was followed by a program of dance music by the Gençer Orchestra; the listings then simply announced a "concert" between 7:50 and 8:15. This is the most likely candidate for Müren's broadcast, and it fits in neatly with the timing of Akın's story. It was followed by classical songs (recordings), music from "a Weber opera," sports news, Turkish classical instrumental music (*fasıl*), piano soloist Popi Panayotidis, Caruso arias, Neapolitan songs, and a final round of news and dance music before broadcasting ended at 11:30 p.m.

3. In very different contexts, Perna 2005 and Waxer 2002 describe music in processes of transformations that might very broadly be described as neoliberal (i.e., driven by elites attempting to transform their societies in response to global markets). Though Latin American circumstances are in some ways very different, these two books ground a historical understanding of the popular genres in question (Cuban *timba* and Colombian salsa, respectively) in terms of embodiment, affect, identities, urbanization and macropolitical transformation in ways that I have sought to emulate here.

1998, 2008; Giddens 1992). Here, too, the Turkish experience resonates with, and provides an important perspective on, the experience of others.

Müren's death also provokes reflection on the broader difficulties involved in understanding Turkish cultural history since 1950. The first multiparty elections in that year initiated a cycle of aggressive economic liberalization, political violence, military intervention, and Islamist reaction. Looked at in a certain way, the cumulative effects of these cycles have been dire (Keyder 1987, 2004). Continuity and stability have been lacking. Public debate has often been stifled. The intelligentsia has routinely been silenced, the press censored, the universities declawed. Factionalized political violence has often reduced public debates to sterile binarisms (left versus right, secular versus Islamist, Kurds versus Turks).[4] Deep cynicism about official public life has become endemic (Navaro-Yashin 2002).

And yet, at the end of the first decade of the twenty-first century, Turkey possesses an uncommonly vibrant public life. Music, art, literature, sport, and journalism, nourished in an atmosphere of energetic debate and civic pride, flourish as never before. Such achievements rest, I would argue, on a transformation of Turkish public life that is more deeply rooted and more continuous than one might expect. If explanations for this cannot be found in accounts of official political process, we must look elsewhere. The simple claim that I make in this book is that mass-mediated popular culture, and popular music in particular, has played an important role in sustaining public life in Turkey. I am particularly concerned in this book with three popular musicians—Zeki Müren, Orhan Gencebay, and Sezen Aksu—who are closely associated with the political transformations of the 1950s, 1970s, and 1990s respectively. Nostalgia for these musicians, I argue, mediates public engagement with Turkey's long liberal "moment." Far from sanitizing the past (as Grainge 2002 and others suggest), this nostalgia continues to pose complex and lively questions about public life at a popular level.[5]

---

4. It should be noted briefly and early on that the Turkish nation-state is home to possibly as many as fifteen million Kurds (i.e., about one-fifth of the total population). They are mainly speakers of the Kurmancı and Zaza dialects. Many live outside Turkey in the large Kurdish diaspora in Sweden, Germany, France and the United Kingdom. Kurds have been subject to forcible assimilation policies through much of modern Turkey's history. The 1980s saw efforts, in step with the liberal experiments of Turgut Özal, to enable a Kurdish media and legalize public use of the language. But such policies have seesawed, and their liberal thrust has been overshadowed by a brutally violent conflict in the southeast of Turkey between state forces and the Partiya Karkerên Kurdistan (Kurdistan Worker's Party, or PKK). The conflict has seen a massive displacement of rural Kurdish populations to the cities in the west of the country, and also to Europe. See Houston 2008. For an English-language account of Kurdish music in Turkey, see Aksoy 2006.

5. I draw historically on Boym 2001 and ethnographically on Stewart 1996 for the more politically engaged concept of nostalgia that interests me here.

The nostalgia also poses complex and lively questions from the point of view of social theory. What role have mass media played in forging nation and modernity, particularly on Europe's fringes?[6] How do we theorize emotion and affect in such contexts?[7] How do private and public spheres relate in late capitalism, globally speaking? How do we imagine the fragmentation of the public sphere, and the proliferation of alternative formations ("counterpublics")? These days, such questions are underpinned by a sharp sense of the limitations of a social theory that assumes a singular modernity fashioned in the West and leaves the rest of the world in the "imaginary waiting room of history," to use Chakrabarty's memorable phrase (Chakrabarty 2000).[8] Such questions also, these days, involve a sharp desire to reengage social theory's sense of optimism and political possibility. In 1976 Richard Sennett declared "public man" dead. As others do today, I feel that "public man" may be down, but he's not out.[9]

---

6. Early to mid-century Marxian critique, particularly that associated with the Frankfurt School, as is also well known, considered mass media to be complicit with political authoritarianism. Adorno's views on popular culture are the focal point of some by now canonical debates in popular music studies. See in particular Adorno 2002 (including Richard Leppert's introductory essay) and Middleton 1990. Other Frankfurtians, by contrast, saw in the collective creative processes of mass culture possibilities for a more democratically accessible public sphere. On Walter Benjamin, see, in particular Middleton 1990; on Negt and Kluge, see Hansen 1994. And many working outside Europe—where literacy and its languages have often been not so deeply rooted, and where official discourses of modernity have often been experienced as being remote from everyday life—have stressed the importance of popular culture in the forging of nation and modernity (Armbrust 1996, 2000; Jones 2001). As Armbrust puts it in the introduction to a collection of essays that has been central to this particular project, popular culture enables "new scales of communication and new dimensions of modern identity" (Armbrust 2000, p. 26) that move fluidly between national and global.

7. Abu Lughod's account of the place of melodrama in articulating Egyptian modernity (Abu Lughod 2005) develops earlier work showing how what has often been labeled as "emotional" and thus marginal has actually been central to modern social processes—chiefly, in this latter context, nation-building, whose theorization has until relatively recently been monopolized by writers preoccupied by print and reading practices (e.g., Anderson 1983). In a rather different though related analysis concerning modern Egyptian cassette sermons, Hirschkind argues persuasively that "the affects and sensibilities honed through popular media practice are as infrastructural to politics and public reason as are markets, associations, formal institutions and information networks" (Hirschkind 2006, p. 9).

8. For Hirschkind, focusing on what he calls the "embedded listener," mass media listening habits fashion what he describes as an "alternative" modernity in Egypt—an "alternative," that is, to a modernity that has often been experienced by ordinary Egyptians as authoritarian and undemocratic (Hirschkind 2006). Hirschkind is appropriately cautious about the terms "counter" and "alternative." They are to be construed as rationally deliberated alternatives to the dominant political discourses of modernity and the public in Egypt, but as ways of grasping processes of public formation that are not recognized in the theoretically dominant Habermassian model. See in particular Habermas 1984, 1991. For critiques, see Calhoun 1992.

9. In political theory, I refer to Warner 2002; in literary theory, Berlant 2008; and in anthropology, Hirschkind 2006. My approach to the theorization of publics is a bricolage drawing heavily

How, then, will this book proceed? This introductory chapter will continue to contextualize the principal theoretical concerns (love and intimacy, the global city, neoliberal transformation), and the place (Istanbul, 1950 to the present day). The next, chapter 2, starts where we began, with queer nightclub star and "model citizen" Zeki Müren, and the nostalgia following his death in 1996. Chapter 3 describes Orhan Gencebay, responsible in the eyes of many for an Arab-influenced popular genre, *arabesk*. Here, I will suggest, a new kind of star-citizen takes shape in aftermath of the political violence of the mid 1970s. Chapter 4 explores pop diva Sezen Aksu's 1995 album, *Işık doğudan yükselir / Ex Oriente lux* (Light from the East) in relation to the radical transformations of Turkey's neoliberal 1990s. Chapter 5 doubles back, taking the reader from the late 1940s to the present day, and tracing a particular song, its multiple versions, and their locations in an urban soundscape. "Aziz İstanbul" (Beloved Istanbul), the title taken from a famous poem by Yahya Kemal Beyatlı, explores the historical circulation, musical elaboration, and civic identity of a deeply fantasized figure in the Turkish cityscape: the wandering melancholic as lover-citizen.

In each chapter I will introduce readers to, and explore, iconic songs by the specific singers involved: Zeki Müren's "Menekşelendi sular" (The waters went purple), Orhan Gencebay's "Batsın bu dünya" (A curse on this world), Sezen Aksu's "Ne ağlarsın" (Why cry?). In the final chapter, a song ("Aziz İstanbul") is at the center of things, and I am concerned with specific recorded performances by Münir Nurettin Selçuk, Bülent Ersoy, and Timur Selçuk. I have chosen this kind of "case study" structure with a view to giving this book, whose arguments may otherwise seem somewhat abstract, a concrete frame of reference. The songs in question are easy to find using online resources, and readers will have plenty of opportunity to contest my characterizations and conclusions. This seems eminently desirable. The "case study" structure also allows me to explain to readers unfamiliar with various genres of Turkish music something about how they work.

This book is, however, intended as more than a set of disconnected case studies and "readings." I have in mind a kind of history—ultimately an at-

---

on these three approaches. Sennett (1976) remains a vital point of reference, not least for of his occasional moments of hopefulness. Speaking of the relationship between eighteenth-century social theory and the revolutionary transformations of that period, he observes that "the attempt to create a social order . . . at one and the same time brought the contradictions of the *ancien regime* to a point of crisis and created positive opportunities for group life which have yet to be understood" (Sennett 1976, p. 346). The publics that interest me in this book are clearly not the public spheres of Habermassian theory, and are "yet to be understood" in social theoretical terms. Considering them "positive opportunities for group life" seems a valid and desirable starting point.

tempt to account for *transformations* of intimacy. This is complicated, since I am reliant on a particular set of representations—iconic songs—that I want to explore as texts (acknowledging the process of "reading" a defined if not entirely stable text-object, and the play of imagination in that process) and also as social and cultural "assemblages,"[10] which I must attempt to understand in their specific and changing contexts. How, then, do I propose to link these case studies? What kind of history do I have in mind?

I do not treat these songs as isolates. They are versions of songs that others had sung before, and others (often in addition to the same singer) would sing again later. In other words, their meanings reside in a historical context of versions and interpretations, both prior and subsequent. In some cases, as we will see, classics have been provocatively reworked or claimed for a new generation. Other songs are more identifiable as compositions of a particular moment, selfconsciously revisited by their creators later in life. Still others have moved between genres and been subjected to radical modification in the process. The songs in question here are, in short, conceived in conversation with others and in constantly evolving musical contexts.[11]

These songs are also articulations of voice. The "uncanny" nature of the recorded voice has been extensively discussed in a psychoanalytically inclined musicology, as well as in musically inclined psychoanalysis, in recent

---

10. I use Deleuze's term, usefully theorized in Born 2005, to refer to the various combinations of mediation—sonic, social, discursive, visual, technical, and so forth—which constitute specific musical "objects." The term reminds us of the complex and social nature of "texts" and their creation, all too easily lost in aesthetic ideologies assuming (as in the case of the dominant Western model) individual creators producing musical ideas, which become texts, which then become performances. For other important critiques of the idea-text-performance ontology see Cook 1999, Bohlman 1999.

11. Silverstein and Urban describe an ongoing dialectic of "entextualization" and "contextualization" in their "natural history of discourse" (Silverstein and Urban 1996). This is very useful to my purposes here. "Entextualization" is the process by which social actors turn ongoing discourse and social interaction into text-artifacts (the traces of which it bears). "Contextualization" is the process, often contested, by which it is returned to discourse and social interaction, thereby generating newly entextualized text-artifacts. Each chapter of this book might be considered as an overlapping case study exploring specific dynamics of entextualization/contextualization—such a process being fundamental, I would add, to any attempt to understand "song." The relationship between text-objects and their subsequent "contextualization" is more closely theorized in Gell 1998. Gell, using Husserlian language of "retentions" and "protentions," reminds us that art objects are like other technologies, designed to be used in particular ways (Gell 1998). They contain within them a history of prior social use and a set of expectations concerning future use. Silverstein and Urban are interested in the "residue of past social interaction carried along with the sign vehicle encoding the semantic, or denotational, meaning in denotational text" (Silverstein and Urban 1996, p. 5). But we might go further, following Gell, in suggesting that such residues "protend" future use and future contextualizations. For instance, a piece of music "entextualizing" patriarchal discourse and social practice *tends to be* contextualized in situations already structured patriarchally, already anticipating such contextualizations, which thus lend themselves to these dominant meanings (naturalizing a patriarchal order). But other contextualizations are always possible.

years (see, notably, Abbate 2001, Barthes 1977, Bohlman 1998, Chion 1999, Dolar 1996, Middleton 2006, Poizat 1992, and Zizek 1996). Two aspects of this uncanniness concern me in these pages, and they bear on the question of what kind of history I have in mind. One is the way in which recording separates body and voice. This one might label a theorization of "acousmatic listening" (see in particular Chion 1999). As many have argued, this separation animates lively fantasies about the now-absent body as the originary site of meaning production in the text. A related point concerns the evasiveness of the voice: its slipperiness in relation to words and their meanings. In Lacanian theory, the voice is a classic "*object a*" (Miller 2005). It is both outside and inside the voiced and voicing subject. As such, it cannot fully be located in, or "quilted" into, the symbolic order. The voice becomes, in this understanding, a quasi-independent object of aesthetic attention and erotic quest. Such an understanding, for all of its drawbacks,[12] focuses attention on the sociable energies involved in *talking about* voices.

The "objectness" of the voices at play in the songs that concern me in this book might be understood in terms of the simple social fact that they generate discourse. Feld, Fox, Porcello, and Samuels have something like this in mind when they say that "the physical grain of the voice has a fundamentally social life . . . speech and song intertwine to produce timbral socialities" (Feld, Fox, Porcello, and Samuels 2004, p. 341). These songs are, then, experienced as "text-artifacts" in relation to others. But they are also, simultaneously, articulations of voice, which I understand as being complex and collective discursive constructions—Feld, Fox, Porcello, and Samuels's "timbral socialities"—that take shape over periods of time significantly longer than the life cycle of the specific songs in question. I attempt to trace the history of discursive constructions relating to particular voices in each chapter.

So, approached in this way, the songs and voices in question enable me to talk historically about extended and overlapping contexts rather than isolated and disconnected moments. They allow me to point to transformations within the broad parameters of the post-1950 liberal "moment" in Turkey (marked, roughly, by the crises of the late 1950s, late 1970s, and late 1990s). At the same time, they productively complicate efforts to interpret this period in terms of the simplistic narratives of progress familiar to readers

---

12. Born 1998 provides a useful guide to the possibilities and limitations of various psychoanalytic theories in music study. Her frustration with the "lack of sociological acuity" of psychoanalytic theories is one I share, particularly with regard to Lacanian theory. I would, however, note recent arguments from social and cultural geography about the fundamentally social and spatial implications of Lacanian psychoanalysis (see, for instance, Kingsbury 2007).

of the regional literature ("democratization," "emancipation of women," "westernization" and so forth).[13] Recordings are not simply inert objects of social scientific or historical inquiry. They are energetic and conversational creatures, alive to us in time and in space. They think us as we think them. I have attempted to recognize this elementary but often elusive fact in the pages that follow, and am aware of the complexity of the task.[14]

This is, in short, a cultural history of Turkey since 1950 told through its popular music. I hope to raise some broader questions about music more generally, though—particularly those genres habitually labeled "sentimental," within which understanding the relationship between "the musical" and "the political" can be both intriguing and problematic. This I propose to do by reference to theorizations of *cultural intimacy*, a topic to which I will return at the end of this introductory chapter. Before going further, though, I should say something about the Turkish context and raise some specific questions about modernity, Islam, and the city—questions that will reverberate throughout this book.

## Turkish Modern

Modern Turkey has routinely been understood as a secular modernizing state imposing reforms on a "traditional" and Islamic periphery.[15] Mustafa Kemal Atatürk, in accord with such understandings, established the modern Turkish state in 1923 out of the ruins of the Ottoman Empire after a bitter struggle with the Western colonial powers. Modernization meant secularization and the forging of a modern sense of national identity, which Atatürk undertook with a firm and occasionally forceful hand. This modern sense of

---

13. David Clarke's discussion of the problems of "seriation" in music history writing might be born in mind here (D. Clarke 2007). Clarke argues persuasively that the effort to think across genres in the analysis of particular music historical moments—for instance 1956, the "moment" of both rock and roll and Darmstadt—might pose productive challenges to the narrative habits of cultural history writing. The "moment" examined in this book is a rather long one, and the genres discussed may be less familiar to many readers than are those represented by Elvis Presley and Darmstadt in Clarke's analysis. But my intentions are similar.

14. Musicological efforts to reckon with the complex cultural life of recordings are still relatively new. For a useful overview of current thinking and a sense of direction in this field, see E. Clarke 2007.

15. On the one hand, classic historical and sociological studies of Turkey frame analysis in terms of a central state leading the reform process (e.g., Berkes 1964, Mardin 1989). On the other, this habit of thought is entangled with Western orientalism, reflected in Ottoman and modern Turkey scholarship in the work of Bernard Lewis (e.g., Lewis 1961). This is not to equate these two intellectual traditions. The critical thrust of the work of Berkes and Mardin is fundamentally at odds with, for example, Lewis's seemingly unquestioned assumptions about the inherent incompatibility of Islam and modernity. They both contribute, however, to a common picture in Turkish studies.

national identity was focused on Anatolia (the landmass of Asia Minor with the new capital, Ankara, at its heart). Claims on former Ottoman territories in the Balkans and the Arab world were quietly dropped,[16] and Istanbul, at the center of the old imperial map, sank into neglect.

Shortly after Atatürk's death in 1938, the country embarked on a period of experimentation with multiparty democracy. The first full democratic elections of 1950 bought the Democratic Party (Demokrat Parti) to power. Its leader, Adnan Menderes, presided over a period of religious reaction, ethnic violence, and massive rural-urban migration.[17] The army, dismayed by the perceived erosion of Atatürkian (or "Kemalist") political commitments, staged a coup d'état in 1960 and hung Menderes alongside two other cabinet members in 1961. The pattern was set. The following half-century was marked by a violent and still unsettled conflict between an authoritarian (secular) center and a liberal (Islamic) periphery, punctuated by military coups on 12 March 1971 and 12 September 1980 and the so-called "postmodern coup" of 28 February 1997.[18]

This habitual understanding of Turkey is still deeply entrenched as, at the time of writing, current debates over Turkey's accession to the European Union and the assassination of Turkish-Armenian journalist Hrant Dink

---

16. The main exception here would be the *sancak* (administrative province) of Alexandretta (known in Turkey as the Hatay), then part of the French-mandated territories of Syria, which was handed back to Turkey in 1939 as a result of changing priorities in the region on the part of the colonial powers before the Second World War. This was the only addition to the territories claimed by Atatürk in the Misaki Milli, the National Pact of 1920. The independent Syrian state that emerged from the French Protectorate in 1946 protested this acquisition as an act of colonial deceit, removing the province from maps of Syria in 1986 at least partly to ensure Turkish participation in the Mediterranean games in Latakia that year. See Stokes 1998.

17. Menderes presided over a period that saw efforts to re-center Islam in public life (including such vital symbols as the Arabic-language call to prayer, which had been sung in Turkish since the time of Atatürk), anti-Greek riots in Istanbul in 1955, and an unprecedented scale of rural-urban migration. According to official statistics, the population of Istanbul rose from 1,166,477 to 1,882,092 in this period—in other words, increasing in size by nearly two-thirds (Başbakanlık Devlet İstatistik Enstitüsü, Türkiye İstatistik Cep Yıllığı 1988). Unofficial estimates by Turkish sociologists and demographers estimate far higher periods of population growth in the undocumented *gecekondu* squatter towns.

18. A decision by the military's high command on 28 February removed the democratically elected Islamist government of Necmettin Erbakan from power. The coup involved no overt violence, and power was immediately handed over to a secular civilian administration. The term "postmodern coup" quickly stuck, and the event is generally understood as the fourth coup in modern Turkish history. The first coup had bought into existence the weak coalitions that predominated throughout the 1970s. The second eventually bought Turgut Özal, the architect of Turkish neoliberalism, to power as prime minister and then as president. The third coup effectively replaced one Islamist government (that of the radical and flamboyant Necmettin Erbakan) with another (that of the cautious and "moderate" Tayyip Erdoğan) after a brief secular interregnum.

indicate.[19] In this understanding, Islam is associated with civil society and a bourgeois argument for freedom of expression and enterprise. It is only the secular elites in the state apparatus, in this way of looking at things, that keep the country moving toward the West. But this conventional understanding has been under sustained academic assault by critically-minded scholars for at least a decade. Three overlapping and mutually implicated critiques concern me here: one that attempts to interpret the success of the Islamist movement in Turkey, particularly among the urban poor; one that is concerned with the emergence of Istanbul as a "global city"; and one that I will simply describe as the critique of neoliberalism.[20] I will consider each in turn.

The Islamist movement, then represented by the Refah Party, took control of the Istanbul Metropolitan Municipality in 1995 and control of the government in the elections of 1996. Before they were sidelined by the so-called "'postmodern'" coup of 1997, they had created a buoyant parallel Islamic public space within the nominally secular republic, in gated suburbs, in private universities, in consumerism, media, finance, fashion, music, literature, and much else.[21] The new Islamist leaders, political activists, and intellectuals not only questioned the West's monopolization of the idea of the modern but showed themselves to be, in many regards, better at being "'modern'" than the secularists. Whether in their pursuit of education and careers for women, in their tactical astuteness on public media, in their command of the electoral apparatus, or in their intellectual engagement with

---

19. European Union expansion in the east put brakes on earlier commitments to make Turkey a member. On 29 November 2006 the European Commission agreed to put membership talks on hold, overtly in protest at lack of movement over Cyprus. The news was greeted furiously in Turkey, which had been granted candidate status at the Luxembourg summit in 1997. Arguments that the country would be better off in alignment with its Muslim and Middle Eastern neighbors, or going it alone, gained considerable ground. See Aktürk 2007 for a recent critical discussion. Hrant Dink, a Turkish-Armenian journalist and editor-in-chief of *Agos*, was assassinated on 19 January 2007 by Ogün Samast, a right-wing nationalist. Pictures of the assassin posing with smiling police officers after his arrest in his hometown caused a major scandal. For many the event marked the resurgence of a militant and xenophobic Turkish nationalism, violently hostile to signs of ethnic diversity and difference within the country.

20. The points I make are not, of course, peculiar to Turkey. In many other parts of the world religious revival, the huge expansion of cities, and neoliberal programming have posed serious if not fatal challenges to social-scientific thinking about what used to be called "modernization"—orderly national development, industrialization, urbanization, and the forging of liberal multiparty democracies in the "third world." For an early critique of modernization theory with reference to the Middle East literature, see Gilsenan 1990.

21. On 18 April 1999 Merve Kavakçı became the first female deputy to turn up at the Turkish parliament wearing a headscarf, albeit only for a few hours (Göle 2000, p.102), thus broaching the very citadel of Turkish secularism. Islamist successes of this sort traumatized the secularist intelligentsia, throwing into question their hitherto unquestioned role as leaders of Turkey's march to the West, and to modernity.

Western traditions of social thought, the Islamists often seemed a step ahead of their secularist counterparts.[22] An orderly set of binarisms—West/East, secularism/Islam, reason/tradition, state/civil society, center/periphery—that produced a simplistic picture of Turkey as a textbook case of nation-state modernization has thus been thoroughly unsettled.[23]

The emergence of Istanbul as a "global city" has also significantly changed the theoretical landscape. The expression is in part popular and nostalgic, referring to the Ottoman imperial metropolis sitting astride the continents. For Turkish Islamists "global Istanbul" endorses a nostalgic vision of an Islamic social order supervised by Turks, free from petty ethnic squabbles and the ravages of modern capitalism. For secularists it resurrects Istanbul as the cosmopolitan and polyglot intellectual center it was before secular modernists relocated the capital to Ankara, imposed their drab vision of a nation unified by its folk culture, and—deepest of ironies—ensured a uniform Muslim society by means of the Balkan "population exchanges" and other policies which ensured that ever-increasing numbers of the city's Christians and Jews left the country (Scognamillo 1997–78; Keyder 1999).[24] Celebrations of "global Istanbul" informed by these kinds of cosmopolitan

---

22. On Islamist feminism in Turkey and its pitfalls, see White 2002. On the new Muslim intelligentsia, see Meeker 1991. On Islamist modernity, see Göle 1996 and 2000. The gender politics of the Islamist movement have been particularly unsettling for secularist radicals. Secularist Kemalist elites promoted women's rights as citizens and as public beings but did so in a patriarchal and authoritarian manner, one that feminist scholars would later refer to as "state feminism" (Kandiyoti 1991). This would ensure that most women, despite conspicuous exceptions to the rule, remained tied to private, reproductive, and domestic roles. The Islamist movements of the 1980s and 1990s were able to draw on strong feelings amongst women that secular modernity had not done them any favors. Whether in grass-roots electoral politics or in debate in newspapers or on television, Islamist politics, as Göle puts it, "enable[d] Muslim women to participate in public life, to organize meetings, to publish articles, to establish associations, to abandon the private domestic sphere and its traditionally defined roles" (Göle 2000, p. 99). Such impulses did not go unchallenged by men in the Islamist movement. But a fundamental argument of Kemalist political mythology—that secular modernity would be good for women and bring them into public political life—was exposed as myth.

23. Bernard Lewis's *The Emergence of Modern Turkey* (Lewis 1968) might be taken as one of the strongest endorsements of a modernization theory–driven view of Turkey's (successful) embrace of modernity, with a Western-oriented state holding traditional and Islamic civil society in check. Şeref Mardin's *Religion and Social Change in Modern Turkey* (Mardin 1989), by contrast, insisted on an understanding of modern Turkish Islamist movements (specifically the followers of Said Nursi, the Nurcu movement) *as modern*, critically engaged with Western thought, and forged in print and other modern technologies of intellectual exchange. Of course the critique of a theory of modernity dependent upon these kinds of binarisms, and driven by state-centric analytical models, has a history that predates the literature on the current Islamist movement.

24. On the new kinds of "consumer civility" focused on neighborhoods and entertainment districts to be enjoyed for the flavor of earlier times, of CDs, journals and coffee-table books celebrating the city's cosmopolitan heritage, see Bartu 1999, Yalçın 1997/98.

fantasies came to a head in the publicity surrounding the Habitat II conference in Istanbul in the spring of 1996.

Such celebrations of Istanbul's "global" status not only implicitly rejected a vision of development emanating from the capital, Ankara, but also reflected a growing acceptance of the power of the market rather than the state as the engine of progress. But globalization had its discontents.[25] As Keyder shows, a black economy of drugs and money laundering and an under-regulated industry manufacturing textiles for Russian suitcase traders fueled dramatic economic growth and promoted the global integration of the financial sector during this period.[26] Hotels, casinos, luxury shopping malls, fast-food outlets and high-rise office buildings mushroomed. "Istanbul in the 1980s lived through its own version of casino capitalism and yuppie exuberance" (Keyder 1999, p. 15). Sharp discrepancies were soon to be noticed between "the two Istanbuls": one oriented to the global economy and the world outside Turkey, a world of shopping malls, gated suburbs, the new business districts of Maslak and Levent, study abroad, vacations, and partying in a newly gentrified Beyoğlu; the other a world of squatter towns and run-down suburbs oriented to the city's rural hinterlands and the dwindling redistributive mechanisms of the state. Istanbul experienced the effects of globalization, Keyder argues, without fully becoming a global city.

Global transformation of the city and the Islamist capture of the state apparatus are both related to the steamroller dynamic of neoliberalism, which has, worldwide, reduced the role of the state to that of administering markets and facilitating the flow of global capital (Balakrishnan 2003). In countries like Turkey with strong traditions of state capitalism, such transformations take place through pressure externally and political violence internally. In such a frame of analysis, state corporatist models—which in Turkey rely on the idea of a benign, modernizing, secular center—are increasingly implausible. The political symbolism associated with this center, the "unified and uniform Kemalist holy cosmos," as Seufert and Weyland put it (Seufert and Weyland 1994, p. 85), has imploded. The state media that once ensured the ubiquity of this "holy cosmos" are now dwarfed by satellite channels,

---

25. For loosely related critical perspectives, see Robins and Aksoy 1995, Sönmez 1996, Yerasimos 1997/98, Somay 1997/98, and particularly Keyder 1999.

26. The facts and figures are of course hazy at best. Keyder suggests that the extraordinary growth of the Turkish financial sector in the 1990s was not unrelated to its foot-dragging in meeting international finance-industry standards. As he puts it, "Istanbul is not unique in accommodating dirty money, but the government has been remarkably slow in responding to pressure from international agencies to comply with emerging world standards of transparency and financial sector responsibility . . . the bloat and high profitability in the financial sector are due in part to capturing a share of the billions of dollars of unknown provenance that daily circle the globe" (Keyder 1999, p. 21).

the Web, and local radio. State salaries, pensions, and benefits lag behind the cost of living. State institutions hold little appeal for young people considering careers. Military service no longer structures the passage to adulthood for all young men. Corporations physically and psychologically dominate the landscape. Following the Susurluk incident, as Navaro-Yashin points out (Navaro-Yashin 2002), the state "survives" only in a cynical mode, in compensatory and often violent efforts to shore up something that, common experience suggests, has ceased to exist, at least in the once-familiar forms.[27]

Özyürek, in a recent book (2006), suggests yet another twist in the far-reaching cultural logic of neoliberalism. Nostalgia for the Kemalist 1930s has been a conspicuous feature of Turkish public culture in recent years. Hieratic representations of Atatürk the revolutionary leader and statesman are slowly being replaced by a more intimate imagery in public places, an imagery of Atatürk the man, portrayed in everyday and domestic situations. Responsibility for this is often assumed by *vakıf* foundations and, perhaps most conspicuously, banks.[28] In other words, the injunction to love the nation no longer emanates from the state itself, whose carefully crafted images of family and domesticity were vital tools in its early struggle to naturalize and internalize the institutions of the secular republic. Instead it emanates from private agencies that represent intimate identification with the state as being freely internalized, an act of consumer choice (Özyürek 2006, p. 6). The relationship of citizen to state is thus, Özyürek points out, mediated by public imagery saturated with a symbolism that reflects the market-driven priorities of neoliberalism. This discussion of Özyürek's characterization of

---

27. Navaro-Yashin aptly describes the car crash of 4 November 1996, known as "the Susurluk incident," as "the truck that crashed into the 'state'" (Navaro-Yashin 2002, p. 171). Four people were found dead in the car: a right-wing Kurdish parliamentarian, a mafia boss known for his involvement in fascistic pan-Turkish politics, a prostitute with a false identity card, and Istanbul's former vice-head of police. The event was reported in outraged terms by the Turkish press as a sign of the endemic, deep, and systemic corruption of the state; it was also, as Navaro-Yashin notes, quickly and cynically "normalized."

28. *Vakıf*-s are pious trusts, now administered by the state. As regards banks, Özyürek (2006, pp. 72–92) discusses the *To Create a Citizen* exhibition, curated by the Yapı Kredi Bank in 1998, in detail. This was a prominent exhibition on İstiklâl Caddesi in Istanbul's central business district, showing photographs of, as Özyürek puts it, "mundane transformations in the daily lives of citizens in the 1930s" (2006, p. 72). The "Representations of Life Styles in Turkey" exhibition hosted in 2006 by the Osmanlı Bankası in Karaköy and curated by two sociologists, Meltem Ahıska and Zafer Yenal (see Ahıska and Yenal 2006), contrasted with these displays of "official" intimacy. It presented a history of Turkey since the 1980 coup through food, language, music, dance, fashion, media, and advertising. The rocky progress of the country from the coup years to hyperliberalism is subtly and humorously on display. There is clearly a struggle taking place over the intimate and the everyday as a space of social and cultural critique. See also Stokes 2002b.

the "intimate state" concludes a brief review of some recent critical currents in the study of modern Turkey, and anticipates the last section of this chapter, which is directly concerned with the central issue of cultural intimacy. But before turning to this, I should say something about the overarching musical context of this book.

### Popular Music in Turkey

The chapters of this book are part of a broader history of Turkish music. They actually exceed it, in the obvious sense that they depict artists who are listened to outside Turkey, by non-Turks, and who thus are part of other people's music history.[29] They also exceed it in the more complex sense that they often escape well-worn habits of narrating Turkish music in terms of genre, region, ethnicity, class, and historical periodization. Despite their huge popularity and significance Zeki Müren, Orhan Gencebay, and Sezen Aksu have figured prominently neither in the non-Turkish ethnomusicological literature nor in Turkish musicology. This section suggests an alternative framework within which their broad popularity and significance might more readily be understood.

Genres familiar to urban audiences in Turkey today include what I refer to here as "Turkish art music" ("*Türk sanat müziği*" or "*sanat musikisi*"),[30] "Turkish folk music" ("*Türk halk müziği*"), and various kinds of popular music (*fasıl*, *arabesk*, *aranjman*, *Anadolu* rock, pop). Problematic though these genre distinctions are, for reasons that will become clear, some preliminary characterization may be useful for readers unfamiliar with Turkish music. "Turkish art music" is generally understood as a monophonic vocal and

---

29. At various times the voices of Zeki Müren, Orhan Gencebay, Sezen Aksu, and certainly Münir Nurettin Selçuk have been popular in nearby Balkan, Middle Eastern, and Central Asian countries. They have also taken their place in the migrant soundscapes of western European cities: Berlin, Paris, Stockholm, and London in particular. To limit their significance to "Turkish music history" would be quite wrong.

30. The wide range of orthographic conventions for the word *musiki*, particularly the question of whether one chooses to use accents to indicate long vowels, denote relative degrees of faithfulness to Ottoman (Arabic) or Greek orthography. Usually these orthographic choices index religious conservatism, scholarly fastidiousness, or antipathy on the part of the author to everything evoked by the French-derived *müzik*, its main rival in modern Turkish. A footnote in O'Connell 2005a is worth quoting at length, since it captures the main orthographic issues with precision: "Turkish classical music is known by a number of different names in Turkish. Generally speaking, this ancient tradition is called osmanlı mûsikî and fenn-i mûsikî in Ottoman sources and türk sanat müziği and türk klasik musıkisi, alaturka and (more colloquially) ahenk. The choice, spelling and even pronunciation of specific terms in many courses reveal aesthetic preferences and ideological attitudes reminiscent of the alaturka-alafranga debate. . . ." (O'Connell 2005a, p. 17).

instrumental chamber repertory dating at least from the earliest years of Ottoman rule and mostly concentrated in the urban centers. Since the end of the nineteenth century a great deal of it has been notated, theorized, and adapted to the concert stage and the recording industry.[31] "Turkish folk music" is generally understood as a repertory of monophonic rural song and dance accompanied by or played on the saz (a long-necked folk plucked lute) and other instruments, varying from region to region, subject to institutionalization in the early years of nation-state building, and now well-known through radio, television, cassettes, and CDs.[32] "Popular music" is a more inchoate category, referring in general usage to a great variety of vernacular and mass-mediated genres which range from nightclub popularizations of the art music repertory (*fasıl*), to Arab-oriented hybrids (*arabesk*) and Western-style pop and rock. Most of these use an eclectic array of local, regional, and global instruments (a unison string chorus often being prominent) and engage an equally eclectic array of musical styles.[33] Academic writing about Turkish music usually prioritizes art or folk music. Political sympathies as well as aesthetic sensibilities are often at play.[34]

A history that attempts to reckon with the voices of Zeki Müren, Orhan Gencebay, and Sezen Aksu is one that is obliged to move somewhat differently. As we shall see, these singers and their songs have slipped between genres, locales, and historical moments. To anticipate a key term (again), these are voices of *cultural intimacy*. As few other public institutions have

---

31. For the most important scholarship on the key institutions and historical transformations of the Ottoman repertoire, see the work of Behar (for instance, Behar 1992, not yet translated into English), Feldman 1996, and Wright 2000. For a systematic explanation of art music modal practice (*makam*), see Signell 1977.

32. See, paradigmatically, Bartok 1976 and Picken 1975. Their sense of the radical difference between urban and rural music, motivated by rather different intellectual agendas, had an impact on Turkish musicology.

33. For English-language discussions see Beken 2003, O'Connell 2003 and 2006, Solomon 2005a and 2005b, Stokes 1992 and 2002, and Seeman 2007. For Turkish see, inter alia, Meriç 1996, 1999a, and 1999b; Dilmener 2003; Dorsay 2003; and Paçacı 1999.

34. In the mid-1980s when I was first studying Turkish music, identifying with folk culture usually involved a leftist political orientation, generally supportive of the secular state, while identifying with art music often involved a conservative political orientation, hospitable to the recuperations of the Ottoman past and Islam in public life that were being promoted by the dominant conservative parties. Even then, though, in my own circle of friends these identifications were often complex and contradictory. For a historical account of the relations between the Turkish left and Turkish folklore research, see Öztürkmen's recent account of the 1948 trial of eminent folklorist Pertev Naili Boratav (Öztürkmen 2005). It is also worth pointing out the existence of other musicological traditions in which distinctions between folk and art music have never been axiomatic. See O'Connell's useful discussion of Mahmut Ragip Gazimihal (O'Connell 2005a), a musicologist whose published work in the 1920s in certain ways confounds and complicates these distinctions.

done,[35] they shape an intimate, as opposed to official, idea of the nation. This section briefly sketches a context for such a history, considering in turn the music reforms, the dynamics of officialdom, popular musical cosmopolitanism, vernacular religiosity, and the urban spaces in which popular music circulates in Turkey today.

Beyond Reform

"Official history" making has been a consistent project in the modern Turkish Republic. Its key ideological components are, as is well known, the emergence of national consciousness and the drive for self-determination amongst the intelligentsia in the declining Ottoman Empire, the national struggle following the First World War; the humiliations of imperial aggression, the enormous sacrifices of the people of Anatolia, and the heroic leadership of Mustafa Kemal Atatürk. It has consistently stressed Atatürk's pursuit of a national modernity—a modernity by definition European and secular (see Lewis 1955, Ahmad 1993).

Music has played an important role in the promulgation of this official history. Early republican ideologues such as Ziya Gökalp saw music as a peculiarly revealing challenge for the developing nation, one echoed by Atatürk in a speech to the National Assembly on 1 November 1938.[36] A quotation from that speech has been inscribed on the entrance to the main recording hall in the Turkish Radio and Television buildings in Harbiye, Istanbul: *"Bir ulusun yeni değişikliğinde ölçü, musikide değişikliği alabilmesi, kavrayabilmesidir"* ("The ability to accept, to grasp change in music is the measure of nation's progress"). In orienting the music of the nation to the Turkish folk and to a European modernity, reformers like Gökalp were rejecting what they regarded as the most deeply internalized identifications of the Ottoman social and political order: with Islam, with Arab civilization, and with cosmopolitan city life.

The music reforms were, however, problematic from the outset. Intense

---

35. Film and television have not constituted the kind of core, stable facts of national experience as they have done, for instance, in Egypt (Armbrust 1996; Gordon 2002; Abu Lughod 2005). Radio broadcasting was, however, a central tool of government from the outset. The Turkish recorded music industry has also had a broad national reach from its earliest days. The topic has been neglected, and facts and figures are hard to come by (but see Kocabaşoğlu 1980, Tura n.d., and Özbek 1991). The "acoustics of national publicity," to borrow Brian Currid's useful phrase (Currid 2000), may occasionally be hard to pin down, given the current state of media research in Turkey, but they are clearly of fundamental importance to an understanding to Turkish modernity.

36. For Gökalp on music, see Stokes 1992a, O'Connell 2005a. For Atatürk on music, see Oransay 1985.

and often debilitating debates continue today about the place of Anatolian folk music; the role of Central Asian music ethnography; the relevance of the urban art music tradition; the wholesale importation of Western practices, pedagogies and institutions; rival techniques of counterpoint and polyphony; and the relationship of the reform process with the market and popular tastes. Nonetheless, the state invested heavily in the production of a new national music. Such efforts might be dubbed, to borrow Andrew Jones' apt term (2001), "phonographic realism": music to reveal the nation. National radio and television were its vehicles.

The rural Anatolian tradition initially prevailed in efforts to build national institutions and media policy.[37] Muzaffer Sarısözen's *Yurttan Sesler* (Voices from the Homeland) Chorus, initiated in 1948, was an early institutional product of the music reforms and a central point of reference with its large, well-drilled orchestras of folk instruments and mass choral sound. For many reformers the urban art music tradition was too tainted by its past, its urbanity, and its Middle Eastern cosmopolitanism to be "properly Turkish." This argument was, however, systematically countered during the 1950s and 1960s.[38] Turkish radio director Mesut Cemil forged an art music style that was in many regards the classical equivalent of Sarısözen's rural-oriented phonographic realism: disciplined, rationalized, orchestral, and choral. When the new state conservatory was established in Maçka, Istanbul, in 1976, a new status quo was established when art music, folk music, and Western music were officially placed on an equal footing. Fol-

---

37. The Darü'l-Elhan conservatory, often referred to as the Istanbul Conservatory or the İstanbul Belediye (Istanbul municipal) Conservatory, was established by the Ottoman state in 1917 under the auspices of the Ministry of Education. It was the first conservatory to open in the education system (as opposed to the military system), superseding a number of private institutions that had checkered histories due to the First World War. With the declaration of the republic, Ankara became the favored site for new Western-oriented musical institutions—such as the Riyaset-i Cumhur Filarmonik Orkestrası, the Riyaset-i Cumhur Bandosu, and the Riyaset-i Cumhur Fasıl Heyeti, all of which drained the Darü'l-Elhan of personnel and funds. In 1926 the teaching of Turkish art music was discontinued at the Darü'l-Elhan at the command of the Ministry of Education. Anatolian folk music was increasingly prioritized, a move signaled by a series of folk music collecting trips organized and undertaken by the new Darü'l-Elhan director, Yusuf Ziya Bey (Demirci) between 1926 and 1929. With the closing of the Sufi lodges in 1925 and the ban on radio broadcasting of art music between 1934 and 1936, the formal art-music pedagogy apparatus had been dealt lethal blows. Transmission of repertory was ensured by the notational efforts of the Şark Musikisine Ait Tarihi Eserleri Tedkik ve Tesbit Heyeti (Committee for the Examination and Codification of the Historical Works of Eastern Music), the length of whose name alone indicates the extent of official anxieties about this musical tradition—during these early years. It also continued in the popular domain, where it was increasingly dominated by the recording industry and nightclubs. I draw here on Paçacı 1999 and Behar 1992.

38. See Arel 1969. This reflects the intense polemics of the 1950s, for which one might also turn to any issue of the influential *Musiki<sup>oo</sup> Mecmuası*, edited by Laika Karabey, published in these years.

lowing the 12 September 1980 coup, which inaugurated a three-year period of economic austerity and political repression, the art, folk, and Western classical ensembles of the Turkish Radio and Television Corporation (fed almost exclusively by graduates from the state conservatories) dominated the soundscape.

Turkish musical officialdom underwent significant transformations in the 1990s. The TRT had to compete with private television channels, FM radio, and later the Web as media were progressively deregulated. The state conservatories evolved into more generalized environments of tertiary education and research.[39] Those who continued to work at the TRT did so for security rather than the burning sense of mission that seemed to characterize those I knew there in the 1980s. "Official" musicological discourse had a significant afterlife, but no longer made quite the same kind of sense. Liberalism has demanded alternative narratives of national intimacy. In recent years these have taken self-consciously cosmopolitan and "global" forms.

Turkish popular musical cosmopolitanism has usually looked west. Operetta was enormously popular in Turkey during the later Ottoman, constitutional, and early republican periods. *Kanto* adapted operetta and Western music hall for the "old" city's theaters.[40] Tango took root in Turkey in the 1920s; jazz shortly after.[41] Erol Büyükburç ("the Turkish Elvis") recorded "Little Lucy" in 1961, but rock and roll cover bands had been in existence for at least a decade.[42] Eurovision and Sanremo ensured the enduring influence of the Mediterranean chanson.[43] Rock radicals looked to the Anglo-Saxon world for inspiration, even when searching for an authentic Turkish

---

39. The evolution of Müzik İleri Araştırma Merkezi (MİAM, the Advanced Music Research Center) from within the state conservatory at the Istanbul Technical University in Maçka, Istanbul, is instructive in this regard. The state conservatory had formerly provided a steady stream of graduates to TRT stations across the country. With media privatization in the 1990s, new directions were sought. The musicology department at the state conservatory had formerly been the home of a strong scholarship that was expressly designed to serve the collection, archiving, and exemplary performance of folk music in the state media. MİAM, by contrast, resembled an American or European music department, oriented to international research horizons, with specializations in composition, music theory, ethnomusicology, and music history.

40. On operetta and *kanto*, see the Yapı Kredi recordings of operettas, *kanto*-s, and *fantezi*-s from the early decades of the twentieth century, including a recording of the long-running *Leblebici Horhor* (Horhor the chick pea seller), originally written in 1875. On *kanto*, see Hiçyılmaz's popular but useful book (Hiçyılmaz 1999).

41. On Turkish tango, see the final chapter of Akgün 1993. On jazz in Turkey, see Meriç 1999a.

42. On the history of Turkish rock and pop, see Ok 1994, Hasgül 1996, Meriç 1996, Meriç 1999b, and Dilmener 2003. For a brief English-language account that owes much to the above, see Stokes 2002a.

43. On Mediterraneanism in Turkish popular music, see in particular Özer 2002; Dilmener 2003 and 2006 discuss Eurovision and Sanremo in Turkey.

rock practice. *Anadolu* (i.e., "Anatolian") rock flourished from the late 1960s until the coup in 1980.[44] Turkish rap and hip-hop (originally popularized by German-Turkish rappers and DJs in the mid-1990s) continue to borrow energetically from North American models while a new generation of rock and pop musicians pick up the threads that were broken by the 1980 coup.[45]

Turkish popular music comopolitanism also looked east. Arab musical practices have been a long-standing influence in Turkish popular culture. Though disparaged, Egyptian cinema and popular music practices were pervasive and powerful in Turkey.[46] Turkish instrumentalists, composers, singers, and recording industry personnel traveled to Egypt to learn the ropes in the 1930s and 1940s.[47] In the early 1950s, the pages of media journals like *Radyo Magazin* were still dominated by the vocal and cinema stars of the age: Umm Kulthum, Mohammed Abd al-Wahhab, Yusuf Wahbi. In the 1960s, "Arab," Turkish popular classical, Turkish folk, and Western pop and rock were mixing in a hybrid popular music style later dubbed *arabesk*. Belly dancing, or *oriyental,* borrowed freely from Egyptian models. Many of the great Turkish *oriyental* stars learned and developed their art in the Arab world.[48] The Roma ("gypsy") musicians associated with Egyptian-inflected popular music and dance styles in Istanbul further degraded it in the eyes of critics (see Seeman 2007, Potuoğlu-Cook 2007), but also introduced Balkan, Mediterranean, and north Indian elements to Turkish audiences as well as disseminating this Turkish-developed hybrid further afield.[49]

44. On *Anadolu* rock, see specifically Hasgül 1996 and Aya 1996.

45. On the earlier generation of Turkish rap and hip-hop, mostly based in Germany, see Robins and Morley 1996 and Stokes 2002a. On the second generation of mostly Istanbul-based rap and hip-hop artists, specifically Nefret and Fresh B, see Solomon 2005a and 2005b. Fatih Akın's film *Crossing the Bridge* (2005) portrays the continuation of the Anatolian rock tradition well. It also exemplifies the new and rather more serious (verging on reverential) attitudes towards popular music history that currently prevail in Turkey.

46. See, for instance, O'Connell's discussion of the issue in the early republican period (O'Connell 2002 and 2005).

47. The list includes violinist and bandleader Haydar Tatlıyay, vocalist Münir Nurettin Selçuk, and composer Artaki Candan.

48. Mehdia Cemal—born in 1938, and thus one of the first generation of mass-media belly dancers in Turkey—learned dance at Samiye Cemal's school in Beirut (Cemal had been a student of Egyptian film belly dancer Tahia Carioca), building a career in the *gazino* and nightclub world of the early 1950s. Yonca Yücel, born in 1948, made her name as a dancer in Turkish musicals but developed her art, as had many others, in the nightclubs of the gulf and north Africa. Dilara, more recently, learned belly dancing and first appeared on stage in Israel. For interviews and biographies with a number of the major Turkish belly dancing stars, see Ok 1997. The influx of Russian dancers in recent years, as elsewhere in the Middle East, has renewed in Turkey a sense of this practice as national heritage, as it is now perceived by many to be under threat.

49. On Roma-mediated "Turkish" influence in Balkan popular music, see Rice 1996, Buchanan 2006, and Seeman 2006.

This is cosmopolitanism "from below"—to be distinguished from initiatives from above, within the official music education system, to graft Western compositional techniques to Turkish musical content. It has readily acknowledged the vital role of Istanbullian Greeks, Armenians, and Jews in mediating non-Turkish musical styles and adapting them for Turkish audiences.[50] It has acknowledged the complex powers and pleasures of the copy, the imitation (Taussig 1993). To create a Turkish jazz (or tango, or hip-hop, or electronica) is not simply to import something (and thus recognize a lack), but to exercise and enjoy mastery in rendering it Turkish. To anticipate, once again, a term I will discuss in more detail later, popular musical cosmopolitanism has then shaped an *intimate* sense of national identity, and has done so through its validation of everyday lived and experienced social, cultural, and historical relations rather than of an officially fabricated past.[51]

## Popular Music and Islam

Popular musical culture and popular religion have shared space in complex ways in Turkey. This ambiguous relationship has been vital to popular music's meanings. The architects of the secular republic sought a clear demarcation of public and private spheres, in which religion would be emphatically confined to the latter. This clear demarcation was never fully achieved. Population exchanges early in the life of the republic bought large numbers of Greek- and Bulgarian-speaking Muslims into the country, creating a large Muslim majority, and collective habits of self-identification as Muslims that were never successfully erased. Reaction to the Kemalist reforms of the 1930s often took the form of religious conservatism wedded to economic liberalism (Berkes 1964; Ahmad 1977). The state might always have been secular, but modern Turkish nationalism has always had a strongly religious undercurrent.

This situation is reflected in popular musical culture. Until the establishment of the republic, the Sufi lodges constituted the major institutional site of transmission for the art musical tradition. They were closed in 1925. But

---

50. There has been a proliferation of archival recordings released in Turkey of the musical traditions of "the minorities." See, for instance, Kalan's recent *Ermeni bestekarları* (Armenian composers) series. For published academic discussions, see Sarhon 2003, Estukyan 2003, O'Connell 2006, Aksoy 2006, and Seeman 2006.

51. Turino argues against the habit of understanding cosmopolitanism and nationalism to be in conflict, with reference to the forging of a national popular music in Zimbabwe (Turino 2000). Musical nationalism, he suggests, presupposes the existence of a cosmopolitan intelligentsia that is familiar with the nationalisms of others and is able to claim a particular cosmopolitan formation, a particular conjuncture of local and transnational musical styles, as its own.

those responsible for instituting the new conservatory system learned and notated a great deal of the art music repertoire from Mevlevi sheikhs, and retained close ties with the order.[52] Early recording stars such as Sadettin Kaynak and Hafız Burhan learned music in traditional religious environments, made extensive recordings of religious repertory, and continued to hold day jobs as religious functionaries.[53] Kani Karaca, a touchstone of classical authenticity, made recordings of the Qur'an and the Mevlid-i Şerif in the 1960s and 1970s that continue to be revered by older music lovers today.[54] The conservatories insisted on a clear boundary separating sacred and secular, but it has generally been irrelevant in popular practice.[55]

52. The Mevlevi order, known to many in Europe and America as the "whirling dervishes," were established in Konya, central Anatolia, by Celaleddin Rumi (Jalal al-Din Rumi) in the thirteenth century. They cultivated music assiduously, as do the Cerrahi and Halveti orders in Turkey today. Their "lodges" (meeting places) were built around *semahane*-s (ritual halls) where complex musical suites (*ayin*) were performed to accompany the *sema* (whirling dance ritual), a form of *zikr* or "remembrance" of God. The Şark Musikisne Ait Tarihi Eserleri Tedkik ve Tesbit Heyeti (see note 37 above) was staffed by Zekaizade Ahmet (Irsoy) Efendi, Rauf Yekta Bey, and Ali Rifat Bey (Çağatay). Its principal sources were Celaleddin Dede, sheikh of the Mevlevi lodge at Yenikapı; Ataullah Efendi, sheikh of the Galata Mevlevi lodge; and Hüseyin Fahrettin Dede, sheikh of the Bahariye Mevlevi lodge. See Paçacı 1999 and Behar 1992.

53. Sadettin Kaynak, born in 1885, was the son of a prominent Istanbul mosque *müderris* (i.e., a state appointed religious official). He graduated from the Darü'l-Fünun Theology Faculty, traveled extensively, became a major recording star, recorded Turkish music for Egyptian film soundtracks, and provided the music for some of the İpekçi Brothers' first Turkish film musicals. He also recorded a great deal of religious repertory, including the first recording of the Turkish-language call to prayer, which was included on Kalan's archival CDs (*Kendi sesinden Hafız Sadettin Kaynak*). He maintained state appointments in mosques throughout his career, ending up as second imam of the Sultanahmet mosque in Istanbul. He died in 1961 (see İnal 1958). Hafız Burhan (Sesyılmaz) (1897–1943), reputedly of Roma ancestry, received a musical training in the Ottoman military music academy, the Mızıkay-ı Hümayun. He quickly began a career singing the Mevlid-i Şerif (a devotional poem celebrating the birth of the Prophet) and recording *gazel*-s for the popular market in the 1920s, many of which are still celebrated today.

54. The "Mevlid-i Şerif" is the name given to the fifteenth-century poem in Turkish by Süleyman Çelebi narrating the birth of the Prophet. Kani Karaca (1930–2004) was born in Adana and studied with Sadettin Kaynak (see note 53). He made a large number of recordings of Qur'an, *mevlid*, *kaside*, *ezan*, and items of religious repertory associated with the Mevlevi order. He also recorded extensively for Turkish Radio after his arrival in Istanbul in the early 1950s. Two sets of archival recordings—*Kani Karaca* and *Kani Karaca dini musıki*, released by Kalan in 1999 and 2001 respectively—document the two interlinked halves of this important musical career. Non-Muslim musicians in Turkey also made popular recordings that combined religious and nonreligious repertory. İsak Algazi, for instance, performed Jewish devotional music and Turkish *şarkı* and *gazel*-s, as well as secular Ladino (Levantine Spanish) repertory maintained in the Turkish Jewish community, before emigrating to Uruguay (Seroussi 1989).

55. The attempt to secularize folk music also ran into difficulties, especially in relation to Alevi music. The Alevi are a Shia minority in Turkey (i.e., spiritual and political succession in the Muslim community is considered in terms of the Prophet's family, and the Shia are particularly devoted to Ali, the Prophet's son-in-law). Music from Alevi regions has always been treated axiomatically as folk repertory in official circles, but it has circulated in urbanized popular forms for a long time. The

The military coup of 12 September 1980 heightened anxieties about the relationship between religion and secularism in modern Turkey. The junta cited the threat of communism as a rationale for the coup, but they were also concerned with the rising power of the Islamists, who had recently led major demonstrations calling for the return of *şeriat* (Islamic religious law). Atatürkian secularism was enforced in public even though, as subsequently became clear, covert support and encouragement was given to Turkish Islamists in Germany as a means of diverting potential leftists.[56] A new climate of anxiety about the signs and symbols of public Islam came to prevail, and this had important ramifications for musical life. Urban Sufi practice was driven underground or abroad. Religious or religiously inflected repertory disappeared from the mass media. The cassette sermons of Fethullah Gülen, involving mass weeping and other forms of public emotionalism (cf. Hirschkind 2006), circulated covertly. *Arabesk* hinted at these suppressed archives of popular religious emotion, though it never spelled them out explicitly (Stokes 1992a). The organic connection between popular Islam and popular musical culture was severed; what "survived" did so as something repressed, under erasure.

The Islamist movement sought to resuscitate these connections in the 1990s, and did a great deal to encourage the emergence of an Islamic popular culture with a strongly national flavor. Musically this has taken the form of various kinds of "green pop," a great deal of which adopted the music and lyric formulae of *arabesk* for overtly spiritual purposes.[57] Representatives of the new Islamic popular musical culture have little connection with the past. They are the products of a generation for whom the musical culture of the Sufi lodges is somewhat distant. Their musical orientations are proletarian rather than classical. Their intentions are not only to entertain

---

first recording I have of an Anatolian Bektaşi-Alevi folk *deyiş* in an urban popular style is Perihan Altındağ-Sözeri's famous 1953 recording of "Haydar Haydar" (which can be found on a compilation CD, also entitled *Haydar Haydar,* released in 2003 by Rounder Records as part of its Masters of Turkish Music series. Of course there may also be much earlier examples. By the early 1980s both the TRT and the cassette market were catering to a lively popular interest in Alevi folk music, which was represented within the TRT by Ali Ekber Çicek and outside it by Arif Sağ. See Markoff 1986 and 1990/91.

56. For English-language accounts of the so-called "Rabıta affair," in which investigative journalist Uğur Mumcu uncovered details of the junta's sponsorship of Turkish Islamist organizations in Germany and was subsequently assassinated, see Akın and Karasapan 1988 and Stokes 1992a, p. 110.

57. Green is the traditional color of Islam for Muslims, hence the name, though there are many others: *yeni ilahi, zikr pop,* and so forth. These genres have often used very similar vocal techniques to *arabesk,* and a similar musical and lyric language. In them, the secular-sounding string choruses and *darbuka*-s of *arabesk* are usually replaced by the *ney* and the *def,* instruments with spiritual overtones.

but also to instruct a generation of listeners spiritually cut adrift by the secular republic.⁵⁸

Secularists have been both bewildered and outraged by the speed with which this Islamist popular culture has taken root. An article in the secularist *Milliyet* pointed to the persistently high sales figures for sermons, Islamist pop, and *arabesk*. Early in 2006, for instance, the Minik Dualar Grubu ("Mini Prayer Group," an ensemble of singing children) sold 285,000 copies of *Teşekkür ederim Allahım* ("Thank you God"), significantly outselling Sezen Aksu's *Şarkı söylemek lazım* (148,500), for instance.⁵⁹ The tone of anxiety in the article is unmistakable. The recent wave of Islamic pop has forced on secularist commentators (like Tuğba Tekerek, *Milliyet*'s correspondent) an uncomfortable awareness of the deep strands of religious experience that shape Turkish life. Popular religion is an anomaly in a secular state, at least according to official historical logic.

The new Islamist pop seems to have been designed, at least in part, to force secularists to confront the impossibility of the secular-modernist project. It might be described, as radical experimentalism within the Islamist movement once was, in terms of a cultural politics of consciousness raising (White 2002). But this music also appeals to an intimate logic—to an everyday, commonsense view of things in which Islam is understood as an integral component of Turkishness, and in which efforts to separate them are futile.

---

58. Mehmet Emin Ay, a prominent representative of this genre, was born in 1963 in Van, in the predominantly Kurdish southeast of Turkey. I draw here on a September 2007 interview with him. He received his education in an İmam-Hatip Lycee, one of the religious high schools developed during these years at least partly to soak up and distract disaffected youth in the provinces at a time of high anxiety about communism. This system of religious high schools was to be greatly expanded in the 1980s and 1990s. One of Mehmet Emin's celebrated recordings, "İmam-Hatiplim" (My İmam-Hatip student), is now to be found on the websites of a great many İmam-Hatip schools. Mehmet Emin sang Arabic and Turkish religious repertoire as well as Qur'anic recitation in a voice strongly inflected by folk and popular styles. Late-1980s cassettes such as *Taleal bedru* (an early Islamic *kaside*) were best sellers. Islamist websites claimed sales that would appear to have rivaled those of Tarkan at the height of his popularity (Songül Karahasanoğlu, personal communication). Mehmet Emin is still enormously popular, and was evidently the mentor of many of the new generation of "green"/*zikr*/Islamist pop singers such as Cemal Kuru, Abdürrahman Önül, Hasan Dursun, and others, though he distanced himself from them.

59. Tuğba Tekerek's article in *Milliyet* can be found at http://www.milliyet.com.tr/2006/12/17/ekonomi/axeko01.html. It draws on figures provided by the Turkish Music Industry Federation (MÜYAP). Amongst other interesting figures that emerged in this article was the prominence of cassette sermonizer Fethullah Gülen, deemed 2005's seventh best-selling recording artist. I am grateful to Cihangir Gündoğdu for pointing this article out to me.

### Spaces and Places

A history of Turkish popular music is also necessarily about urban spaces and places. Broadly speaking, it is useful to distinguish the spaces of bourgeois public leisure in the European parts of Istanbul, where Western genres from operetta to rock and pop have taken root, from the old city venues (specifically, the Direklerarası, the "Arcades," today's Şehzadebaşı Caddesi) where lower-class hybrids emerged, catering to the predominantly Muslim middle and working classes. Both might be distinguished, in turn, from sites of officialdom: the music conservatories, the *halkevleri* ("people's houses"), and the radio and television stations.[60]

Turkish popular music must be understood in terms of a very specific site of national intimacy: the *gazino*. *Gazino*-s emerged from the *meyhane*-s and *kahvehane*-s (roughly, bars and cafés, run by Christians and Muslims respectively) of the later eighteenth century.[61] The classical style took a particular form here, known generically as *fasıl*, increasingly focused on *şarkı* song form, *taksim* improvisation, and instrumental *peşrev*-s and *semai*-s. Court patronage declined, and composers and performers started to explore a lucrative new market. These new sites of recreation and entertainment were increasingly referred to as "*gazino*-s," after the casinos in vogue in the Pera district of Istanbul during the reign of Abdülhamit II (1876–1909) (Feldman 2002). These were, by all accounts, sites of easy interethnic musicking, increasingly dominated by Turkish Roma as the numbers and influence of the other minorities declined during the early decades of the republic.[62]

By the later 1940s the *gazino* catered increasingly to a new class of rural-urban migrants anxious to celebrate, simultaneously, their rural roots and the promise of the modern. The classical genre adapted accordingly, with the help of the recording industry and savvy entrepreneurs such as

---

60. The Darü-l Fünun conservatory was located close to today's Istanbul University, between Beyazit and Aksaray. The State Conservatory (Devlet Konservatuarı) was eventually attached to Istanbul Technical University in Maçka in 1976, where it remains. It is within walking distance from the main TRT radio station building in Harbiye and the television studios in Kuruçesme, just a short cab ride north from the main entertainment districts of Taksim and Beyoğlu. On the *halkevleri* (people's houses) movement, see Karpat 1963.

61. On the origins of the *gazino* see Feldman 2002—particularly pp. 16–17, on which most of this paragraph draws. See also Güngör 1990 and Beken 2003.

62. Many modeled themselves on the design and entertainment program of the Tepebaşı *gazino*, close to Beyoğlu, which was established in the 1930s (Beken 2003). Once central to the careers of many of the musicians discussed in the earlier part of this book, it has long since disappeared. A major road project in the late 1980s linking the Taksim area with the old city turned the whole area into a noisy thoroughfare, though by the time I first got to know this area in the early 1980s it was already a notorious slum and a red-light area.

the "*gazinocuların kralı*," ("king of the nightclub owners"), Fahrettin Arslan. Zeki Müren (as we will see in chapter 2) gave shape to new consumer desires for glamour and intimacy with a flamboyant act, a T-shaped stage, and a mobile microphone, all of which staged a moment of encounter and physical proximity between fan and star. Orhan Gencebay (as we will see in chapter 3) popularized a hybrid of *gazino* art music, folk music, rock, and pop for these new audiences, later known as *arabesk*. He remained somewhat aloof from a world that could clearly be exhausting and demanding, avoiding live performances. In the 1980s an evening in a *gazino* was prohibitively expensive for working-class folk, despite the proliferation of cut-rate varieties.[63] So Gencebay's refusal to participate had some popular justification. But the fact that he was, and continues to be, criticized even by his fans for this aloofness shows just how central the *gazino* had become as an idealized site of intimate and peculiarly Turkish musical pleasures.

The singers at the heart of this study might all be described in terms of ambivalence towards the state music reform project, a vernacular cosmopolitanism, and a folksy mysticism that has occasionally shaded into a cautious religious conservatism. They are also singers in and of Istanbul—its sites and histories of popular cultural production, its spaces of leisure and entertainment, its topographies of fantasy and desire. They are neither of the country nor fully of the city. They are neither creatures of officialdom nor fully in opposition to it. No wonder they have so consistently eluded scholarly appraisal, and no wonder they have been such a crucial focus in Turkey for intimate identifications of self and of nation.

### The Republic of Love

A glance at the Turkish mediascape today suggests that a number of influential voices in the country think love is in a state of crisis. The matter is considered to be of national importance.[64] Consider, for instance, a recent ar-

---

63. Matinee performances, intended specifically to attract female audiences, were common in the 1950s. Lower-class alternatives to the *gazino* developed, some of which were essentially places to pick up prostitutes (*pavyon* and *gece klüpleri*) while others were designed to attract working-class families (for instance, the *aile gazinosu*). The more recent moniker *müzikhol* distinguishes the food-and-entertainment format from the more folksy and "democratic" environment of the *türkü bar*, where patrons can drink beer and listen to live (usually folk) music without having to pay for a meal. See Kayhan 2003.

64. One could refer to many examples. The ubiquitous 2006 Turkcell mobile phone advertisement joked about the forthcoming football season, which was sponsored by Turkcell. A young cartoon couple is shown sitting on a hill overlooking the Bosphorus. The moon shines over this lyrical scene (see chapter 5). A Turkish flag is visible in the background, as if to remind viewers, should

ticle in the Islamist daily *Zaman* by secularist author Elif Şafak (Şafak 2006). Young people in Turkey are taught from an early age to revere love (*aşk*), she points out. Everybody in Turkey, she writes, knows the characters in the great medieval and folk romances—Aslı and Kerem, Leyla and Mecnun, Ferhat and Şirin—a fact that is daily demonstrated in the names people give their children. But love, constantly represented and referred to, is puzzlingly absent in everyday behavior. Şafak wonders: is love now forbidden? Where has it gone? What has changed?

Şafak suspects that Turks have simply become unable to bear the demands that love makes on them ("Why have we changed? Have we become incapable of endurance?"). Her final emphases convey a powerful anxiety: "Love is the very thing itself. And love is something valuable enough to make sacred, to celebrate, to preserve, to embrace."[65] We must secure "the thing itself" and then shore up its representations. The problem is, she suggests, that Turks seem to be committed to doing the opposite. Somewhere along the way, love has disappeared.

The crisis, for Şafak, is one of civility. Reverential talk about love seems only to produce its opposite: violence and coercion. It renders Turks oppressive (*baskıcı*) and harsh (*katı*). It is "love" that produces the fathers who kill their daughters for the sake of the honor crimes that Turks read about with such depressing regularity in the press. It is "love" that makes parents imprison their children. "Love" seems to render Turks incapable of getting on with others—particularly where it most matters for Şafak, in the domestic sphere. The point was picked up by an online commentator, "İnsan" ("Human"), a few weeks later: "A basic answer to (Şafak's) difficult question: in our view, the character (*mahiyet*) of love has changed. We have spoken of

---

they need reminding, of the national frame of reference. The young woman sighs, romance on her mind, and says: What a beautiful moon! The young man turns towards us, sighing for a different reason. The words below—"*Türk Süperligi başlasın artık!* [Let's get the Turkish Superleague started already!]"—indicate what is on *his* mind. The idea of love as a condition of national dysfunction supports the joke. Perhaps most striking is Orhan Pamuk's recent novel, *Masumiyet müzesi* (Pamuk 2008), an ironic take on popular and sentimental culture that depicts mismatched love as an allegory of national identity. A wealthy urbanite falls in love with a poor relative and encounters, in his pursuit of her, all that Western-looking Turkey has repressed or marginalized. Needless to say, the affair ends in disaster. The book—the first novel Pamuk published after winning the Nobel Prize for literature in 2006—has already been a sensation in Turkey.

65. "*Aslolan aşktır. Ve aşk; kutsanacak, kutlanacak, korunacak, kollanacak kadar kıymetlidir.*" The term for "love" here is the Arabic-derived *aşk*, not the Turkish *sevgi*. There are subtle shades of distinction between these two words, just as in many cases where speakers have a choice of words with Arabic or Turkish roots. Here I would argue that the Arabic-derived term elevates the concept, distancing it from localized expression. I do not believe these subtle shades of meaning affect my general argument, but they are occasionally worth noting.

love to somebody not in love, we have done things for people for the sake of love who are not themselves capable of love, we have extracted the insides and worn the shell, and now that's all we have left of love; this is what we have come to know. We have become suspicious of people who say they are in love. That's the long and short of it" ("İnsan" 2006).[66]

This brief exchange is notable for at least three reasons. First, love is understood as a national issue. Turks are taught to revere love from childhood, and come to understand their Turkishness in terms of this reverence. *Ours*, Şafak says, is a culture that respects and assigns importance to love. *Our country has produced a unique treasury of love songs and love stories. Love is inscribed on our landscape in the names we give to sites of natural beauty, place names, and street names.* To talk about love being in crisis is, then, to talk about a peculiarly *Turkish* crisis.

Secondly, the crisis of love is understood politically, in terms that complicated the relationship between public and private spheres. For Şafak, "love" is publicly celebrated, yet the very terms of this celebration impose impossible pressures on domestic life, which in turn create dysfunctional families whose various crises are returned to the public sphere in the form of honor killings and so forth. "İnsan" is more explicit about the corrosive effects of this situation on public life, but his point simply extends Şafak's. Turks assert their ideals, but no longer live up to them. Cynicism is the inevitable consequence.

Thirdly, we might briefly observe that Şafak's article appeared in the main Islamist daily, *Zaman*.[67] That *Zaman*, a paper with liberal and intellectual aspirations, might solicit an article from a well-known secularist and feminist writer was, at least at that time, not in itself unusual. Rather, we might note that even for a secularist and feminist like Şafak, discussions of love are automatically understood to have a spiritual dimension.[68] Poor people in Turkey, she points out, offer prayers for the lovers on television soap op-

---

66. "*Zor soru basit cevap: aşk denenin mahiyeti değişti bizce. Aşk olmayana aşk dedik, aşka yakışmayanı aşk uğruna yaptık, içini boşalttık kabuğunu giyindik, sonra böyle kaldı bizde aşk, böyle duyduk, böyle gördük. Aşığım diyene güvenemez olduk. Bütün mesele budur.*" For this and more online discussion of Şafak's article, see http://satirarasi.wordpress.com/2006/12/21/turkiyede-ask-yasak-midir/ (accessed 23 January 2007).

67. *Zaman* has generally represented the Gülen movement and its cliques in government and academia. On the Gülen movement, see Yavuz and Esposito 2003.

68. The issue was contentious. The Islamist movement had been rocked by conspicuous sex scandals in the 1990s. For some these indicated opportunism and cynicism within the Islamist movement. For others they suggested problematic rifts between male leadership and female rank and file. Turkish Islamist novels thematized the issue. See Göle's discussion of the 1997 sex scandal involving a sheikh of the Aczmendi sect (Göle 2000, pp. 108–10). See also Ahıska and Yenal 2006, p. 203, for a discussion of more recent journalistic anxieties about "the explosion of sexuality amongst the Islam-

eras. Turkish mystical traditions call those seeking truth "lovers" (*aşıklar*). "Love" is one of the names Turkish Muslims give to God. Love provides a shared public idiom for talking about the nation and religion. These are contentious and divisive issues in Turkey, obviously enough. Şafak is speaking across the Islamist/secularist divide, and must pick her words carefully. Everybody might be persuaded to agree that love is "in crisis," and that this crisis touches secularists and Islamists, leftists and rightists, Turks and Kurds alike. Everybody might be persuaded to agree that, whatever else separates them, a definably Turkish "culture of love" brings them together.

From an outside perspective, of course, the exclusively "Turkish" nature of this "culture of love" is open to question. Its connections with a pan-Islamic culture of love stretching from Spain to India are striking. It is certainly very closely shared with Turkey's near-neighbors in Iran and the Arab world. And from another angle, the role of love in fashioning selves and other identities has been theorized, globally, as a distinctly modern phenomenon (Giddens 1992) shared by all who construct modern senses of self. But let us dwell for a moment on the specificities of the Turkish case.

A historical understanding of cultures of love in the region necessarily relies heavily on the literary record. In the Ottoman case, the record has been extremely rich. Andrews and Kalpaklı dub the period from 1550 to1622 "the Age of Beloveds" on this account (Andrews and Kalpaklı 2005). This period is marked by the consolidation of Ottoman rule in the Balkans, by the development of a courtly culture in Istanbul, migration from the provinces, by the expansion of the Sufi orders and *medrese* education, by the institutionalization of *meyhane*-s and coffee houses, and, above all, by poetry.[69] As Andrews shows in an earlier study (Andrews 1984), the lyric (*gazel*) poetry of this period drew on earlier Persian models representing intimate scenarios characterized by time and place (the garden, the nighttime gathering), sensory saturation (wine, food, perfumes, spices, and musicians), and intense emotionality (the suffering lover, conversation amongst friends and fellow-sufferers). *Hicran*, a bittersweet state of loneliness, suffering, and vulnerability, dominated all.[70]

---

ists," and see Göle 2000 and Çayır 2006 for thought-provoking discussions of Islamist novels. Most readers, like myself, would have had this general, anxiety-laden background in mind.

69. As Holbrook, in a study of a later period, points out: "The extent of Ottoman poetic production appears today extraordinary; everyone 'scribbled'—bureaucrats and pedagogues, pashas and sultans, as well as professional poets. . . . One thing that every member of the ruling classes, from Şeyhülislam to village imam, from Grand Vizier to governor's protégé, was 'reading' and 'writing' poetry" (Holbrook 1984, p. 111).

70. An extensive vocabulary describes the suffering of the lover (*gam*, grief; *ah* and *figan*, the lover's wail; *yaş* and *'eşk*, the tear; *bela*, *derd* and *cefa*, states of torment and helplessness; *kan*, *tığ* and *hun*,

Andrews and Kalpaklı read the lyric poetry of this period in conjunction with contemporary courtly poetry from Renaissance Europe, noting the ways in which absolutism in a variety of contexts generated "very similar deployments of desire and very similar cultural products" (Andrews and Kalpaklı 2005, p. 269). These deployments of desire were homoerotic, mystical, and reflections of and on courtly power relations. Power relations were "persistently eroticized" (Andrews and Kalpaklı 2005, p. 28). As they observe, courtier and courtesan ("addicts of love") ". . . quite literally cannot imagine their lives outside the metaphors and actualities of love" (Andrews and Kalpaklı 2005, p. 250). In addition, the religious culture of the time understood both *"mecazi"* ("metaphorical," i.e., worldly) and *"hakkiki"* ("real," i.e., divine) love as being necessary components of the spiritual life. Only later did Neoplatonist conceptions of love come to prevail, and with them a sense that metaphorical love was to be understood "only" as metaphor—divorced, that is to say, from the matter of physical desire and bodily urgings.[71]

But much was changing during the Age of Beloveds. Andrews and Kalpaklı show how the Ottoman lyric bore the marks of broader political transformations. Population growth and inflation across Anatolia created political instability. The period was increasingly marked by peasant revolts and a climate of anxiety about unruly young men (mercenaries, *medrese* students, mendicant dervishes) in the Ottoman capital. A growing bureaucracy and a climate of puritanical reformism began to alienate the poets. Elites turned to markets to ensure their livelihoods as the palace became increasingly cash-strapped. The execution of Osman II in 1622 marked the end of an era. The poetic system in the Age of Beloveds accommodated, but was also pressured by, new currents of violence, emerging forms of political authority, and economic stratification.

However much marked by the structures of absolutism, the culture of love in this period was incipiently egalitarian for Andrews and Kalpaklı. Tales of affection across the religious divide of the early modern Mediterra-

---

signs of woundedness; *ateş, nar,* burning; and so forth. Andrews provides a vocabulary of about seventy such terms (Andrews 1984, p. 45). For detailed discussion of *hicran*, see Andrews 1984, p. 136.

71. In a later period, Victoria Holbrook makes a somewhat similar point in relation to modern Turkish readings of Şeyh Galib's 1782 mystic romance *Hüsn ü aşk* (Beauty and love). There are multiple ironies at play here, as Holbrook skillfully notes. Literary modernism has generally validated the aesthetic as an autonomous domain, yet Turkish modernists found Ottoman lyric and mystical poetry lacking in realism and thus lacking an organic connection to social and political process. It took sustained and systematic efforts, in other words, to banish complex and playful works like *Hüsn ü aşk* from the realm of the modern or the protomodern in Turkish literary study. See Holbrook 1994, p. 120.

nean implied that love knew no bounds and leveled all. The homoerotic element in Ottoman poetry expressed the possibility of love between equals; such a relationship was considered unlikely at the time between men and women. Though the beloved is always ultimately the ruler, and the lover the courtier, the poems stage subtle role reversals and table-turnings.[72] In many parts of the early modern world, the language of love expressed an emerging dispensation of sympathy that was later to be explored philosophically by Adam Smith and David Hume, and politically in the American Revolution. Its central question was: how might it feel to be in another person's shoes? What might be involved in setting up a society organized around affectionate sensibilities? This (sentimental) question was fundamental to republican political philosophy. Evolving historical conditions dictated a variety of answers. In America, for instance, the quest for territory and industrial growth quickly pushed sentimentalism to the ideological margins. It was to be resuscitated in the twentieth century only in ways that blunted or masked its inherent radicalism.[73]

However tempting it might be to regard it as simply an extension or echo of Andrews and Kalpaklı's Ottoman "Age of Beloveds," Turkey's culture of love today is marked by distinctly modern circumstances. These are also broadly shared. The republics of the postcolonial world, amongst which Turkey might be ambiguously counted, deployed a sentimental language of affection and intimacy in the forging of independent national identities.[74] This independence would often prove tenuous, provoking retrenchments into fantasies of racial purity and the (always threatened) authenticity of national cultural heritage. Authoritarian political cultures presented their heads of state as benign father figures, and the duty of citizens as first and foremost one of affection. Turkey has not been exceptional in this regard.[75]

More recently, late capitalism has pressed sentimentalism globally into the service of the "market state," in Turkey as elsewhere.[76] Public provi-

---

72. As Andrews and Kalpaklı note of the early seventeenth-century story of Tayyib and Tahir (two lovers who were captured by Christians and eventually fell in love with the captors, who then secured their release), such stories culminate "in a series of reversals from which the lovers and beloveds emerge into a new, more equal distribution of power" (Andrews and Kalpaklı 2005, p. 267).

73. Julie Ellison describes in these terms the evocation and manipulation of Smithian sentimentalism by the right-wing Cato Institute in America (Ellison 1999). See also the final chapter of this book.

74. See Kandiyoti 2002 for an argument about Turkey's "postcolonial" status.

75. Lisa Wedeen's analysis of the Asad cult in neighboring Syria (Wedeen 1999) bears comparison, and my brief observations here owe much to her systematic and rigorously theorized study. On republican intimacies in Turkey, see Özyürek 2006.

76. I follow Balakrishnan's (2003) usage of the term "market state," though he himself is not particularly interested in questions that fall under the category of "cultural intimacy."

sioning and warmongering are franchised to increasingly unaccountable private agencies. States project themselves as guardians of private morality. Relationships between public and private are subject to complex inversions; their original (liberal) meanings collapse. Sentimentalism has mediated the process. In Turkey, as elsewhere, the production of sentimental public discourse and imagery is increasingly in private hands, not those of the state (Özyürek 2006). The broader question here is, then, one of sentimentalism in late modernity and modernism.

There are three critical positions that strike me as being particularly important in this regard. The first is associated with Roland Barthes. With the secularization of Western concepts of love, and modernism's commitment to "an erotics of unfulfilled and unfulfillable desire as the condition for amorous and linguistic experience" (Clark 1991, p. 209), sentimentalism becomes, in Barthes's terms, an "unwarranted discourse." "This discourse," he says, "is spoken, perhaps, by thousands of subjects (who knows?), but warranted by no one; it is disparaged, or derided by them, severed from authority but also the mechanisms of authority (sciences, techniques, arts)" (Barthes 1979, p. 1). "By a reversal of values, then," Barthes concludes, "it is sentimentality which today constitutes love's obscenity" (Barthes 1979, p. 175).

For Barthes, the challenge posed by the "lover's discourse" is to understand how it works as a system of signs. Disparaged, derided, and severed from authority, it takes convoluted forms. "To try to write love," he says, "is to confront to the *muck* of language: that region of hysteria where language is both *too much* and *too little*, excessive (by the limitless expansion of the ego, by emotive submersion) and impoverished (by the codes on which love diminishes and levels it)" (Barthes 1979, p. 99). Like all meaning-producing systems for Barthes, this confrontation engages the body, with its constitutive lacks, desires, and suffering. In sentimentalism the general issue is simply more accented, more quickly identified as a kind of *écriture feminine*.

I am interested in the post-structuralist characterization of sentimentalism as "unwarranted discourse," and the language Barthes uses to describe its challenges. He evokes its embarrassment, its elusiveness, its pleasures, its threats, its unruly politics. But he is reluctant to engage with its social, political, and historical specificities. I am interested here in *how* such unwarranted discourses are marginalized, by whom, to what ends, and with what consequences for which people. These are, at root, questions about *distribution* in a social economy of affect—questions demanding a historical and ethnographic approach.

The second position addresses precisely such questions of distribution.

In a series of articles and books on literature, sentiment, and sexuality in the North American public sphere, Lauren Berlant and Michael Warner discuss "cultural intimacy" in ways that connect closely with Andrews and Kalpaklı's theorization of "cultures of love."[77] In a stark claim that reverberates throughout this book, Berlant and Warner describe cultural intimacy as "the mechanism by which a core national culture can be imagined as a sanitized space of sentimental feeling and immaculate behavior, a space of pure citizenship. . . . A familial model of society displaces the recognition of structural racism and other systemic inequalities" (Berlant and Warner 1998, p. 549).[78]

A simplistic reading of these sentences would suggest cultural intimacy as a conventional Marxian problematic of "false consciousness." But they and other contributors to the *Public Culture* special issue on cultural intimacy (Berlant 1998) also understand it as a space of tension, of competing and antagonistic claims. Contradictions in the ideology of nuclear family and romantic love have been exposed by contemporary conditions, presenting those who understand the world in these terms with problems and dilemmas. What kinds of family life are afforded by global conditions of labor migrancy? What kinds of love can survive the overcrowded domestic conditions of life in the shantytowns of the modern metropolis? What happens to marriage when the expenses associated with it become impossible to achieve? The central institutions of intimacy survive and adapt, but not without cost to the ideological coherence of the modern nuclear family and the institutions of companionate heterosexual love so insistently championed by the managers of the new market state. The cracks are seldom difficult to perceive—which, for Berlant and Warner and their fellow contributors, accounts for the society-wide currents of anxiety that surround intimacy, the ever-intensifying efforts to secure its meanings, and the repetitious evocation of threats to it.

A third position is associated with Michael Herzfeld's *Cultural Intimacy: Social Poetics and the Nation-State* (Herzfeld 1997). It uses different language but describes intuitions similar to those of Lauren Berlant and Michael War-

---

77. See Berlant and Warner 1998; Berlant 1997, 1998, and 2008; and Warner 2002. For my own efforts to connect this writing to theories of sentimentalism, see Stokes 2007a, a "reading" of Adam Smith's *Theory of Moral Sentiment* (Smith 1984) in an Egyptian context, thoroughly informed by Griswold 1999.

78. Later, in a similar vein, they describe cultural intimacy as "the endlessly cited elsewhere of political public discourse, a promised haven that distracts citizens from the unequal conditions of their political and economic lives, consoles them for the damaged humanity of mass society, and shames them for any divergence between their lives and the intimate sphere that is alleged to be simple personhood" (Berlant and Warner 1998, p. 553).

ner. This book is particularly useful for my purposes here, since it is ethnographic and derives from Herzfeld's work in Turkey's neighbor Greece. For Herzfeld, cultural intimacy is a "recognition of those aspects of a cultural identity that are considered a source of external embarrassment but that nevertheless provide insiders with their assurance of common sociality, the familiarity with the bases of power that may at one moment assure the disenfranchised a degree of creative irreverence and at the next moment reinforce the effectiveness of intimidation" (Herzfeld 1997, p. 3). And later: "Embarrassment, rueful self-recognition: these are the key markers of what cultural intimacy is about" (Herzfeld 1997, p. 6).

Herzfeld is not narrowly concerned with discourses of love, but Şafak's article might well be understood in his terms. The failure of Turks to live up to their own high ideals about love is truly a source of embarrassment for Şafak and others. To be Turkish and thus a second-class citizen of the world is one source of (implied) humiliation, eliciting well-known jokes and other kinds of self-deprecating but ultimately reassuring humor. To be lousy lovers, on the other hand . . . a truly sorry state of affairs! But one, at least, that everyone—Islamist and secularist, leftist and rightist, Turk and Kurd—might be persuaded to agree is a real issue. Discursively speaking, it evokes common ground, core values, Herzfeld's "assurance of shared sociality."

Herzfeld's definition of cultural intimacy also alerts us to the distinctly critical tone of Şafak's article, one with which most *Zaman* readers, though hardly "disenfranchised," might be in agreement. Throughout its short history the Turkish state has spoken to its citizens in the persona of a benign paterfamilias who has loved his nation to excess and demanded nothing less in return. To observe at the most general level that love is in crisis in Turkey is to note a deterioration of the republic's fundamental social contract, to hint at the political violence and authoritarianism that the culture of love has licensed. Şafak's comments about love perform a "familiarity with the bases of power" in the modern Turkish republic, in particular those ideological mechanisms that order and coerce in the name of love and affection. So talk about love engages power directly, not evasively.

What follows in this book might be described as a cultural history of Turkey's "liberal period" (1950 to the present). It would be reasonable to argue that this is, politically speaking, a simplistic characterization of a turbulent period—one that has, moreover, seldom been particularly "liberal." But religion, political pluralism, the market, and an orientation to "outside" forces we would now label "globalization"—all set within the context of a hitherto authoritarian, secular, and generally inward-looking political culture—have structured the entire period. "Liberal" is certainly a debatable word, but it might perhaps be justified if my premises about the underlying continuities of Turkish public life are accepted. Whatever its drawbacks, the term "liberal period" is intended to draw attention here to the broader patterns of Turkish culture between 1950 and the present day. In particular, it enables me to point to the ways in which a sustained public discourse about love has mediated the underlying tensions and contradictions of the whole period.

What follows is also a rather specific argument about music and musicians. I argue that Turkish musicians have played a vitally important (and hitherto neglected) role in the liberal period's public discourses and transformations. I propose an understanding of these transformations in the next three chapters as a kind of sequence: Zeki Müren, Orhan Gencebay, Sezen Aksu. These three figures have, each in turn, dominated the popular cultural landscape in Turkey. They have done so not simply as inert objects of verbal discourse, but as *music makers*. The next chapters of this book will explore how musical meanings and practices have been central to the broader configuration of the Republic of Love and its transformations.

# 2

# Zeki Müren:
# Sun of Art, Ideal Citizen

When queer nightclub star Zeki Müren died in 1996, the nation mourned and commentators and fans contemplated a complex legacy. In the years immediately following his death, old recordings and films slowly materialized and broader stretches came into view of a remarkable career, until then largely remembered in terms of the kitsch and camp of his latter years. A consistent theme emerged: Zeki Müren as "model citizen." This chapter explores that characterization and its entanglement with issues of cultural intimacy.

The theme began to emerge in the very first obituaries. The nation, many declared, had lost not only a great Turkish artist but also a great *citizen*. Müren cared about the national development of his art and advanced it as nobody else had. He donated half of his fortune to the Mehmetçik Vakfı, a foundation that serves army veterans, and half to the Turkish Education Foundation. When he sang, he spoke to inhabitants of the Turkish Republic as a fellow citizen. The entire *millet*, the national community, felt the pain of his death.[1] The citizenship narrative became, if anything, more emphatic over time. For example, Emine Aşan's biography of the singer, published in 2003, ends with a chapter entitled "He Was the Model Citizen" (*Örnek yurttaştı o*).

---

1. Obituaries from all of the major papers are collected at http://www.sanatgunesi.com/.

This is, on the face of it, a counterintuitive assertion given Müren's flamboyant (though never verbally declared) queerness.[2] Responses to his queerness have been ambivalent in Turkey. "Fear of the effeminate man" runs deep there, as Elif Şafak suggests (Shafak 2004, p. 27). Many simply chose to ignore this aspect of Müren's personality, or to affect innocence.[3] Yet relatively few people objected publicly,[4] and in the years following his death the theme of his queerness emerged as an explicit topic of public conversation. It could be read as a sign of spirituality, of identification with the male-male friendships canonized in Turkish Sufism. It could be taken as a sign of sincerity in an insincere, cynical age or, conversely, of worldliness, wiliness, and urbanity in an age that prefers crass moral simplicities. It could be read as love uncoupled from family and reproduction, and thus given freely to the nation. As we shall see, these kinds of interpretations played a significant role in Müren's designation as "model citizen". We must contextualize them, though, in an account of his life and his music, and show how they are entangled.

## A Brief Biography

Zeki Müren was born in the provincial city of Bursa on 6 December 1931,[5] the son of a moderately wealthy tobacco and timber merchant. Bursa nur-

---

2. Queer culture and camp are usually considered as critical operations, as a commentary on the heteronormativity central to modern institutions (see Cleto 1999). In the United States in recent years, as is well known, questions about homosexuality in public life have repeatedly orchestrated nationwide moral panics. Turkish society is a little different in this regard. It has for a long time made space for queer culture, not only in music and dance (see Ellingsen 1997, Altınay 2008), but also in many scattered areas of public life (see Kandiyoti 1994). See also Shafak 2004.

3. Perhaps the most common response whenever the topic of conversation comes up, particularly amongst people my own age or a little older (i.e., people in their forties or fifties), is, "Would you believe it; when I was a kid we never used to think of him as gay." Such declarations of ignorance quickly unravel in further conversation. I take entirely seriously here the point that "queer" was not a public and labeled social category in the 1950s and 1960s in Turkey. There were, however, many ways in which his queerness was publicly (though tacitly and euphemistically) negotiated at the time. See the last section of this chapter, where the issue is discussed in more depth.

4. An article on fetishism in Turkey in *Haftalık dergisi*, 15 July 2004, describes it as "the second biggest issue to make all hell break loose in Turkey, after Zeki Müren [*Zeki Müren sonrası Türkiye'de gerçekleşen en büyük ikinci 'başımıza taş yağacak' denemesi*)] (quoted in Ahıska and Yenal 2006, p. 204). It begins, "Good luck to a country that had difficulty stomaching Zeki Müren [*Zeki Müren'i zor hazmeden milletimize hayırlı olsun*]." One rarely comes across such directly negative references to Müren's sexuality in the Turkish press. Passing comments such as these suggest that one should be cautious about assuming a climate of unquestioning tolerance.

5. In his well-known poem "Biyografim" (1965, p.127), Müren gives his own birth date as 6 December 1933. It is difficult to know whether this rewriting is a matter of authorial vanity or a re-

tured a large number of well-known popular classical musicians. The city's prosperity rested on its rich agricultural hinterland, its industrial development during the early republican years, and its proximity to Istanbul's markets. This nourished an energetic and urbane bourgeoisie with close ties to cultural life in Istanbul.

Business contacts from Bursa took Müren under their wing in Istanbul, where his father sent him to complete his education, initially as a boarder at the Boğaziçi High School (1946–47) and then at the Fine Arts Academy in Istanbul.[6] Soon he was taking lessons from Şerif İçli, Kadri Şençalar, Refik Fersan, and Sadi Işılay, notables at the Turkish Radio station nearby. An early composition, "Zehretme hayatı bana cananım," was broadcast in 1949 or 1950 (the date seems difficult to ascertain), sung by Suzan Güven. Later in 1950 Müren successfully auditioned for a salaried post as a vocalist there.[7]

His first big break was a live broadcast on 1 January 1951. This has been the subject of numerous retellings (Aksoy 2002; Hiçyılmaz 1997; Aşan 2003) and of various reminiscences by Müren himself (Müren 1996). Most accounts relate that Perihan Altındağ, one of the leading female classical singers of the time, had been taken ill. Refik Fersan phoned Müren and asked him to take her place, apologizing for the short notice. Another version, related by Hiçyılmaz (1997, pp. 40–41), drawing on an interview with Müren shortly before his death, asserts that Altındağ was ill and sent a message suggesting that one of her recordings for the commercial market be played instead. Then, as forty years later, the radio station placed a high premium on live performance. Turkish Radio's director at the time, Zahir

---

flection of the confusion engendered by the common practice of announcing dates of birth later than their actual occurrence. The overt rationale for this practice is that it enables families to have the productive and emotional resources of their male children in the family for a longer period of time than would otherwise be the case. Adulthood begins when military service begins. The date 1931 comes from Rona 1970, and is accepted by most biographers.

6. Aşan notes that Bursalı tobacco merchant Hayri Terzioğlu took Müren under his wing while at the Güzel Sanatlar Akademisi. She also mentions that Müren died in possession of three trillion Turkish liras worth of Bursa Cement shares, suggesting that he maintained close ties with Bursalı elites (Aşan 2003, p. 118). (Three trillion Turkish liras would have been nearly two million U.S. dollars at the time Aşan was writing. It is difficult, though, given inflation, currency devaluation, and so forth, to know exactly what this figure represents today, other than a very large sum of money). Agapos Efendi and Udi Kirkor were Müren's first music teachers.

7. According to Kocabaşoğlu (1980, pp. 296–97) Turkish Radio devoted around 30 percent of its airtime and a significant proportion of its budget (relative to other musical genres) in this decade to Turkish art music—the largest of any programming category. Istanbul Radio's art music section therefore would have been recruiting during this period.

Törümkümey, was apparently furious. "Why do we have to put up with this nonsense from soloists? They pile insult on insult. What does she mean, 'Play my record?' I won't do it. Find me a soloist instead."

Müren was recommended, and after some frantic phone calls with friends and Turkish radio musicians about repertoire, the choice of *makam* (mode), and so forth,[8] Müren turned up at the radio studio. He had the good fortune to be playing with a particularly experienced instrumental group.[9] But the program selected was demanding.[10] By all accounts there had been only the briefest of rehearsals before the program started, and the concert was being broadcast live. Müren and the musicians had forty-five minutes to fill. To general consternation, their planned program came to an end eight minutes early. Şükrü Tunar, the clarinet player, produced a short *taksim* (an instrumental improvisation), giving the vocalist and the other musicians a moment to consider their options. Entirely unrehearsed, Zeki Müren launched into a *maya* (a vocal improvisation in a rural idiom), "Yürü dilber de yürü, yolundan kalma," accompanied by the clarinetist.[11] This still left them with a minute of potential dead air. Müren then leapt in for a second time with a perfectly timed fragment of a folk song, "Hem okudum, hem de yazdım," without missing a beat. Or so the story goes.

Accounts of the 1951 radio concert are indeed clouded in dense layers of mythology, many added by Müren himself. But a number of things seem clear in retrospect.[12] Müren was, from the outset, remarkably surefooted in

---

8. The *makam*-s chosen were a sequence of songs in *hicaz*, then *bayyati* and *uşşak*. Details of these *makam*-s can be found in Signell 1977. Suffice it to say here that they were popular rather than abstruse, and that *uşşak* shares much with the modes of folk music, in terms of intonation and modal process—especially in its lower tetrachord. A fuller explanation of *makam*, for those unfamiliar with the concept, will be found in the next section, where I discuss "Menekşelendi sular."

9. According to Hiçyılmaz, the ensemble comprised Hakkı Derman (violin), Şeref İçli (oud), Necdet Gezen, and Şükrü Tunar (clarinet) (Hiçyılmaz 1997, p. 42). Aşan (2003) adds Refik Fersan (*tanbur*). Aksoy (2002), however, in a more detailed set of quotes from Zeki Müren himself, suggests that ensembles of three members were the norm at the time, and that only İçli, Derman, and Tunar were playing.

10. It ranged from Sadullah Ağa and Dede Efendi (eighteenth-century classical repertory) to Şevki Bey (late nineteenth century), to Salahattin Pınar (who died in 1960, and many of whose works Müren sang later in his life).

11. Aksoy's interview material (Aksoy 2002) gives "Yiğidin alnına yazılan gelir" as the title of this *maya*.

12. Live broadcasts were evidently not taped during that period, so this highly mythologized moment is not available for direct musical consideration today. The earliest of Müren's Turkish Radio recordings that are now publicly available date from 1955 (Aksoy 2002). From these, one can get some sense of the voice that stunned listeners in 1951.

his handling of *makam*,[13] repertoire,[14] and diction.[15] His voice was even and controlled from baritone to high tenor range, and entirely individual despite being firmly and clearly rooted in the classical vocal art of the immediately preceding generation. It is also clear in retrospect that even at this early stage Müren could keep his cool under pressure and lead a performance. He filled an unexpected silence with an entirely apposite fragment of music, continuing the folkish theme of the *maya* improvisation and providing an appropri-

---

13. Some *makam*-s are understood today to be complex, difficult, and "academic" while others are relatively easy and "popular," which is not to say that difficult or academic songs or instrumental pieces exist in the repertoire. On the "difficult" side, a compound (*birleştirilmiş*) *makam* combines the characteristics of two, requiring detailed knowledge of how each works and how they are combined. Transposed modes (*şedd* or *göçürülmüş*) involve knowledge of the different rules and cadences appropriate to specific transpositions. *Makam*-s might be described as "complex" also in the sense that their performance is associated with detailed rules or with difficulties, such as lying high in the tessitura. Müren made a number of radio recordings in "difficult" *makam*-s, many of which can be easily located today (note, for instance, the 1955-63 recordings issued by Kalan, which cover *dilkeşhaveran, neva, hisarbuselik, acemkürdi, suznak,* and *şedaraban,* amongst others). Over the course of his career, *nihavent, hicaz, hicazkar, rast, uşşak* and *segah* could all be described as lying on the "common" or "popular" side of the continuum. On the emergence of *nihavent* as a particularly important and popular signifier of melancholy, see below. *Makam*-s have gone in and out of fashion, evolving and falling out of favor according to slow historical processes well described by Feldman (1996) and Wright (2000).

14. The earlier pieces in this and other surviving radio concert recordings employed a complex Ottoman vocabulary with longer vocal lines in, or modulating to, more obscure and compound *makam*-s and in longer and more complex rhythmic modes; these range in time roughly from Dede Efendi (1778–1846) to Hacı Arif Bey (1831–1885). Lyric song, by contrast, would be represented in these early recordings by the more or less contemporary works of Lemi Atlı, Salahattin Pınar, Sadettin Kaynak, and Müren himself. Many of these are in familiar and simple *makam*-s (see note 13 above), and in relatively simple duple, triple, or compound rhythmic modes, using a language closer to everyday spoken Turkish.

15. He was later to comment that those listening that day found themselves in the presence of "a childish voice; but [one] utterly soft [*yumuşak*], utterly lyrical [*lirik*]. It articulated a bunch of wild [*vahşi*], hard-to-pronounce words with great ease [*sükunet*]. An affective [*etkili*] voice. Everyone was amazed" (cited in Hiçyılmaz 1997, p. 41). Even allowing for Müren's habit of genteel hyperbole, the correct pronunciation of complex Ottoman texts in musical performance was evidently highly prized. Consider, by way of a later example, the following recollection from Amir Ateş, a distinguished classical musician and composer associated with TRT. "We were listening [together with Müren] to his version of a song in *nihavent*, 'Bir kere bakanlar unutur derdi günahı.' When we got to the section containing the line '*Görmem gözümün nuruna daldıkça sabahı,*' I was just amazed [*adeta hayretler içinde kaldım*]. Because Zeki Bey interpreted this section like one who knew Qur'anic cantillation [*tecvit*] and old Turkish [i.e., Ottoman]. Whereas the vocalists of the day would pronounce the word 'nuruna,' Zeki Bey would pronounce it 'nuuruna.' The dearly departed was, anyway, somebody who would pronounce words giving individual attention to each; that was really his speciality" (Ateş 2008, p. 51). The point being that Müren not only knew the older and more orthographically correct pronunciation ("spelling out" the long vowel as distinguished in the Ottoman script but not the modern Turkish), but would have been aware of its relation to the *aruz*, or classical metrical scheme.

ate closure. He had already struck up a remarkable musical understanding with the clarinetist Tunar, without whose quickness and adaptability these last improvisations could not have worked. The two were to work together for the rest of Tunar's life.[16] Even in this thoroughly administered and bureaucratized space, Müren could improvise, work with the ensemble, and make a performance his own. Within a year his Saturday evening concert slots were an institution.[17]

Müren followed up with moves into the worlds of sound recording, film, and *gazino* (nightclub) performance. He often rationalized his commercial sound recordings and films as ways of making himself available to "the common people" (the *halk*), who didn't have the chance to see or hear him in Istanbul. His first commercial recording was "Bir muhabbet kuşu," a composition of Tunar's.[18] Thus began a successful association with RCA Victor (HMV/Sahibin Sesi) and later Grafson. Some 120 of Müren's 45 rpm singles from these early years, mostly newly composed pieces by the classical composers of the day, are listed in Hiçyılmaz's discography.[19]

These were heard across the country. In his obituary for Müren, Ayhan Katırcıkara gave an interesting picture of the conditions of radio and record listening habits at that time in a remote province.

> I grew up in Kilis [on the Syrian border]. Next to the Great Mosque was the "Little Market," where our house was. At the beginning of the

---

16. Şükrü Tunar died onstage while accompanying Müren at Cumhuriyet Gazinosu in 1962. See Rona 1970, p. 538, for a brief biography of Tunar.

17. Early in 1953 Müren's regular slot, 9:20 to 10:00 p.m., was identified with his name in the radio listings in *Radyonun Sesi* (The voice of the radio)—a distinction reserved for a relatively small handful of Turkish radio stars. He was not, at least in the early years, a "*kadrolu*" member of the TRT—on a full-time salary, in other words—because he was a student. This restricted the amount of radio work he could do (Işık 1951, p. 12). Much later, during an interview in *Hey* 2 (5) 1971, pp. 34–35, he was taken to task by the (anonymous) interviewer for the diminishing frequency of his radio and television performances. Müren replied: "I sang every Saturday at 9:00 p.m. for fifteen years. . . . One day they said I could only have a fifteen-minute slot. By then I was singing for about fifteen minutes in advertisements. What, then, was the point of singing for TRT?" The details may be inaccurate, but they reflect a period of time in which his radio broadcasts became nationally prominent.

18. As he was to observe later, "Istanbul Radio couldn't be heard well across Anatolia. Those were the years in which Ankara Radio dominated Anatolia. One sees now just what a coincidence it was, the musician Şükrü Tunar picking me up from school, taking me to a record company in Yeşilköy, and having me sing his own piece, 'Muhabbet kuşu'; this introduced me to the whole of Anatolia" (Müren 1996).

19. Systematic discographic information on Müren is hard to find. Hiçyılmaz 1997 contains a discography (without dates) of his Grafson recordings. A non-comprehensive but still useful overview of his recordings can be found at www.sanatgunesi.com.

1950s there were few radios in people's homes. But most of us in the "Little Market" had radios. Particularly when the market was busy, the houses were opened up and people could listen to the songs.

Because Ankara Radio's signal was weak, people used to listen to Radio Damascus. They always used to play Safiye Ayla, Suzan Yakar, Perihan Altındağ, and Celal Şahin pieces on their Turkish program. And also Zeki Müren's. . . . A voice like velvet [*kadife gibi bir ses*] . . . it flows, sparklingly [*pırıl pırıl akıyor*]. . . . Turks having property in Syria, in those days people would could come and go with a safe conduct pass [*pasavan*]; those who owned land would in this way visit relatives, wives and friends. They would move from Aleppo to Kilis and from Kilis back to Aleppo as though it was nothing. And everyone who came to Kilis carried with them Zeki Müren records.[20] Because these were the most valuable presents.

There were two names in the area. One only had to mention the Egyptian Umm Kulthum or Zeki Müren from Turkey.[21] People would be enchanted [*mest*] when they heard them. . . . (Katırcıkara 1996)

It was commercial recordings, not radio, that made Zeki Müren's voice a national institution. Radio's range in those days was limited. Radio Istanbul did not extend much beyond the Marmara Sea region, and even there it could be hard to hear.[22] Radio Ankara evidently did not extend far into the east or the border regions. There were no transmitters east of Ankara. The number of radio sets per capita was still tiny, and mainly concentrated in large cities.[23] This, however, was obviously not true of record players.

Riding high on the success of his first radio broadcasts and recordings, Müren made his first musical film, *Beklenen şarkı,* probably in 1953. One of his father's partners in the tobacco industry, İhsan Doruk, was a success-

---

20. The anecdote implies, then, that Turks bought their recordings of Müren—along with those of Umm Kulthum, one assumes—in Aleppo, Syria, and then bought them back across the Turkish border to Kilis. Aleppo would indeed have been the nearest large city at that time. Information on Aleppo radio broadcasting in the early 1950s is hard to come by.

21. Müren could be, and often was, identified as "the Turkish Umm Kulthum." He was positioned, in other words, as Kulthum's rival, or at least equivalent, in a related world of musical "enchantment" (*tarab*; see Racy 2003).

22. In 1950 a note in *Resimli Radyo Dünyası* 1 (1), p. 19, indicated that Radio Istanbul then broadcasted at 5,000 watts, Radio Ankara at 120,000 watts. Müren himself remembers listening to Radio Ankara in preference to Radio Istanbul even in Bursa.

23. Kocabaşoğlu suggests 1.7 percent in 1950 and 4.9 percent in 1960. Despite this increase in the number of radio sets, the proportion of such sets concentrated in cities remained constant at around 70 percent; see Kocabaşoğlu 1980, p. 289.

ful Istanbul businessman married to fledgling film star Cahide Sonku. The film, the first made by Doruk's own production company, depicted Müren (here playing a character named Zeki) as a struggling artist falling in love with Sonku. Unbeknownst to all parties, Zeki's father, also a musician, had once been in love with the mother of Sonku's character and had composed a song for her: the *"beklenen şarkı"* ("awaited song") of the film's title. Half of the written notes for the song are in her possession, and the other half in Zeki's. Through various twists and turns, the song eventually brings all of the elements of the plot together. The music was composed by Sadi Işılay.[24] Biographers often note Müren's insistence on speaking his own part (see, for example, Aşan 2003, p. 35). At that time, spoken parts were normally dubbed by professional Istanbul actors. Müren's refusal to conform to this convention suggests an early effort to control his public representation in a period during which the division of labor in the Turkish film industry, and the place of stars within it, was apparently still unsettled.[25]

*Son beste* (1955), produced by Erman Kardeşler, seems to have hit a more successful commercial formula, with the singer more firmly in the center of the picture. The music was composed by Müren, and a song repeated as a refrain in several parts of the film became one of his most highly selling and best known: "Manolyam." This film portrays Zeki Müren as a struggling musician, sharing a bachelor household with two riotous friends.[26] An invitation to sing at an aristocratic musical gathering is made possible when an

---

24. Sadi Işılay, a violin player teaching at the Istanbul Conservatory and a seasoned composer and performer in various branches of the Turkish popular music industry, lived a life typical for many jobbing professional musicians in the early republican period. Born in 1898 in Istanbul, he learned his musical skills in the café his father ran in Laleli, in Ismail Hakkı Bey's Musiki-i Osmanî music society, and alongside Tanburi Cemil Bey and Ziya Bey at aristocratic household gatherings before the declaration of the republic. He worked briefly as a primary school music teacher, then in France making recordings for the Turkish recording industry for three years. Later in life he became a member of the Istanbul Conservatory. He died in 1969. This was a highly cosmopolitan musical life, embracing official and popular music-making in the cultural order of the Ottomans and the new republic. See Rona 1970, pp. 453–54.

25. Much that has been published on Turkish cinema is concerned with art cinema. For a more socially inclusive year-by-year account of Turkish cinema, see http://www.sineport.com/turk/6170.html. For a detailed filmography of Müren, see Hiçyılmaz 1997, pp. 193–95.

26. The similarity between this film (based on a novel by Kerime Nadir) and Abd al-Halim's 1955 film *Ayamina al-hilwa* (costarring Omar al-Sharif), as well as the relationship between these films and Henri Mürger's *Scènes de la vie de bohème,* which formed the basis for Guiseppe Giacosa and Luigi Illica's libretto for Puccini's *La bohème,* is not coincidental. There was significant popular cultural traffic between Egypt and Turkey in this period, and it particularly included local literary versions of the sentimental classics of eighteenth- and nineteenth-century France. Both *Son beste* and *Ayamina al-hilwa* involve riotous bachelor households in the orbits of consumptive women (Fatin Hamama in al-Halim's film, and Belgin Doruk in Müren's film) who die tragically after the initially lighthearted plots take one heart-wrenching turn after another.

orphan, Nermin (Bedia Doruk), working in the local pawnshop, takes pity on him and lends him a tuxedo. They fall in love. But at the gathering Zeki meets the spoiled Semra (Neşe Yulaç), who snares him into giving her music lessons at her family's country estate and does all she can to make Zeki forget Nermin and love her instead. As the two true lovers struggle unsuccessfully to reconnect in Istanbul, Nermin succumbs to an illness. She collapses and dies while watching Zeki, now a star, performing "Manolyam" onstage for a rapt audience. The formula for this story was further developed in the seven films Müren made in the late 1950s and throughout the 1960s with Seden Films, one of the first companies to own their own production facilities in these early years. Müren continued to play the role of "Zeki" in sentimental romantic dramas: a young musician struggling to do the decent thing and find love against the odds.[27]

Müren made a total of sixteen films between *Beklenen şarkı* and *Aşktan da üstün* (1970). Though a number of the later ones involve more extravagant plots—with religious (*Berduş*, 1957), orientalist (*Hindistan cevizi*, 1966) and historical (*Katip*, 1968) themes very much of their time—the purpose of these films with their formulaic sentimental storylines was consistent and steady: to be an additional means of publicity, and provide a repetitive narrative component to the public myth of Zeki as the serious and sensitive artist. Both of these were crucial to success in that central arena of Müren's reputation: the *gazino*, an institution the singer was practically to make his own in the later 1950s and 1960s.

The 1950s and 1960s were a time of increasing market-fueled prosperity and rural-urban migration. Istanbul's nightclubs (*gazino*-s) were places of conspicuous consumption.[28] Nightclubs maintained orchestras of highly paid musicians (many of whom also worked at Turkish Radio),[29] and offered enormous salaries to the stars of the day. Müren signed contracts with two

---

27. As his first scriptwriter, Sadık Şendil, put it: "Before writing the script, I wondered what would Zeki be best at. He was still too young to play a father or a music teacher. Neither could he be a murderer or a smuggler. The best thing was for him to remain the same person the people had already fallen in love with. In other words, a young singer who enchanted people's ears with his voice. So Zeki remained Zeki." (Aşan 2003, p. 34)

28. *Resimli Radyo Dünyası*'s reporter, Tarık Gürcan, noted the lack of good live music venues in Istanbul and praised the local municipality's initiative in opening the Taksim Belediye Gazinosu early in 1953 (Gürcan 1953). It could seat 750 people, had good acoustics, was set up to facilitate live radio broadcasts by Radio Istanbul, and was open for matinee performances on Sundays. This seems increasingly to have been the pattern in Istanbul.

29. Hiçyılmaz records the names of the musicians employed by the Küçük Çiftlik Parkı in Istanbul, including Şeref İçli, Salahattin Pınar, İsmail Şençalar, Yorgo Bacanos, Kadri Sençalar, Necdet Gezen, Sevgi Aslangil, and Hakkı Derman—a who's who of popular classical musicians in the 1950s and 1960s.

of the biggest and most glamorous establishments of the time: the Küçük Çiftlik Parkı, run by Mahmut Anlar, from 1955, and Maksim, run by Fahrettin Aslan—the "*gazinocular kralı* (king of the *gazino* bosses)"—from 1960.[30] His 1,200 Turkish liras per night at Küçük Çiftlik and 3,500 Turkish liras per night for his performances at Maksim were astronomical figures even in those inflationary times (Aşan 2003, p. 44). Elaborate battles for prestige and attention in the *gazino*-s among the great singers of the time dominated the popular cultural journals of the period. Müren prevailed through an unrivaled and often innovatory command of performance detail, spectacular high camp, and various astute tactical moves. His rivals in the nightclub world soon began to disappear into the background.[31]

The intense publicity that surrounded these nightclub battles allows one to piece together some details of Müren's early *gazino* performances and thereby understand something of his significance as a performer.[32] The repertoire, for example, would typically follow a three-part pattern. The first would be urban and palace repertoire roughly from the late eighteenth to the late nineteenth century. The second would be "*sanat müziği*"—"art music" primarily for the concert hall, typically from the early twentieth century.[33] The third part would feature more contemporary art, popular, and folk music; Aşan (2003) suggests that it would range from music from popular Hindi and Egyptian film classics to the kinds of rural folk music that were popular amongst wealthy new migrants from the provinces.[34]

30. The main *gazino*-s were Küçük Çiftlik Parkı, Maksim, Tepebaşı, Türküaz, and Besiktaş Bahçesi, all of which were located around the European district of Beyoğlu and the Bosphorus shore. Later in the 1960s *gazino*-s started to expand around the old city districts of Aksaray and Yenikapı, and in and around Bebek, further up the Bosphorus. For a useful history of the *gazino* and the development of a *gazino*-specific musical style, see Beken 2003.

31. Among whom one would note mainly female singers such as Hamiyet Yüceses, Perihan Altındağ, and Mualla Mukadder, but also male vocalists such as Alaattin Yavaşca, and Adnan Pekak. By all accounts, the mere fact that Müren had been hired by one *gazino* had major effects elsewhere in the system. Somewhat later, for instance, the Çakıl Gazinosu became an important venue. When it secured Müren's services for a period, it was reported that other *gazino*-s were obliged to close temporarily, purportedly for restoration. Again, these claims would be exaggerated, but they serve to illustrate the climate of intense competition between the major *gazino*-s during this period. See Boran 1975.

32. For more or less contemporary information on his nightclub performances, see Güç 1996, Rona 1975, Hiçyılmaz 1997, Aşan 2003, Show TV's Aynalar documentary (which can be found at www.showtv.net), and Dedeman Topluluğu's review, *Bir demet yasemin*.

33. This section would often include songs by Selahattin Pınar (1902–1960), a sentimental composer closely associated with Müren.

34. Hindi cinema was popular in Turkey in the 1950s. Rajih Kapour's film *Avare*, for instance, was a major hit in the late 1950s. Its theme song is still known in Turkish belly-dancing circles. See, for example, http://home.earthlink.net/~evacernik/sema.htm. The musical influence of Hindi cinema in Turkey has yet to be researched.

We also learn something about the mechanics of spectacle in Müren's stage shows—in particular, the increasingly important role of costumes and décor.[35] The singer's outfits, many designed by fashion designer Ayla Eryüksel and tailored by Yalçın Say and Muzaffer Çağ (Aşan 2003, p. 89), had names presumably devised as part of the act: "Dağ gelinciği" (Mountain gelincik), "Zirvede açan lale" (The tulip opening on the mountain peak) "Eskimonun sevdası" (The Eskimo's love), "Kar mimozası" (The snow mimosa). Cassette boxes from a slightly later period give some idea (figure 2a). A strict dress code was imposed on musicians, too, down to details such as not wearing watches (and thus not distracting audiences by glancing anxiously at them during performances). Müren's stage persona may (Hiçyılmaz 1997) or may not (Aşan 2003) have taken a decisive turn after he had watched Liberace in Las Vegas early in the 1960s; that issue is still debated.[36] A T-shaped stage, an innovation at the time, allowed him to bring the spectacle closer to his listeners.

One also learns something about the subtle ways in which Müren handled the complex gendered dynamics of urban public life at this moment. To take one example, an elaborate press campaign stoked up the rivalry between Müren and Mualla Mukadder for the 1959–60 New Year's Eve parties in rival establishments.[37] Mukadder was reputedly planning a quasi-dramatic musical in which she would play the part of Venus in Botticelli's painting, rising from the waves on an oyster shell. All manner of camp fireworks must have been expected from Müren in response.

Müren's coup lay in realizing that the Gregorian calendar's new year coincided, in this particular year, with Regaip Kandili, a minor festival connected calendrically to Ramadan and, significantly, observed mainly by women. His program took place in an austerely decorated *gazino*; the music

---

35. *Hey*, then the major popular music journal (see chapter 3, note 24 for a brief history of this influential publication), ran a series of stories told in cartoon form called "Zeki Müren efsanesi" (The Zeki Müren legend), by Mümtaz Arıkan, in 1979. Arıkan was interested in the evolution of Müren's costumery in the 1950s; he includes what are possibly Müren's own words from previously published interviews or from oral tradition. According to Arıkan, the major transformation in Müren's stage show took place after his return from military service in 1956. It was at this point that Müren reputedly took the plunge, appearing on the T-shaped stage for the first time in a miniskirt. Müren had also had a pair of pants made in the same material; he agonized backstage over which item to wear, and waited until the very last moment before making up his mind. He is supposed to have said: "What is important, my dear sir, is the reaction of the people. I would not disrespect that reaction [*Ben o tepkiyi karşı durmam*]" (Arıkan 1979, p. 11).

36. Aşan's efforts to make Müren not look derivative—repeating Müren's own protests that he had started to dress as he did long before hearing of Liberace—are understandable, but Hiçyılmaz's point seems more plausible.

37. The anecdote appears in Hiçyılmaz 1997.

**Figure 2a.** Illustration from Zeki Müren cassette box (*Dilek çeşmesi*, Raks).

was restrained, classical, and severe. Though Müren was associated with camp spectacle, his acknowledgement of religious decorum—already a feature of his films—was also very much of its time.[38] Such sensitivity to women's religious practice, a complex and contradictory field during this period of aggressive secularization and Islamist reaction, allowed him and his managers to cultivate a female audience as no other nightclub singer had previously succeeded in doing.[39]

---

38. According to Hulusi Tunca this was an often-recurring scenario. Müren canceled his appearances at the Izmir fair during the 1976 season because of clashes with the Kandils, and later with the beginning of Ramadan (Tunca 1976). A cynic would note that his rival, Bülent Ersoy, had just appeared on the scene, and was to make an enormous impact that same year at a new prestige venue at the Izmir fair, the Büyük Efes Oteli (see Susoy 1976). So it is also entirely possible that Müren was choosing his battles carefully as usual. Many of his films made much of religious imagery. The death of Belgin Doruk in *Son Beste*, for example, is followed by a lengthy graveyard scene and a closing song functioning as a lament. *Berduş*, a film I have not yet managed to see, apparently shows Müren reciting prayers and sections of the Qur'an.

39. His matinee performances at the Küçük Çiftlik Parkı and Maksim specifically targeted female audiences and quickly became an institution at other *gazino*-s. Küçük Çiftlik Parkı's matinee

In the 1970s, Müren started to withdraw from *gazino* life and other public performances. Health issues began to make these excessively demanding. The music industry and the *gazino*-s, meanwhile, were beginning to cultivate a more proletarian kind of urban audience, to be discussed in more detail in chapter 3. In 1976 the singer released a typically grandiose response in the form of "Kahır mektubu" (The letter of sobs), whose title track was a twenty-minute song with contrasting sections and a recurrent refrain modeled directly on Umm Kulthum's *ughniyat* (Danielson 1997).[40] A number of *arabesk* cassettes followed in the 1980s. Critics generally noted his embrace of this genre with dismay, and most considered his voice to be in decline.[41] Müren retreated to Bodrum, where he spent his final years as a recluse.

His early career was shaped, then, by changing circumstances and opportunities in radio, commercial recordings, films, and *gazino* life. These in turn were shaped by the emergence of a new media and consumer order in Turkey, one that bore the marks of the significant contradictions of the dominant political order (religious reaction in a secular republic, economic liberalism in an authoritarian political culture). The public persona constructed during these early years was, then, capable of absorbing multiple and often contradictory identifications. Müren combined kitsch and high culture, camp and emotional sincerity, modernity and religious conservatism, visual spectacle and aural intimacy, an East-oriented cosmopolitanism and a West-oriented Turkish nationalism. Central to these complex processes of identification was his voice—to which, with the aid of one particular song, we shall now turn.

---

performances were advertised as *içkisiz aile matineleri* (alcohol-free family matinees) and took place on Sundays at 2:30 p.m. Those at Maksim took place on Wednesday and Sunday afternoons.

40. The song was composed by the singer's producer and mentor, Muzaffer Özpınar. It was apparently based on a chance encounter with an Umm Kulthum song heard in an Arab café in Paris (interview with the author and Anne Ellingson, S-Müzik offices, Levent, July 1996). Özpınar was particularly fascinated by its length and its recurring chorus. The shape and form of "Kahır mektubu" suggests that he may well have been listening to Kulthum's 1964 classic, composed by Mohammed Abd al-Wahhab, "Inta omri."

41. Müren's early *"piyasa"* ("commercial") and *arabesk* recordings received some very frosty reviews. The sentimentalism of "Oğlum"/ "Beni terketme," described as a "Western-style effort," was criticized by *Hey*'s (anonymous) reviewers in 1972, and the record was given two out of five stars, even as one of his art-music albums was riding high in the charts (*Hey* 2 (32), p. 17) *Hey*'s review of *Günah defteri* (1975) described Müren's vocal ornamentations (*gırtlak nağmeleri*, literally "throat melodies") as "excessive," for instance (*Hey* 5 (25), p. 58). That album received two out of four stars. Müren's move towards *arabesk* in the later 1970s slowly garnered critical approval, his vocal skills declared by some to be trumping weak material.

## "Menekşelendi Sular" (The Waters Went Violet)

In a corner of the Zeki Müren Museum in Bodrum (Müren's old house), one finds the program for his first concert. A marginal scribble by the singer notes that he often repeated this program.[42] It culminates with "Menekşelendi sular"—a song by a composer with whom Müren was deemed to have a particular affinity, Sadettin Kaynak. It is hard to tell, but the song probably dates from the 1930s and was reputedly written for another singer, Safiye Ayla, whose particular version of it will concern us shortly.

"Menekşelendi sular" (The waters went violet) was clearly an important song for Müren. It is not hard to see why he was drawn to it, as indeed were many others.[43] It is a *fantezi*,[44] artfully combining melancholia and vocal virtuosity. The lyrics describe a darkening evening and the poet as solitary observer, thinking about the absent lover, Ayşe.[45] They can be translated as follows:

| | |
|---|---|
| *Menekşelendi sular, sular menekşelendi* | Violet went the waters, the waters went violet |
| *Esmer yüzlü akşamı dinledim yine sensiz* | I listened to the dark-complexioned evening once again without you |
| *Leylak pırıltılarla bahçeler gölgelendi* | The lilac with its glitter, and the gardens, were enfolded in shadow |

---

42. It is worth briefly noting the details. To start off, seven songs cover early eighteenth- and nineteenth-century classics such as İsmail Dede's "Rast kar-ı nevi" and Nevres Paşa's "Şehnaz divanı." The modes modulate from *rast makamı* to *hicaz*. There is then a ten-minute break before an instrumental set dating from the late Ottoman period, Tanburi Cemil Bey's "Mahur peşrevi," a *taksim*, and Nikolaki's "Mahur saz semaisi." After another ten-minute break there follows the final set: seven contemporary songs, starting, after an instrumental prelude (*peşrev*), with Şerif İçli's "Bir teselli beklerim gönlümdeki bin yareye," then songs composed by Müren himself, and finally Sadettin Kaynak's "Menekşelendi sular." The instrumentalists, we also learn, were Sadi Işılay, İzettin Ökte, Şerif İçli, Vecdi Seyhun, Fikret Kutluğ, and Burhanettin Ökte; some of these names will already be familiar to readers. Siemens is, interestingly, credited with providing microphones and amplification. I have not seen information of this kind elsewhere, so one must assume that this is significant—perhaps as an advertisement for Siemens, perhaps to reassure listeners that what they are listening to is mediated by high quality and reliable technology.

43. I have recordings of the song by Safiye Ayla, Muazzez Abacı, Melihat Gülses, İnci Çayırlı, Emel Sayın, Kutlu Payaslı, and Hande Tekin, ranging from approximately the mid-1940s (Safiye Ayla) to the time of writing (2008). See also below, note 57.

44. Dictionary definitions of the term in, for instance, Rona 1970 specify a "free" and multisectional musical form—one not, in other words, bound by the conventions of *şarkı*.

45. The lyrics were written by Vecdi Bingöl, a lyricist who worked closely with Sadettin Kaynak.

| | |
|---|---|
| *İnledi yine bülbül, olmazmış gül dikensiz* | The nightingale sighed, again<br>There is no such thing, they say, as a thornless rose. |

(Chorus)

| | |
|---|---|
| *Dikensiz gül olmazmış* | There is no such thing, they say, as a thornless rose |
| *çilesiz bulbul, Ayşe* | No such thing as an untormented nightingale, Ayşe |
| *Her kuş bülbül olmazmış* | But not every bird is a nightingale, they say |
| *Her çiçek de gül, Ayşe* | Not every flower a rose, Ayşe. |
| *Ne bülbül gülü sevdi seni sevdiğim kadar* | No nightingale loved its rose as much as I love you |
| *Ne böyle seven gönül, ne de senden güzel var* | Nor was there such a loving soul, nor anyone more beautiful than you |
| *İçli bir özleyişle bırak beni yanayım* | Leave me to my inner longing, for I am burning |
| *Gözlerinde gördüğüm rüyama inanayım* | Allow me to believe in the dream I saw in your eyes |

(Repeat of chorus)

The first verse presents, as far as the lyrics are concerned, a scene of solitude and melancholy. The shadows are gathering, time is passing, but the lovers still are not united. These melancholy observations are thrown into relief in the chorus by a contrary observation, involving stock figures in Ottoman poetics: the nightingale and the rose (see Andrews 1984). But the expected message is reversed. The lovers of poetic tradition may indeed be doomed. After all, every nightingale has its woes, every rose its thorns. However, not *every* bird is a nightingale, not *every* flower a rose. Real human beings (as opposed to figures in poetry) can aspire to, and achieve, real love. The last verse effects a further reversal. Love might be possible, and the chances here seem high. But it is still risky. The poet perhaps is better off alone, with at least his dreams and fantasies intact. Realistic expectations of a fulfilled, this-wordly love are juxtaposed throughout with the bittersweet pleasures of fantasy and solitude.

Musically speaking, the song is multisectional. Each section, as is common in the *fantezi* genre, involves lurching changes of style and affect. In

**2a.** "Menekşelendi sular," opening instrumental section (*sofyan*).

**2b.** "Menekşelendi sular," opening vocal section.

**2c.** "Menekşelendi sular," chorus (*semai*).

this it differs significantly from classical song form (*şarkı*), with its balanced repetitions and its stylistic consistency. In performances of "Menekşelendi sular," the first verse is usually introduced by an instrumental figure with an up-tempo feel, employing the *usûl* (rhythmic mode) *sofyan*. It is usually played loudly. This descends, with embellishments, from the top of the mode *nihavent makamı* (to be discussed in more detail shortly) to the bottom. The figure is often repeated between various sections of the song, though different performers have different preferences (music example 2a).

The song's first verse itself comprises two phrases developing the bottom five notes of the mode *nihavent makamı*. The first of these phrases inhabits, roughly, an ascending and descending arch between G and D, and the second a descending full octave from G' to G. A rhythmic figure related to the rhythmic mode *düyek*[46] connects most of these phrases with each other. It is usually sung softly (music example 2b).

The chorus involves a waltz-like figure, descending sequentially from G', picking up at the cadence (*karar*) the "*düyek*" figure interrupted above at the word "*inledi.*" This is commonly sung, by contrast, mezzo forte (music example 2c).

Verse two (*Ne bülbül*) is usually notated in common time—in other words, with a *C* as a Western-style time signature. (As we have already observed, this can accommodate a variety of Turkish rhythmic modes—specifically, in this case, *sofyan* and *düyek*). It is usually sung in a free rhythm, though, in a performance style somewhere between an urban *gazel* and a rural *maya* in style. A *gazel* would be more extended, and would usually have an underlying instrumental accompaniment vamping on the rhythmic mode. A *maya* would have less in the way of modal modulations than what we hear here. This is another minor stylistic innovation associated with the genre. For the purposes of this discussion, I will refer to it as a *gazel/maya*.

Modally, the *gazel/maya* touches on an *uşşak* tetrachord (D–E comma flat[47]–F–G) at the cadential figure at the word *var*, and on the *hicaz* tetrachord (D–E four commas flat–F four commas sharp–G) at "*ne böyle. . . .*"[48] Turkish notations generally represent this section as follows:

---

46. Düyek is represented in terms of sounds as *düm te-ek tek düm tek* (i.e., low hi-gh high, low high—the hyphenated extension indicating a doubled note value), and in notation as an eighth-quarter-eighth-quarter-quarter note sequence. See Yılmaz 1977.

47. The Turkish tonal system divides whole tones into nine Pythagorean "commas" (the difference between a limma and an apotome). A slightly lowered or raised pitch is usually represented as one comma, and something roughly corresponding to a semitone as four or five commas. Such details emerge in performance in very different ways, with pitches tweaked in ascent or descent, and according to context (nightclub versus conservatory, for instance).

48. See below for an explanation of the broader modal picture of *nihavent*.

**2d.** Notated version of "Menekşelendi sular," middle section. Excerpted from online version to be found at Neyzen.com. Safiye Ayla's recorded versions adhere closely to this notation.

Recorded versions are usually close to this notational representation.[49] Zeki Müren's version is strikingly different, as we will shortly see. At this point, though, we should simply note that the song's abrupt changes in style are an important aspect of its representation of melancholy and the conflicting and inconstant emotions of love.

The song's representation of melancholy is to be considered in relation to another process of signification: mode (*makam*). *Makam* are often considered, in Turkey, to be "empty" syntactical structures in which anything can be said in a variety of moods. This, however, would be a somewhat academic view. For many other people, more in tune with the medieval and early modern sense of *makam* as a system of affect, it signifies mood. That idea underpins the choice of *makam* for the Muslim call to prayer, recent revivals of interest in *makam* as a therapeutic system, and much everyday talk about art music. Though people might dispute what a given *makam* signifies, many assume that it does signify something or other.

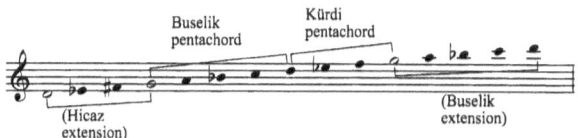

**2e.** *Nihavent makamı.*

---

49. This is essentially a transcription of Safiye Ayla's version using Turkish art music notational conventions. It closely resembles the notated (prescriptive) version published on-line at www.neyzen

Late in the nineteenth century, *nihavent,* formerly somewhat marginal, was becoming very popular.⁵⁰ Zeki Müren, one might say, made this *makam* his own. Many of his most famous compositions and recordings were in *nihavent.* "Menekşelendi sular," in *nihavent,* functioned as his regular end-of-set number. What is this *makam,* then? What is it held to signify, and why?

Textbooks, like Yılmaz 1977, explain it primarily in terms of linked tetrachords (*dörtlüler*) and pentachords (*beşliler*). To be more precise, it is described as a *buselik* pentachord at the bottom transposed from A to G (i.e., G–A–B five commas flat–C–D), with a *kürdi* or *hicaz* tetrachord attached at the top (i.e., D–E five commas flat–F–G or D–E four commas flat–F four commas sharp–G).

Theoretically speaking, this puts *nihavent* into the rather capacious category of "transposed" *makam*-s (known in Turkish as *göçürülmüş* or *şedd*). The *seyir* (predominant melodic direction) is also theoretically specified, in this case as "ascending and descending" (*inici-çıkıcı*), as are cadential formulae (*karar*) and possible modulations (*geçkiler*). This constitutes the core of a typical modern textbook definition of *nihavent,* which would occasionally add a model instrumental improvisation (*taksim*) and a song or instrumental piece by way of example.

In everyday practice, away from the conservatories, *nihavent* is taught with a slightly different set of principles in mind. I am now remembering how I was taught this *makam* by my *kanun* teacher early in the 1980s.⁵¹ Three features of his explanation are still very clear in my mind. First, after being presented with the textbook definition, I was told that *nihavent* was "really just the same as the Western minor scale." It was, in other words, not quite a *makam* like others. Rather it was a hybrid creature, somewhat Westernized. Second, unlike other *makam, nihavent* was one in which the performer really could play around and show off: chromatic scales, arpeggios, glissandi, using

---

.com; I have attempted in this transcription, though, to describe the post–Safiye Ayla common practice and performance tradition.

50. A glance at a website representing the contemporary art-music song repertory, Neyzen.com, illustrates the point. Numbers are an imprecise guide but they do convey an impression. The compilers of this popular website have well over three hundred songs in *nihavent*; *hicaz* is the only other category to come close. *Rast* and *uşşak* each have around half this number. Others of the eighty-nine categories listed—a good map of contemporary modal practice—are represented by less than one hundred songs.

51. My *kanun* teacher, Tunçay Gülersoy, was a retired military man who played *kanun,* often at that point with his son (a *darbuka* player), in nightclubs around the city. He attended classes at the Üsküdar Musiki Cemiyeti nearby and understood scholarly discourse on *makam* well. But he was also in touch with popular aesthetics and discourse, often registering the conflict between the two, as here. He was, particularly for my purposes but in other regards as well, a brilliant teacher.

the entire gamut of the instrument, and so forth. Third, and most significantly in this context, it was associated with melancholy.

I had an experience of this latter association a few weeks later. After one lesson, I found myself stranded at my teacher's house during an intense snowstorm. All buses and boats had ground to a halt, so I stayed the night. I woke up a little early, as I often do in strange houses. I picked up the *kanun* and was practicing my newly acquired *nihavent* moves quietly. The snow was still falling from a leaden sky, though gently by now. A little later my teacher's son was up and about, saying that lying in bed he had been struck by the combination of the snow, the quiet of the city streets, and the sound of *nihavent*. A perfect and melancholy (*hüzünlü*) combination, he said as we sipped tea at breakfast. I remember taking it as a compliment and feeling that some threshold in my own understanding of the intimate aesthetics of *makam* had been crossed.

This is a *makam* defined by many, then, in terms of its "Western" feel, its opportunities for virtuosity, and its melancholy (*hüzün*). In a popular musical world defined by its Western orientation, a regard for virtuosity, and a growing national preoccupation with melancholy,[52] *nihavent* came to signify in new ways. Zeki Müren was, I would suggest, an important contributor to this process. "Menekşelendi sular" was replete with these new significations.

*Nihavent*'s melancholic and virtuosic meanings also inhere in its place in a performative sequence. Many of Müren's concert performances would start off modally in one area and move towards *nihavent* as a final destination. The issue of modulation should be discussed in a little detail. Modulation is an important aspect of *makam* practice in Turkey as elsewhere in the Middle East (see, for instance, Nettl 1998). It has at least two distinct dimensions. Specific items of repertory (songs, instrumental preludes, or postludes) contain internal modulations. This kind of modulation is usually rule-based to the extent that it is often specified in textbooks as part of a *makam*'s definition (see, for instance, Yılmaz 1977). Modulation also takes place between items, usually by means of an instrumental *ara taksimi* (interval *taksim*) leading, for instance, from one group of songs in one *makam* to another group in a different *makam*. The mixing of these *makam*-s is usually done with the care and attention of a chef planning a menu. There are few specific rules. Judgments of taste are very much to the fore, though, in the balancing of contrasts and continuities.

---

52. The question of national melancholy (*hüzun*) is explored in detail in Orhan Pamuk's recent portrait of the city (Pamuk 2005). See chapter 6 of this book for a more extended discussion.

A good illustration of how this worked in practice can be found in Müren's "first public performance," mentioned above. The first set of songs modulated from *rast* to *hicaz*. This was followed by an instrumental interlude in *mahur*. The final set then modulated from *acemaşiran* to *nihavent*. Much could be said about the symmetries and parallels one might detect in these modulations. Suffice it to note, briefly, the interlocking movement of their respective "tonics" (G–A; F–G) and the overarching movement from a *makam* popularly associated with robustness and theoretical centrality[53] in the *makam* universe (*rast*) to one associated with melancholy and theoretical hybridity (*nihavent*).

Melancholy is therefore signified in "Menekşelendi sular" in two contrasting ways. On the one hand the formal structure, *fantezi*, involves the listener in restless changes of musical tempo and style. As we have seen, these might be correlated with the changes in perspective offered in each verse by the singer on his own condition as a lover (absorbed by his beloved's absence, optimistic about the possibilities of a "realistic" love, imploring the beloved to leave him to his dreams). The instrumental introduction and interludes add a further level of contrast. On the other hand, a listener even moderately informed on the subject of *makam* is drawn into another system of meanings constituted by the modal system, *nihavent* signifying melancholy through the various evolving properties attributed to it as described above. One might speculate in passing that one of the things that made the song "Menekşelendi sular" stand out to Müren and his listeners was its unsettled quality, bought about by the fact that two different processes for signifying melancholy musically were in play simultaneously.

We must also consider Müren's recording of "Menekşelendi sular" as a commentary on another singer's particularly authoritative version. As already mentioned, the song was reputedly written for Safiye Ayla. We should note that Ayla was particularly popular amongst the republican intelligentsia and political classes in the 1930s and 1940s, and her first recording of this song must date from that period, perhaps towards the end of it.[54] Her treatment of this moment of the song was followed carefully by many others who performed it later.[55] There is also a very close fit between her recorded version and the notations that still circulate. This is particularly noticeable in the third

---

53. Most theoretical treatises start off with *rast*. See, for instance, Yılmaz 1977. I remember my teacher describing it as having a "manly" (*mert*) character.

54. The number of the Columbia recording is BT 22163–CTZ 6333, close in numbers and in sound to a recording on Kalan's archival CD of Safiye Ayla, "Katibim," bearing the date 1949.

55. The recorded televised versions by Muazzez Abacı, Melihat Gülses, and Kutlu Payaslı closely follow Safiye Ayla. What must—to judge by the lower voice and more classicized accompaniment,

verse, the *gazel/maya*, in free time (see music example 2d above). Ayla adds a descending scale connecting the G of "Bülbül" to the D below it, thus outlining a descending *uşşak* tetrachord. This simply registers a fleeting modal excursion. In other words it is short and, modally speaking, to the point.

Müren's version has a very different feel. It is slower throughout. The orchestra is bigger. Western instruments (including the prominent piano, with its occasional harmonic flourishes) have disappeared. But the most significant differences materialize at verse three, the *gazel/maya*. Consider the contrast.

**2f.** Zeki Müren's recording of "Menekşelendi sular," middle section. The transcription follows notational conventions in Turkish art music for *nihavent makamı*, and thus is transcribed an octave and a fifth above the pitch levels on the recording.

---

without piano and slower—be a later performance can also be quickly located, at the time of writing, on YouTube.

We can see here that Müren's version of the *maya/gazel* extends Ayla's version significantly, turning a prosaic G–D descent into a meandering melisma. At a general level this is in tune with the more pronounced melancholy of the Müren version with its dreamy intimacy, its self-absorbed and seemingly endless twists and turns. It also divides up the phrases more emphatically, with carefully placed cadential flourishes. In part, these cadences are achieved by a sudden intensification of movement towards the modally prominent pitches at the end of each line. Notice how, for instance, the first phrase ends with a rather abrupt descent from G to D, and how the E–D movement speeds up at the end of the fourth phrase. There is an element of technical display here: these phrases (note particularly phrases one and five in this regard) can only be bought off in a satisfactory manner if the singer possesses great breath control, stamina, and concentration. Listeners consider the singer's physique at such moments as they would that of a gymnast attempting a tricky move.

Such moments, in the performance of improvised vocal music in Turkey as elsewhere in the Middle East, also involve a consideration of the singer's interactions with his or her audience. The concept of *qaflah* (plural *qaflat*) in Arab art music, the bravura performance of cadential flourishes (see Danielson 1997, Racy 2003, Shannon 2006), has no precise equivalent in Turkish classical music but is entirely appropriate in this context. *Qaflat* not only signify technical mastery and detailed knowledge of *makam,* but also signify an ability to generate an emotional and vocal exchange with listeners—a quality Racy (2003) theorizes as *tarab* (roughly, "enchantment"). A *qaflah*, then, produces a brief moment of recognition of what singer and audience together have wrought: a state of collective emotional warmth and heightened creative alertness.

It is inevitably hard to know exactly how this recorded version of "Menekşelendi sular" relates to the versions Müren sang at the end of his performances. But a comparison of the Ayla and Müren recordings is still instructive. One gets a general sense of Müren's ability to mesmerize a *gazino* audience and establish an emotional rapport with it.[56] The cadential figures

---

56. Müren's concerts could, by all accounts, be lively affairs with much give and take between performers and audiences, like the ideal *tarab* gatherings described by Racy (2003). Aşan 2003 reports that nightclub performances could be rowdy. The more rural-inflected proletarian atmosphere of the later 1950s made for an atmosphere that could be confrontational, as unruly clients demanded songs and took offence when denied. *Kanun* player Hilmi Rit, accompanying Müren, was wounded by a flying knife during one such event. Müren evidently became skillful at calming and then enchanting such crowds, although, interestingly, his mentor Müzeyyen Senar commented that rough edges and inexperience showed in his *gazino* performances in the early 1950s. Turkish singers of the previous

of his *gazel/maya* section evoke the singer's physical presence and the live moment of encounter. This evocation rests on what we might describe as a metaphysics of voice, a collective conception of the voice as a dynamic and productive agency at the heart of events, situations, and social relations. Though neither new nor peculiar to Turkey, the particularity of Müren's voice was increasingly understood in these terms.[57]

## The Virtues of the Voice

Zeki Müren's voice compelled verbal engagement. People liked writing about it (including Müren himself), and still enjoy talking about it. These representations constitute a web of metaphors that articulate the aesthetic experience and link it with other social domains. First, some general conceptions, which I take mainly from the obituaries and other writings that appeared around the time of his death in 1996 (e.g., Katırcıkara 1996, Ok 1996), will help me frame some of the more specific issues later in this section. Müren's voice was routinely described as "soft" (*yumuşak*), "like velvet" (*kadife gibi*). This "softness" combined with, or was itself an attribute of, a certain disciplinary power. "Wild" (*vahşi*) lyrics would be tamed, uttered with ease and facility (*sükunet*). Yet there was no violence or force in this disciplinary operation. It was a voice that simply flowed with the ease and grace of a stream (*pırıl pırıl akıyor*).

It was, above all, a civil voice. Müren's voice tone possessed "*nezaket*"; it was "decent," "polite." And yet it commanded attention: it was "*etkili*," simultaneously "affective" and "effective." It would put people in a state of "enchantment," of "*mest*," part melancholy, part joy, part spiritual intoxication (see above). Müren's voice was often described as "*füsunkâr*," enchanting. This term was frequently used in Turkey in the 1940s and 1950s to describe the voices of the Egyptian stars, particularly Mohammed Abd al-Wahhab, thus establishing an aesthetic kinship with the sentimental singing of the Arab world. Müren's was, then, a voice that set out not to "burn" or otherwise assail listeners (qualities valued in *arabesk*, for example; see Stokes

---

generation had routinely cultivated their art in the Arab capitals, and the cross-border continuity of *tarab* culture between Turkey and the Arab world at this particular moment should not surprise us.

57. Who influenced whom, particularly when one comes to the matter of specific songs, can be difficult to figure out. Archival footage, apparently from the TRT, of İnci Çayırlı's rather similar version of the song can quickly be located, at the time of writing (2008), on YouTube. The other version that bears comparison in this regard is Emel Sayın's, which is long and *tarab*-like, and unlike the earlier Safiye Ayla version. Sayın, though very much younger than Ayla, was perhaps one of the last of the major art music stars who toured extensively in other Middle Eastern capitals. His version can also be found on YouTube.

1992a) according to traditional Turkish folk music criteria, but rather to caress, to cajole and persuade.

It was a voice that was also held to possess a quality of *uyum*, a term embracing the English words "conformity" and "consistency." This expression has citizenly connotations, implying reasonableness, thoughtfulness, and social-mindedness. In the context of discussion about Müren's voice, the term has two particular dimensions. One concerns what one might think of as a citizenly vocal ethic. Clarity, both musical and textual, and the avoidance of error that might obscure this clarity were the cardinal virtues, as we have already seen. These were simple enactments of citizenly respect for the principles of intelligibility and transmission, as well as for listeners and bearers of musical tradition.

Müren's singing also demonstrated *uyum* over time. The vocal virtues he cultivated were held to have changed very little over the course of his career. Recently available archival recordings from the 1950s strengthen this claim. Early in his career his voice was higher—arguably possessing, as the friend who introduced me to these recordings put it, a little more sparkle (*parlaklık*) than it had in the 1980s. But Müren's consistent care with words, diction, texts, intonation, and clarity in his rendition of *makam* remained constant. This became particularly important when he turned to *arabesk*. So *uyum* also signified for Turkish commentators an ability to move in and out of different styles and to conform to the demands of the market without sacrificing one's vocal integrity.

"Vocal integrity," in Müren's case, revolved around diction. In the Turkish idiom, one "shows respect" to diction. As we have already seen, this attitude of respect and diligence (*özen*) involved the far from simple ability to deliver complex Ottoman texts with due respect for prosody, vowel harmony, and the pronunciation of vowels and consonants in archaic Ottoman words of Arabic and Persian derivation. It also involved an ability to sing the words with the appropriate emotional conviction. To put it simply, one had to know the meanings and emotional registers of the non-everyday language of Ottoman and modern Turkish classical song to be able to sing it effectively. But above all, it involved control: the ability to convey words and musical expressions clearly and correctly, in different and often quite demanding musical contexts.

For example, the third line of text, the so-called *meyan* section in classical song (*şarkı*), would be located in a higher register and often in a different *makam*. This could pose problems for singers whose command of register was weak, a problem compounded by the convention of turning up the emotional heat (and thus the volume and intensity of vocal ornamentation) when delivering the *meyan* in performance. Done with conviction—as by important older contemporaries of Zeki Müren, such as Müzeyyen Senar—the effect could be electrifying. However, words could get lost, as Müren himself noted, reflecting later in life on his earliest experiences of listening to radio at home in Bursa.

> I knew the songs sung by the singers of the time by heart. I had a great big songbook. But when listening to most of them, I couldn't understand the third line, particularly—what we call the *meyan*. It used to irritate me, not being able to understand. When listening to the same song sung months later by a different singer, I would struggle to understand, but still not get it. I used to say that if I were to be a singer one day, that those listening to me should understand the words in these lines, that they should be able to write them down.... (Aksoy 2002)

This judgment on his contemporaries may have been a bit harsh. But listening to the early radio recordings, which feature demanding songs from the Ottoman repertoire, one realizes just how seriously he took this project. In performances in *makam* in which extremes of register could be explored, such as *nihavent*,[58] his handling of vocal ornamentation and text is precise and clear. Most Turkish-speaking listeners can easily identify what he is saying, and most reasonably fluent musicians can easily interpret his handling of musical lines in terms of classical *makam* conventions.

Zeki Müren was considered by many to have a new kind of voice. It was a voice that resisted traditional musical processes of reckoning in relation to teachers and mentors. Mass mediation meant that the one-on-one mentor relationships typical of the Ottoman *meşk* (repertoire transmission) system (Behar 1993) were disrupted, however much they continued to be idealized, at least by some. So when Müren approached Şerif İçli and Kadri Şençalar for lessons soon after he arrived in Istanbul, after a short audition he was asked the obvious question, "Who taught you?"—a question designed to clarify how and where Müren situated himself in established *meşk* networks. The presumably unexpected reply was: "My father, my grandfather, the radio, the singers at the tent theater in Bursa, records...." (Aşan 2003, p. 19). This implied, in other words, that he as an individual had developed his

---

58. For another interesting and readily available *nihavent* example, see the *fasıl* (suite) beginning with Lemi Atlı's "Bin gül çıkarırdım" and ending with Faiz Kapancı's "Gel güzelim Çamlıca'ya" on Kalan's 1955–65 Turkish Radio archival recording—an early recording, in other words. The *meyan* (central) sections operate here in a high tenor register (the octave above middle C). It is worth noting that vocalists then, as now, transpose *makam* to suit their own vocal registers.

vocal skills and assembled his repertoire from diverse sources. His voice was not, then, at least according to him, the product of a chain of *meşk* transmission.[59]

So part of the newness of Müren's voice was registered in terms of this broad institutional change in Turkish vocal culture: singers increasingly learned repertoire and technique from media and other sources, rather than from institutionalized musical authorities. It was also registered in terms of technological changes. For some contemporaries, Müren was the first to use the microphone as an expressive device, holding it at varying distances to capture different vocal nuances, and using it as a stage prop.[60] Iconic images—for instance, pictures seen on postcards on sale at the Zeki Müren Museum, as well as the statue outside—invariably show him posing with a microphone. Such images tell an interesting story to the technologically minded. The earliest show the singer standing before not one but several microphones; later they show him as classic crooner, his face almost permanently attached to some version or another of the RCA 44A or Shure Unidyne;[61] yet later they show him striding about the stage with one of the lightweight, portable condenser microphones of the 1960s and 1970s in hand.[62] Microphones today are such a naturalized and unobserved element in the production of sound that they are easily overlooked (Théberge 2003). But Müren's use of the microphone was often noted.[63]

Given these technological and institutional changes, some felt the need

---

59. Müren's own statements concerning how one might place his voice in the musical landscape are, unsurprisingly, rather complex. The following statement, taken from a conversation with journalist Ayda Özlü Çevik, is rather typical, particularly in the way Müren tries to position himself somewhere between two radically different vocal traditions: one (that of Münir Nurettin Selçuk and Safiye Ayla) very much about literary clarity, the other (that of Muzeyyen Senar) about musical intoxication. In the struggle between the two traditions it is the latter—contrary to the expectation of Müren's interlocutor, perhaps—that wins out. Müren says, "When I was at middle school in Bursa, I only had one of Münir Nurettin Bey's recordings and one of Safiye Ayla's, [but] I had thirty-eight of Müzeyyen Senar's. This is the kind of voice that makes the hairs on the back of your neck stand up, that makes you have a drink to relieve your sadness, that's Müzeyyen Senar's voice. They say Bülent Ersoy's voice is like Müzeyyen Hanım's. True, the style is the same, but the sound is quite different. If you put a Müzeyyen Hanım LP on the turntable and play it at a slower speed, you get Hafız Burhan. His old 78s still move me [*hala beni duygulandırıyor*]. Münir Nurettin Bey never did" (Hiçyılmaz 1997, p. 113).

60. Interview with Cem Karaca by Anne Ellingsen and Martin Stokes, July 1996.

61. See pictures in Dikici 2005. This suggests that the RCA 44A, or some version of it, was used in concerts in Paris as early as 1947. It may have become the norm in Istanbul shortly after.

62. On crooning, see McCracken 2001, Petkov 1995, and Shaw 1995. On the microphone, see in particular Théberge 2003. On crooning and the microphone elsewhere in the Middle East, see Stokes 2007a and 2008.

63. Müren's T-shaped stage is discussed, for example, in Arıkan 1979 and Güngör 1990.

**Figure 2b.** At the Zeki Müren Museum, Bodrum. Photograph by the author.

for a completely new language to describe Müren's voice. This was precisely the project of popular composer, singer, and music critic Edip Özışık. His *Musiki sanatı* (Özışık 1963) attempts, amongst other things, to provide a critical and aesthetic vocabulary for Müren's vocal qualities and effects (see in particular Özışık 1963, pp. 187–91).[64] For Özışık, Müren's voice posed a significant puzzle. It was lacking in certain conventional regards. He had no particular powers of "prolongation" (*imtidat*), "range" (*irtifa*) or "strength" (*şiddet*). He was "no Caruso." In what, then, did the undoubted, "God-given" (*Allah vergisi*) beauty of this voice reside?

Özışık distinguishes "internal" and "external" characteristics. "Internal" characteristics refer to what one might call this voice's *sentimental* effects. Müren's voice is "natural" (*tabiî*), "well proportioned" (*mütenasip*), "warm" (*sıcak*), and "sweet" (*tatlı*), as well as more obviously being a technically superior voice (possessing *"üstün bir kabiliyet"*). It produces its effects in the listener through "sympathy" (*sempati*), through its amorous qualities (*aşkı hattırlattığı için*) and its capacity to captivate people (it was *"tesirli"*). Somehow it takes us prisoner whether we want it to do so or not. These "internal"

---

64. The book is dedicated to Müren and to the author's brother, composer Ayhan Özışık. Müren was a champion of Özışık's music. This book was presumably a way of returning the favor. I am grateful to Serkan Delice for pointing this out to me.

characteristics involve an explicitly sympathetic principle: Müren's voice enfolds us in a familiar embrace because it awakes within us an internal voice ("*içimizden olduğunu hissetiğimiz bir ses*"). It is this sympathetic resonance that produces the "pleasure and happiness" (*zevk ve saadet*) we experience while listening to him (Özışık 1963, p. 189).

Özışık's "external" characteristics have an objective character. These are not qualities that necessarily resonate within, like the "internal" characteristics he mentions. Müren's is above all an original voice: the voice of an individual, one hard to imitate.[65] He introduces, according to Özışık, new standards of diction and pronunciation (*telâffuz*). The voice has unrivaled "powers of association" (*tedai kudreti*), by which Özışık means both that it allows the imagination to wander, and that it conjures up other musical ideas. It has, in other words, powers of reference within the Turkish listener's *musical* universe. And finally, it is a voice that possesses unrivaled "powers of interpretation" (*tefsir kudreti*). The term is a weighty one, with theological connotations. It denotes the skill that enables the singer to turn rough diamonds into shining jewels—a skill that can be achieved only by a singer possessing a "delicate soul" (*hassas ruhu*), "exceptional abilities" (*müstesna kabiliyetleri*) and a capacity for "higher-order pleasures" (*yüksek zevkleri*) (Özışık 1963, p. 191).

Özışık's book is remarkable for the explicitness with which he identifies the newness of Müren's vocal art. He directly connects these vocal qualities with new imaginations of the sentimental subject, a subject understood as natural, delicate, sensitive, intimate, and sympathetically in tune with others. These are, equally clearly, civic virtues, the product of the liberal reaction of the 1950s to the authoritarian political traditions of the early republic.

Müren's voice was, finally, often perceived as being androgynous. As the singer himself once commented about the reaction to his first radio concert in 1951, "some people (who were listening) appear to have argued about whether this was a male or female voice. A young student with a tenor [*tenor*] voice might sing in a delicate [*ince*], crisp [*gevrek*] manner. I wasn't much fussed by the question of whether this was female or male voice" (cited in Aksoy 2002). The two terms he used relating to the perceived "feminine" qualities of his voice, *ince* and *gevrek*, imply tone quality and diction, not simply high pitch. High pitch on its own did not necessar-

---

65. He was, and continues to be, constantly imitated by comics. At the time of writing, Erol Evgin's impersonations of Müren and others (including Sezen Aksu) are notorious. Comic imitations of this kind ironically underscore the inimitability and individuality of a voice. They accentuate the impossibility of borrowing the vocal techniques in question for serious aesthetic purposes.

ily imply "female."[66] Folk singers finding a space in the urban music market of the immediately preceding decades had very high voices easily rivaling Müren's in range.[67] But these voices foregrounded physical effort and assertiveness, an unambiguous index of rural and rural-urban masculinity in that period. The *ince* and *gevrek* in the comment quoted above point us in the direction of tone quality and diction, not high pitch per se, as an attribute of femininity. They imply a fastidiousness in pronunciation, in *diksiyon* according to educated, urbane standards. In an urban musical world that even then was adjusting to the tastes and aesthetic preferences of (male) rural-urban migrant musicians and audiences, this fastidiousness in pronunciation—this almost defiant validation of an urbane, educated "Istanbul" Turkish—could be equated with femininity.[68]

Both the evocation and the brushing aside of questions about the androgynous nature of Müren's voice were very much in keeping with his guarded response to questions about his sexuality throughout his life—responses seemingly designed to keep the issues publicly in play. Representations of his voice were, then, thoroughly entangled with questions about his sexuality. The next section contextualizes and explores some of these questions.

### Zeki Müren's Sexuality: Three Interpretations

During his own lifetime, questions about Müren's sexuality were mostly framed in hints and euphemisms. His responses were invariably evasive and

---

66. For instance, Rabbi Isaac Algazi, a notable cantor and art-music recording star of the 1920s and 30s in Turkey, sang, as his biographer Edwin Seroussi notes, "with a particularly high tenor voice, called by the Turks [a] "woman's voice" [in the words of Rabbi Refael Aboab]. Such a high voice was praised in Turkey as having a special aesthetic value." (Seroussi 1989, p. 37). Other qualities besides pitch per se, such as Algazi's use of falsetto and his heavy vibrato, may have contributed to his "sounding like a woman," though.

67. Such as Malatyalı Fahri Kayahan, for example, or—somewhat later—Muharrem Ertaş.

68. In Turkey I rarely met men who spoke like Müren. Doing research in the Black Sea high pastures in the late 1980s, however, I did get to know a young man who seemed to make a point of *not* speaking in the impenetrable and regionally ubiquitous local dialect in which almost all the other men took a certain macho delight. His defiant use of Istanbul Turkish was definitely colored by an intonation and diction borrowed from Müren. There didn't seem to be the slightest suggestion that he was gay, and he was clearly a popular figure. He was, though, clearly considered something of an eccentric, and his nickname, "*nazik* Kemal" (polite Kemal) evoked Müren, a consummate figure of *nezaket* (politesse). Sociolinguist Şenel Şimsek, who has made a study of queer argot in Turkey, has also (in personal communication) expressed doubts about the "queerness" of Müren's spoken voice, partly on the grounds that the category was not clearly recognized in mainstream Turkish society during his lifetime, and partly on the grounds that its connotations had much more to do with politeness, civility, and "correctness" as far as most people were concerned. See also note 15.

ambiguous.[69] By 1980, after which I was living in Turkey on and off and following the matter in the tabloid press, he was suffering from severe gout, heart, and liver problems and was living a somewhat reclusive life in Bodrum. Respect and a high measure of public affection for him prohibited public questions that would have seemed crass and disrespectful. This was instantly to change at his death, when questions about his queerness became a matter of public preoccupation.

One can divide the responses to this question crudely into two broad categories of response: those that denied his queerness, and those that accepted it. To this one might add a further category: those that accepted his queerness but took issue with the way he (failed to) express it. Those who were intent on heterosexualizing Müren were quick to get into print—perhaps a measure of the palpable degree of anxiety on the topic. One might refer in particular to Ceyhan Güç's imaginative pseudo-autobiography (written in the first person), *Şimdi uzaklardaysın* (Now you are in a faraway place) (1996), and Ergün Hiçyılmaz's more scholarly *Dargınım sana hayat: Zeki Müren için bir demet yasemin* (I am angry with you, life: A bunch of jasmine for Zeki Müren) (1997). Güç's tactic is to stress Müren's overly intense relationship with his mother (who is, by contrast, almost entirely absent from Hiçyılmaz's book) and a childish, unconsummated love affair in Bursa. These two facts are used to account for Müren's delicate artistic (*ince* or *sanatkâr ruhlu*) spirit and his inability to establish long-term relationships with other women.

Hiçyılmaz presents a more forthright case. He narrates Müren's adolescent visits to the brothels of Karaköy,[70] and accounts for the large number of women with whom Müren reputedly slept. He interprets Müren's long-term relationships with various men as merely "*platonik*," meriting only passing comment. Photographs of Zeki locked in embrace with a variety of well-known female films stars hammer the message home.

Müren's well-documented but understandably evasive responses to prurient journalistic enquiry add credence to these simplistic heterosexualizing tactics. In one amusing exchange, journalist Halit Çapan asked Müren— who by this time had almost completely abandoned suit and tie combinations for sequined robes and costume jewelry on stage—about his choice

---

69. I would emphatically agree with Aşan's comments that he "carefully maintained an ambiguity. It was as though he had signed a contract with the public. Both sides respected this contract...." (Aşan 2003, p. 101).

70. Istanbul's famous red-light area, a huge state-controlled brothel that sprawls down the hill in close proximity to Beyoğlu's nightclubs and bars.

of clothes.[71] The conversation dwelt briefly on the subject of Yavuz Sultan Selim's earring.[72] Müren commented on the absurdity of somebody's claim, on the basis of his androgynous dress sense, that he had already had a sex change: "If women wear trousers, does this mean they are all going to have sex change operations too?" The journalist continued: "But Zeki Bey, if a man goes on stage wearing women's clothes, hasn't he lost something of his manhood?" Müren replied: "But I don't wear women's clothes. I wear the kind of clothes Caesar and Baytekin and Brutus wore." The journalist persisted: "Don't you feel naked [*çıplak*] on stage dressed like that?" To which the singer replied: "I feel like a wrestler going out to wrestle in his swimming costume [*mayo*]" (Hiçyılmaz 1997, p. 51).

Müren sidesteps the question, absurdly, with reference to "Caesar and Baytekin and Brutus," all the while hinting that the presuppositions of his interlocutor—that wrestler-like masculinity can never be lost or compromised—may in fact be entirely sound. He was evidently as much caught up in the contradictory terrain of gender representation as the journalists and commentators who sought to explain or criticize him. Those who sought to heterosexualize his memory, like Hiçyılmaz or Güç, therefore found themselves with plenty to work with, contrary to what one might at first suppose.

Queer arguments provide the more interesting reading, and they raised the more culturally and politically resonant questions after his death. For these cannot, I think, be understood simply as the return of the repressed, as questions that people had wanted to ask before he died but were prohibited to ask for reasons of respect or collusion in an open secret. Rather, these questions were very much entangled with a moment of bewildering change in which broader questions about Turkish identity were being routed through the process of memorializing Müren.

Emine Aşan's popular biography (2003), for all of its airbrushed nostal-

---

71. There are a great many easily accessible websites showing Müren's clothing. See for instance www.sanatgunesi.com (click on "*resimler*," "pictures")—which is interesting for, amongst other reasons, containing a variety of pictures taken at his final television performance and his funeral.

72. The sultan reputedly wore an earring to remember a promise. The expression "*Kulağım küpeli olsun*" (roughly, "I'm going to put an earring in my ear") is still used to tell somebody you mean to honor a promise. In the late 1980s, very few Turkish men wore earrings (Müren is supposed to have been the pioneer here too; see Tunca 1976). If they did, the automatic assumption made by most was that they were gay. I had taken out my own earring (de rigeur in England in the early 1980s) before living in Turkey, but the hole in my ear was still clearly visible and was a constant topic of conversation. The story of the sultan's earring often came up, partly to structure discussions about "modern life" and its foibles in Europe and partly, it seemed to me, to evoke memory of a prerepublican time when different and in some respects more complex gendered expressive styles were legitimate and respectable.

gia, constitutes the most interesting take on the queer Zeki Müren.[73] Her depiction has three important components. One of these locates Müren, albeit cautiously, in a historically identifiable queer subculture in Turkey. This revolved around Beyoğlu's *Klüp 14* and *2019*, favorite hangouts for a variety of more or less "out" gay artists, singers, and designers. Such clubs were reputedly supported by Müren financially, and were also his own favorite places to relax after hours. A second component suggests that Müren was simply unlike other "modern men," whose masculinity rested on their ability to "act like a lout (*kabadaylık yapmak*), swear and climb mountains." Aşan borrows these words from the character Laura in Robert Anderson's 1958 play, *Tea and Sympathy*. In 1960 director Cüneyt Gökçer made a musical film of this play in which Müren played the lead role, the sensitive lad accused of being queer by his oafish schoolmates. Putting the question of sexuality aside, Aşan suggests, like Laura, that proper manhood involves a capacity for sensitivity and emotion but also the strength of character to face down the hypocrisy of the modern order and its self-deceiving sexual imperatives.[74] Third, Aşan portrays Müren as a hermaphrodite.[75] Not by chance, she suggests, did he choose Bardakçı as his favorite place to unwind at the end of the day at his retreat in Bodrum. For here, according to Greek mythology, Salmakis the fairy persuaded the gods to fuse her body with that of her lover, making her Hermaphroditos, both man and woman. Müren's stage and public persona was simply a way, she suggests, of being true to his divided self.

One might note that all three of these arguments keep the categories of male and female firmly in place and are thus, in certain regards, rather conservative. A more radical note, though, is struck by Aşan's insistent appeal to reason and civility. In the first case, Müren's efforts to keep the truth of his sexual choices and preferences private, and to resist prurient journalistic inquiry,[76] conform to the familiar liberal logic in which civility demands

---

73. Aşan identifies herself as a non-journalist and a non-musician, but a trained philosopher.

74. In an interesting critical comment in an otherwise celebratory study, Aşan suggests that his films of the sixties showed him conforming, rather implausibly, to more conventional male film stereotypes.

75. Sema Ok also warmed to this theme in her 1996 obituary (see http://www.sanatgunesi.com/bir_cift_soz_basin10.htm). "*Erkekliğini kadınsı tavırla bileştirmiş kimbilir aynı bedende ayrı bir insan yaratmıştı*" (Who knows . . . he combined his masculinity with effeminate behavior, and created a separate person inside the same body" (Ok 1996).

76. Even if it meant lying. Aşan narrates the brothel visits discussed by Hiçyılmaz (1997) in a very different way. A worldly wise prostitute instantly diagnoses the problem on Müren's first visit, invites him into her room, and closes the door. The two wait inside for an appropriate period of time. Müren then exits, having "passed" this crucial test of manhood in front of his school friends.

the reasoned and civil maintenance of a line between public and private behavior. The second argument, though, suggests in a rather more radical way that the republican political tradition in Turkey failed to keep in touch with evolving sensibilities concerning gender and sexuality. The dominant model of masculinity in Turkey was simply unresponsive to the requirements of a more properly modern gendered civility. The third argument suggests not only that Müren demanded (and received) the freedom to "be himself," but also that the forces that pressed on him to move in one direction or another (to be more of a man and less of a woman or vice versa) were authoritarian and unreasonable. For Aşan these are primarily commercial rather than political forces: singers faced demands to make sexualized spectacles of themselves for public consumption. And nobody, for Aşan, exemplifies what happens when these forces predominate better than Müren's longtime rival, Bülent Ersoy.

Ersoy, a flamboyant transsexual and popular art music singer who emerged as a rival to Müren in the 1970s, will be discussed more fully in chapter 5. At this point I should mention, though, that the two singers were often compared to each other. The comparisons were always loaded, and only rarely about music, but they were highly suggestive of the broader cultural and political stakes of these discussions. For Aşan, Müren represented sincerity and civic-mindedness in stark contrast to Ersoy's crass opportunism and commercial-mindedness.

Others, though, saw things exactly the other way round. For poet and literary commentator Cemal Süreya, Ersoy had convictions about his identity and was capable of acting on them despite a significant level of opposition.[77] Müren was capable of no such thing. As Süreya puts it, "However famous he was, it was just fame. The '*Muhabbet Kuşu*' [the 'Canary,' after Müren's first big hit] lived comfortably, running from success to success. There was no need to display bravery in any area. He wasn't even able to defend his homosexuality" (Süreya 1989, p. 316).

Süreya's comments are to be found in a short book of literary sketches of public figures. In the aftermath of the 1980 coup, Süreya was clearly looking forward to a moment in which citizenship might be thought of

---

77. Ersoy has become a familiar figure in European and American transgendered communities, where Süreya's views are echoed. The ban by a repressive and authoritarian state on his stage performances in the early 1980s has ensured a kind of victim status, and thus citizenship in a global community of transgendered singers (which, to consider only the Middle East, also includes Aderet, Izam, and Dana International) and those who look to them for orientation in a *transnational* struggle. Within Turkey, however, the picture is different: Ersoy is often seen, even by many in the out gay and transsexual communities, as an opportunistic and embarrassing figure.

as being something more than coerced obedience to an authoritarian state. Such a public rethinking would inevitably involve issues of identity, certain of which (specifically Kurdish issues) could not at that point be openly discussed. Süreya's comments about Müren might be interpreted as an effort to find a neutral and in some sense abstract way of broaching these questions. For Süreya, to frame a political claim in terms of identity was acceptable if that identity was declared and negotiated in public in a legible and consistent way. This was both the challenge and promise of the liberal order that was taking shape in these years. Müren, in his view, entirely failed to live up to it.

## Conclusion

For many people in Turkey, Zeki Müren emerged after his death as a figure of distinctly *national* civility and virtue. Why did this happen? In part it happened because the state quickly moved to claim Müren for itself by according him a state funeral—a move entirely consonant with that government's opportunistic populism and its claims to represent the cultural traditions repressed by Atatürk's republic. But the identification of Müren as a kind of model citizen rested on more popular foundations.

I would suggest three elements at play this nostalgic popular identification. First, Müren drew on the regional (and Egypt-dominated) circulation of sentimental films and musical styles identified with revolutionary politics.[78] Impossible love is the very definition of a certain kind of citizenship and civic virtue in this musical-cinematic culture: at odds with a paternalistic social order, and laboring heroically to bring into existence a set of relationships that are just, equitable, affectionate, and democratic.

Second, arguments about Müren's queerness—or denials of it—constituted a way of talking about other kinds of identities and the relationship between identities and citizenship in the 1990s. The only category of belonging recognized by the Turkish state is that of the citizen—the citizen being by definition "Turkish," whatever language he or she speaks at home and whatever religion he or she practices.[79] Yet the state's determination to cling to this formulation of citizenship in the face of a decade of violent

---

78. See in particular Gordon 2002 and Stokes 2008 on Abd al-Halim Hafiz.

79. The assassination of Turkish-Armenian journalist Hrant Dink in February 2007 showed, however, just how quickly and consistently the ethnic-religious category of belonging (racial Turkishness and Islam) trumps the civil category ("being a citizen of the Turkish state") in practice. Police officers, representatives of the state, treated Dink's killer as a hero upon his return to Trabzon. Thousands, Armenian and non-Armenian alike, marched in Istanbul bearing signs that read, "We are all

ethnic strife in the southeast of the country, and the more recent transfer of this violence to the squatter towns of the western cities, has seemed alternately absurd, inconstant,[80] or out of touch with transnational political realities to many Turkish citizens.[81] Contemporary demands to configure citizenship in ways that confer some recognition on categories of identity run up against the persistent inflexibility of official language. Queer identities could, however, be talked about, and thus constituted an important arena for debate and discussion in the later 1990s (presaged, as we have seen, by Süreya's short essay in 1989). Though the conversations are important in their own right, it is hard not to see them also as displacements of the more politically difficult topic of discussion: "ethnic" and class fractures in the modern state. Queer identities could be portrayed as inherently civil, reasonable, and unthreatening, and at the same time as a positive contribution to the cultural life of the nation. They could be seen as the site of an acceptable accommodation between one's responsibilities and rights as a citizen and as a member of a community defined in identitarian terms. Müren, in other words, allowed the question of identity to be publicly construed in a responsible and citizenly way.

Finally, Zeki Müren nostalgia also functions as a palliative to the broad condition of cynicism that prevailed after the Susurluk car crash of 4 November 1996, identified and discussed in detail by Navaro-Yashin (2002, pp. 171–80). As Navaro-Yashin relates it, "The bodies of four people were found in the car: a parliamentarian, Istanbul's former vice-head of police, a pan-Turkist mafia dealer, and a prostitute with a false identity card. . . . The story of the news sounded like the scenario of a gangster movie. . . . Most people in Turkey received confirmation of their suspicions. During the two months following the accident, 'Susurluk' (as the event was called) became the preoccupation and the subject of everyday public conversation in Turkey" (Navaro-Yashin 2002, p. 171). The confirmed suspicions primarily concerned the utter corruption of the government and the collapse of the state into organized banditry. The public response, as subtly analyzed

---

Hrant Dink." Many Turkish reporters noted anxiously that the numbers were impressive but should have been higher.

80. Recording and broadcasting in Kurdish by Turkish media companies is subject to extraordinarily volatile legislation and public acceptability. The ubiquitous print publications and recordings to be seen on the streets of Istanbul in the mid- to late 1990s seem in recent years to have been driven underground once again.

81. European Union legislation demands freedom of expression for ethnic minorities, and the right to education in their own languages. At the time of writing, EU membership is the cause of deep retrenchments in Turkish political culture, particularly following the perceived rebuffs of 2005 (in which Turkey's membership status was effectively put on long-term hold).

in Navaro-Yashin's book, involved a wholesale cynicism and an anxious and compensatory process of "microperforming" the state in everyday life: deploying flags, wearing Atatürk lapel pins and other Atatürk insignia, and engaging in acts of petty violence against perceived antistate protestors.[82]

Nostalgia for Zeki Müren—manifested in the writing and reading of books, the construction and maintenance of websites, the organization of academic conference panels, and the resuscitation and circulation of old films and archival musical repertoire discussed in this chapter—suggests another response to prevalent post-Susurluk cynicism. In this nostalgia Müren appears above all as a figure of sincerity, honesty, and warmth. If his films are narratives of failure, it is a failure that springs from his refusal to recognize the wickedness, shallowness, and general shabbiness of the world around him—a refusal, ultimately, to be cynical. Zeki Müren nostalgia might then be seen as a public assertion that although Müren himself may have passed on in 1996 a few weeks before the Susurluk incident, the citizenly virtues to which the republic aspired had not necessarily died with him.

The military coup of 12 September 1980 introduced a period of economic austerity as well as political repression. Economic conditions, coupled with the growing war against a Kurdish insurgency in the southeast, accelerated the move of villagers to the cities, particularly Istanbul. The urbane citizenly virtues represented by Müren quickly found themselves under pressure. Cosmopolitan urbanites developed not only contempt but real fear of the villagers in their midst (Öncü 1999). A new kind of national conversation began to take shape over newly perceived rifts between rich and poor, city and village, east and west. At its heart was a strikingly different figure of musical-citizenly virtue: Orhan Gencebay. It is to him that we will turn next.

---

82. See Özyürek 2006 for a related critique, specifically an analysis of the privatization and miniaturization of state imagery in this period.

# 3

# The Affectionate Modernism of Orhan Gencebay

The political repression that followed the military coup of 12 September 1980 left marks on Turkish society that still defy comprehension but increasingly compel public attention.[1] This period was also marked by an intense public discussion about national emotionality, focused on a popular music genre called *arabesk*. That discussion also continues to reverberate, though now in an atmosphere of nostalgia.

The "*arabesk* debate," as some have called it,[2] was from the outset a one-sided affair; in other words, it was not much of a "debate." The intelligentsia initially saw *arabesk* in unambiguously negative terms and monopolized representations of it. For them,

---

1. A recent article in *Radikal*—one of an increasing number in recent years marking the anniversary of the coup, produced the following figures: 650,000 detained; 1,685,000 placed under surveillance (*fişlendi*); 230,000 people, in 210 court cases, charged; 7,000 death sentences demanded (by state prosecutor); 517 death sentences awarded; 50 people executed; 98,404 people charged with "membership in illegal organizations"; 14,000 stripped of their citizenship; 30,000 people out of the country as "refugees"; 300 people dead under suspicious circumstances; 171 people dead as a result of torture; 299 people killed in jail; 14 people dead from hunger strikes; 16 people killed while "attempting escape"; and 95 people killed in "exchanges of fire" (Saymaz 2008, p. 9). Protests on university campuses and in public spaces in the major cities, demanding that those responsible for the coup be held to account, are an increasingly prominent feature of these anniversaries.

2. See Stokes 1992a. The term I used as the title of this book was a direct translation of the Turkish *arabesk tartışması*, the common expression for the issue at that time.

it revealed an inner Orient in a supposedly Western country, and a cultural tangle of insufficiently suppressed "Arab" influences and traditional elements that flourished amongst poorly integrated rural migrants in the squatter towns.[3] It showed the painful limits of the Turkish state's efforts to become "modern."[4] Early in the 1990s these certainties began to waver, and alternative positions were mapped out.[5] Critical commentators began to question the modernist assumptions and appropriated orientalist discourse that sustained earlier representations. And they began to talk to—rather than simply at or about—the key musicians. Orhan Gencebay, an avuncular figure of irreproachable decency, soon emerged as *the* public voice of *arabesk*. The "sly civility" (Bhabha 2004) of this voice concerns me in this chapter.

## A Brief Biography

To redress the negativity that has habitually surrounded discussions of *arabesk,* let me attempt a brief fan's-eye introduction to Gencebay and his music. Two brief and somewhat typical encounters stick in my mind, the first of which took place in the summer of 1995. In those days Istanbul's Gül-

---

3. The term *arabesk* had come to be associated with rural-urban migrants and *gecekondu* (squatter town) neighborhoods by the mid-1970s. In a review about Gencebay, Oğuztan describes *arabesk* as the product of poor neighborhoods in Istanbul, listened to particularly on informal neighborhood minibuses (*dolmuş*) (Oğuztan 1975, p. 17). By 1977 Gencebay, who had always been anxious about these identifications, was also playing up the idea of the genre's association with misery. "Sarhoşun biri" (A Drunkard) was advertised in the following terms: "If you don't know what love is, if you don't drink, if you haven't suffered troubles, DO NOT BUY THIS RECORD" (in *Hey* 7 [39], 8 August 1977, p. 23). By this stage, the term *arabesk* had clearly gathered together the connotations of foreignness, misery, and poverty that were to define the "*arabesk* debate" of the 1980s.

4. Öztuna 1987 provides the most direct (and directly nationalist) critique from the point of view of associating the genre with Arab music influence. The term *arabesk* had long been rather vaguely associated with Arab music. Özışık, for instance, in a book that reflects the language and cultural politics of the 1950s, defines *arabesk* as "highly wrought ornamentations [*girift tezyinat*]" in composition or performance. It is used to describe not only "Arab style" (*Arab usûlü*) but anything that reminds one of that style. It is definitely "not Turkish" (Özışık 1963, p. 208). Eğribel 1984 and Güngör 1990 are Frankfurtian critiques, loosely speaking, though overt references to Marxian cultural theory had to be veiled or cautiously expressed in this period. *Arabesk* is associated in these two books with a warped modernity, problematic processes of urbanization, and the hyper-liberalism of the early Özal period. See Stokes 1992a for a full discussion of literature on *gecekondulaşma* (a Turkish neologism that might be translated as "squatter-town-ization") and its relationship to *arabesk*.

5. For two published academic rehabilitations of *arabesk*, see Özbek 1991, Işık and Erol 2002; both might be seen as responses to this moment. The Turkish translation of my own study of *arabesk* (Stokes 1992, the translation of which appeared in 2000) may have had a role to play. Özbek's important study will concern me later in this chapter.

hane Park hosted a municipally sponsored music festival during the summer months.[6] Major *arabesk* stars would give free concerts for the inhabitants of the *gecekondu*-s (squatter towns) and outlying neighborhoods of the city—people who in general were unable to afford a night out in the big clubs and *gazino*-s where the major stars habitually performed. These appearances were eagerly anticipated. In fact, they were seldom advertised far in advance for fear of the large and unruly crowds that might turn up. Occasionally word circulated about an appearance by one of the big names: Ferdi Tayfur, Müslüm Gürses, İbrahim Tatlıses, Bülent Ersoy. Street kids would claim the front seats and sleep in them for the next several days and nights, waiting for the concert to start. Others, like me, tended to turn up early on the day of the concert, expecting a couple of hours' wait even before knowing who was going to be performing, and ready for possible disappointment.

On this occasion I had turned up exceptionally early and was sitting in an open-air café close to the performance area—a pleasant, shady spot under large plane trees. There was a lull in business. The youngish waiter, clearly bored, pulled up a chair to find out who I was and what I was doing there. His name was Ali. Noticing an Orhan Gencebay cassette on the counter, I turned the conversation towards *arabesk*. I quickly discovered that Ali was a fan and had much to say.

For Ali, Gencebay (born in 1944) was to be distinguished from the "youngsters" one saw so often around Gülhane. Even then he was seen as a mature, avuncular figure rather than a member of the rising generation of popular musicians. Gencebay had made his name first on the TRT in the early 1960s as a young saz (long-necked folk lute) virtuoso. He had also composed some celebrated numbers for well-known popular folk musicians outside the TRT's ambit (notably for Ahmet Sezgin in the mid-1960s). He soon left the TRT, finding its cultural policy restrictive and opportunities in the commercial market attractive. His first hit song, "Bir Teselli Ver" (Console me), came out in 1969; it was attached to a musical film a couple of years later, and a great many other musical films followed over the next

---

6. Gülhane had been a site of public festivity since Ottoman times. It is close to the Sirkeci train station and the Eminönü transport ganglion, and thus easily accessible by public transport and *dolmuş* (shared taxi) for people living in the poorer districts to the west of the old city. At the time of writing, the Gülhane Park festival has been discontinued. It was apparently first postponed after the 1999 earthquake. I am not sure when the last such festival took place. It is a distant memory for most people today. Shortly after the earthquake, the proliferation of live concert venues for paying audiences around Istanbul's Taksim area (such as the open-air theaters in Harbiye and Kuruçeşme) may have reduced the perceived need in Sirkeci for an event of this kind, which must have been tremendously costly and troublesome for the local *belediye* (municipality).

decade.⁷ After a brief hiatus during the military coup, the later 1980s saw uninterrupted and energetic productivity by Genecebay, geared increasingly to sound recordings rather than films. His recording company, Kervan, was by now well established, producing cassettes (and, by the mid-1990s, CDs) for a thriving market then based in Unkapanı.⁸ Gencebay's intense productivity continued unabated through the first years of the new century, until a role as a commentator on *Türkiye Popstar Yarışması* (a Turkish television program based on the format of *American Idol*) began to occupy his time and energy in the middle of the decade.⁹

Ali reminded me that Gencebay was from Samsun, a large industrial city on the central Black Sea coast. This fact—one that everybody in Turkey knows—was worth stressing for Ali, who, it turned out, was from that area himself. As he knew, *arabesk* was associated by its critics with poor and uneducated migrants to the big cities from the rural southeast. From a metropolitan perspective, Samsun may well have been a remote province, but it was also in its own way a thriving, modern, and cosmopolitan city. Gencebay's musical education there, received mostly from his father and from family friends, encompassed Western classical music as well as Turkish art and folk music. It continued when the family moved to Edirne (a city in Turkish Thrace) and eventually Istanbul. To Ali, Gencebay's Black Sea roots, cosmopolitanism, education, and general cultural seriousness meant that he could enjoy Gencebay's *arabesk* while distancing himself from sterotypes created by the intelligentsia.¹⁰

---

7. For useful discographic information, on which much of this chapter relies, see http://www.diskotek.arkaplan.com.tr. It includes pictures of original 45 rpm records and record sleeves. Dates given for "Bir teselli ver" vary greatly, often to as early as 1968. Record numbers and the dates of reviews published in *Hey*, though not infallible, would seem to suggest the later date and the general accuracy of this website. The date of the film (1971) is easier to establish. *Orhan Gencebay klasikleri* gives both the first recording date (1969) and the film date (1971); this should probably be taken as authoritative.

8. Gencebay established Kervan in 1972, parting company with İstanbul Plak, which he had co-owned and with whom he recorded all of his early hits. Kervan's first Gencebay recordings hit the market early in 1973. Gencebay proved exceptionally adept at promoting his new company. The pages of *Hey* and *Ses* in these early years attest to one publicity stunt after another; Gencebay had a knack for keeping himself in the limelight. Celebrity goalkeepers recorded for Kervan. Forty-one women named Zühdü (a slightly unusual name) were invited to a *gazino* to celebrate the release of an album by Gencebay entitled *Zühdü*. And so forth.

9. On *Popstar*, as on *American Idol*, amateur singers compete and a professional panel evaluates them. A phone vote by viewers eliminates candidates and eventually selects a winner. Gencebay and Bülent Ersoy are the regular panelists.

10. For the intelligentsia, *arabesk* listeners were uncouth proletarians who from the mid-1980s were satirized in the figure of the unshaven, prayer-bead twirling *maganda* who appeared in cartoon magazines such as *Fırt* and *Leman* (and notably in a cartoon strip Turkish readers of that generation

One thing rankled Ali, though, as it did many of Gencebay's other fans. Gencebay was rarely to be seen. Where other *arabesk* stars considered brief appearances at Gülhane crucial as a way of demonstrating their gratitude to fans who did not have enough money to see them in concert, Gencebay had never shown his face there. In fact, he has hardly ever appeared live on the concert stage—a topic that never fails to come up in published interviews.[11] Throughout his career, Gencebay has made a variety of excuses for this, all of them vaguely plausible.[12] Ali told me he would wait night and day for a front seat at Gülhane if Gencebay were to perform there. Half of Istanbul would be there, he said. Does the guy really know just how popular he is, just how much he means to people like me? Ali's comments seemed to have a slightly resentful tone, but there was also unmistakably a note of admiration for the single-minded self-fashioning that Gencebay's absence implied.

For fans, Gencebay has always had an aura not only of intelligence and cosmopolitanism but also of self-sufficiency. For many, this is quite simply encapsulated in the way he looks. Pictures of this "look" are ubiquitous; few

---

will quickly remember: *Grup Perişan*). See Öncü 1999 for a more detailed genealogy of the *maganda*. I am also grateful for conversations with Pierre Hecker, an expert on the topic, about the relationship between metal and *arabesk* fans in Turkey during this period.

11. A large advertisement in 1973 for the new Kervan initiative (see *Hey* 3 [28], 30 May 1973) struggled to make a virtue of this fact as early as 1973. Announcing the presence of "the creator of a new school of Turkish music" in breathless terms, the advertisement continued: "'Why don't you appear on stage?' they sometimes ask. It is people who don't know him who ask this question. Those who don't know are not able to imagine that he thinks of his listeners and fans as 'worthy as water' [i.e., gold]. He has no—and I mean *no*—intention of breaking his links with his fans, with those he loves." Though he often tried to make a virtue of what was clearly a deeply rooted reluctance—and to construct an intimacy with fans in other ways, as here—the need to prove himself "live" obviously nagged Gencebay. See Akyıldız 1974 for coverage of a rare appearance at the İzmir Fair, and suggestions that he was explicitly trying to deal with claims that his voice was not up to live stage work.

12. In a phone interview that appeared in *Müzik Magazin* in 1986, one fan, Ahmet Eman, asked Gencebay: "There are four main *bağlama* players in Turkey. I think you are the best, as a virtuoso. Have you ever thought about doing this kind of thing in concert?" Gencebay replied: "Right now, one of the things I am thinking of doing is giving a *bağlama* recital, and to do a concerto. Of course, since this will involve hard work on the orchestration, it's going to take a long time" (*Müzik Magazin* 2 [1], 29 December 1986). When I eventually met Gencebay, I was unable to resist putting the same question to him. His answer hinted at a rather engaging insecurity: "Why haven't I done live performances? I much prefer composing and thinking about music. In this business one has to have showmanship [*şövmenliği*], stage showmanship. I'm not good at that. I don't do stage stuff because I prefer writing music. I keep putting it off, saying I'll do it one of these days, I'll do it one of these days. Twenty-seven years have gone by. I'm still putting it off! (laughs) Just too much . . . ! It's as though if I appear on stage, I won't be able to compose; it's like I've got this fear that I won't be able to produce [*ben bir şey üretemem gibi geliyor bana, benim bir korkum var*]" (interview by author 4 August 1995; unless otherwise stated, all subsequent citations are from this same interview and have been translated by the author).

in modern Turkey come close in terms of sheer familiarity. A second brief anecdote: I remember bringing a copy of the latest Gencebay cassette back to a friend's flat after a shopping trip on one occasion in the mid-1980s. My friend hated *arabesk,* and I was looking forward to antagonizing him when he asked—as I knew he would—what was in my plastic bag. His sister, Yasemin, then about eighteen, had joined him from the village that year. She enjoyed teasing her elder brother and generally deflating his musical and other pretensions. She seized the moment, not only to engage me in enthusiastic pseudo-fan talk about Gencebay's films and earlier songs, but also to comment on his good looks. To twist the knife, Yasemin came up with a phrase that stuck in my mind: *"Ama ne güzel pozları var!"* (Roughly, "Don't you just love the way he *stands!*") For her, Gencebay's publicity pictures were the very definition of *poz* (pose).[13] Like publicity shots of most popular media stars in Turkey, these were mainly pictures of a face, brightly lit against a neutral background. Gencebay usually leaned in towards the camera, engaging the viewer directly and suggestively with his eyes, head slightly lowered, chest out and shoulders back. The clothes (usually a smart leather jacket or a matching T-shirt and sweater combination), hairstyle, and mustache suggested proletarian decency but no pretensions. People like Yasemin and Ali were familiar with the iconography and would recognize and enjoy its subtly varying moods. For Yasemin the connotations of *poz* were positive: machismo, pleasure in the gaze of others, a certain familiarity and intimacy. For her brother, of course, they were the very definition of the broader problem: provincials taking over, winding back the clock of Turkey's efforts to be Western and modern. But Yasemin had chosen her words well. Her brother did not, as I remember, have much of a reply.

Gencebay's fans know him in a variety of ways. Unlike the lives of other *arabesk* stars, which have been shrouded in mystique or mythology, Gencebay's life story is a matter of unremarkable public record. Sought out by journalists and academics throughout his career, his views on many subjects are well known. There is an intimacy to this knowledge. The visual imagery is ubiquitous; most people recognize that *poz* with a smile. His films, tales of unhappy love and bloody revenge, are easy to get hold of on VCD or the Web. Even in the early 1980s, when cassette sellers mainly stocked current hits, Gencebay's 1970s "classics" (as they were already called) could readily be found. Fans, as a consequence, know his music with a detailed intensity

---

13. A good source of chronologically arranged visual information is to be found in the Gencebay discography at http://www.diskotek.arkaplan.com.tr.

**Figure 3a.** Cover of Orhan Gencebay cassette box (*Beni biraz anlasaydın*, Kervan)

unusual in the *arabesk* world. I will try to demonstrate this in the next section with reference to an early song, "Batsın bu dünya" (A curse on the world), one that has been central to subsequent efforts to understand the politics of Gencebay's *arabesk*.

## "Everything Is Darkness"

"Batsın bu dünya" (1975) is widely considered a Gencebay classic. Kervan marketed it as such in the early 1980s.[14] For academic commentators, the song marked a moment of authenticity. Fans and others have evoked it passionately in conversation with me, often with reference to personal circum-

---

14. My own collection of early Gencebay tapes dates from around this time; they were mostly bought from a man who ran a small cassette booth near the bus stop on Şehzadebaşı Caddesi, a street where I once took saz lessons and still occasionally buy musical instruments. He prided himself on his service to the *arabesk* cognoscenti, and the Gencebay "classics" were always neatly on display.

stances.[15] Gencebay himself included it as the first number on his 1998 CD *Orhan Gencebay klasikleri* (Orhan Gencebay classics).[16] Others, prompted no doubt by his new role as commentator and judge on *Türkiye Popstar Yarişması*, have paid homage by rendering the song in pop, rock, and hip-hop idioms.

"Batsın bu dünya" marked the emergence of a musical style that changed little in subsequent years.[17] It was the first of Gencebay's songs to be recorded in stereo and to exploit its effects.[18] It marked a stage in a shift towards instrumental rather than vocal artistry;[19] fans often describe this instrumentally oriented style as "*fantezi*."[20] It also marked a shift in the tone of Genecbay's lyrics and vocal style. His later songs involved a kind of conver-

15. This, for example, from a Turkish friend in Chicago, loosely translated: "When I first came here as a student [i.e., to the University of Chicago], I made money driving packages around for a firm, driving throughout the night. I'd put 'Batsın bu dünya' on the tape deck and listen to it constantly [sings, rather tunelessly, 'Batsın bu dünya . . . !' and laughs]. That was how I survived."

16. He selected these on the basis of votes; "Batsın bu dünya" was apparently an easy winner, and thus appears first on the compilation.

17. One of the principal agents of this consistency in modal, rhythmic, and even harmonic matters has been composition on the saz, the long-necked folk lute. Gencebay can switch rapidly on this instrument from linear, improvisatory melodies derived from art music to the patterned plectrum movements peculiar to folk music (*tavır*). Chords and thus certain harmonic conceptions are also possible. See Stokes 1992b on saz chording and *tavır*. The art of saz chording was peripheral on the acoustic instrument, but essential on the *elektrosaz*.

18. The full-page advertisement for "Batsın bu dünya" in *Ses* 52, 14 (1975), makes much of the technical features: "*Bu plak* 'full-frequency-range four-phase system' *ile kayıt edilmiş ve* 'Dolby noise reduction' *ilavelidir* [This record is recorded with the full-frequency-range four-phase system and includes Dolby noise reduction]." It stands between "Bir teselli ver," which was recorded in mono in 1969, and "Hatasız kul olmaz," which was recorded on four channels in 1976 (Özbek 1991). "Bir teselli ver" was essentially an ensemble performance captured by microphone. "Hatasız kul olmaz" involved elaborate orchestrations (including oboe and trumpet), and a clear distinction between foreground and background (*altyapı*, as studio engineers used to call it, comprising drums and percussion, electric bass, and keyboard, usually added last). Gencebay now works with an assistant, with whom he produces a *şablon* (chord chart) and then a *partisiyon* (instrumental arrangement) for studio work, at which point the *altyapı* is added. The harmonic structure of the song is added separately, almost as an afterthought to tunes that are conceived melodically on the saz from the outset. "Batsın bu dünya" marked, in other words, a stage in the evolution of a concept of acoustic "space" (Moore 1993) and a division of labor in the studio production of *arabesk* songs.

19. Gencebay's voice was often considered problematically "weak." This claim has a long history. References to the issue start to crop up in the mid-1970s. His first appearance at the Izmir Fair, for example, was understood by some as an attempt to respond to "rumors" that his voice was "inadequate" for the stage (Akyıldız 1974). Reviews of "Batsın bu dünya" raised the issue, as we see later in this chapter.

20. *Beni biraz anlasaydım* (1986) and *Cennet gözlüm* (1987) stand out in this regard, including songs such as "Elhamdüllilah," "Dünya dönüyor" and "Cennet gözlüm." Gencebay often refers to these in interviews as "*deneysel*" (experimental). The term *fantezi* (fantasy) has some of the same musical implications of its earlier usage (see Rona 1970 and chapter 2, note 44)—in other words, freedom from the metrical and formal constrains of *şarkı* form. As used with reference to Gencebay, though, the

sation with the beloved and the external world and, correspondingly, a more muted, modulated vocal style. From that point of view, "Batsın bu dünya" seems to look back to his earlier songs. It depicts a protagonist absorbed by his own pain and suffering at the hands of fate (*kader*). Gencebay's voice is correspondingly choked and emotional—to use the Turkish expression, "burnt" (*yanık*).

"Batsın bu dünya" is remembered by many as a powerful song, a howl of protest at an unjust social order. This interpretation draws on the narrative of the film in which the song appears. The film (*Batsın bu dünya*, 1975) was made by Osman Seden, based on a story by Vedat Türkali. It owes much to the conventions of the music cinema popularized by Zeki Müren (see chapter 2) a generation earlier, but also a certain amount to the rural-themed cinematic realism popular in Turkey at the time.[21] It costars Müjde Ar as Seher, a village girl. Gencebay plays Orhan,[22] a motorboat ferry owner. For reasons only partly explained in the film, Orhan has a patron who has evidently looked after him in the past and to whom he is deeply indebted. This patron has political aspirations but his feckless son is causing him problems. Tearing around the countryside on his motorbike, the son and a group of his friends come across, harass, and finally rape Seher. Orhan, though in no way involved, is obliged to take responsibility for the rape, all charges being dropped if he agrees to marry her. This he does with deep reluctance; he has no choice since his patron commands absolute authority. Seher is shunned by the villagers and treated with increasing coldness by her new husband. To make matters worse, the patron's son continues to harass her. Finally she attempts suicide. The suicide attempt kindles Orhan's pity and affection, and true love blossoms. But the patron's son continues to bother Seher, and Orhan's deep sense of humiliation grows. Seher, now pregnant, looks anx-

---

term also signifies instrumental play (at the expense of vocal and lyrical sophistication), and a certain idiosyncrasy in the use of *makam*.

21. Seden trained with Lütfi Akad, who made a number of Zeki Müren films; the kinship between his work and Akad's sentimental films is direct and obvious. The popularity of Yaşar Kemal's novels and Yılmaz Güney's films (serious, left-leaning revenge narratives dramatizing the "Eastern question" in rural settings) should be borne in mind, along with the popularity of films by Charles Bronson and his Turkish counterparts (e.g., Cüneyt Arkın). See Stokes 1992a, pp. 93–96, for a brief discussion of developments in popular cinema during this period.

22. In most *arabesk* films the lead actor uses his own real name and essentially plays "himself"—which is to say a personality that remains stable in character, if not in employment and other narrative details, from film to film, and is recognizably the actor's public character. The lead actress, meanwhile, assumes a fictional name and plays a role more obviously relating to, and restricted to, the narrative of a particular film. Online discussions amongst Turkish fans these days tend to blur the issue; any female character played by Müjde Ar is, for example, usually referred to as "Müjde."

iously at Orhan, who is lost in dark thoughts; he sings "Batsın bu dünya." Orhan, speaking to Seher, promises his unborn child "a present," and disappears in his boat. Seher watches anxiously from the quay. Later he returns with the body of the patron's son swinging from the boat's mast.

The interpretation of "Batsın bu dünya" as a social protest piece also draws on the song's lyrics. Formally speaking, these are divided by syllable count, rhyme scheme, grammatical construction, and rhetoric into four distinct sections. Gencebay himself uses art music terminology to describe the song's sections, but one has to adapt this terminology since not everything "fits" into what is in fact a hybrid of art song (with *zemin* and *zaman* constituting the first and second lines respectively and a contrasting *meyan* section constituting the third), folk song (with lines determined by syllable count rather than poetic meter), and the verse-chorus structure of Western pop. The first section might then be thought of as an "opening," the second as a "*zemin*," the third as a "*meyan*," and the fourth as a "chorus" in Western popular music terms.

(opening section)
*Yazıklar olsun, yazıklar olsun*     A pity, a pity[23]
*Kaderin böylesine, yazıklar olsun*     That fate should do such a thing, a pity

*Herşey karanlık, nerde insanlık*     Everything is darkness, where is humanity?

*Kula kulluk edene, yazıklar olsun*     Shame on those who make a slave of the slave.

("*zemin*" section)
*Batsın bu dünya, batsın bu dünya*     A curse on the world, may this dream end

*Ağlatıpta gülene, yazıklar olsun*     Shame on those who laugh and make others cry

*Doğmamış çileler, yaşanmış dertler*     Do I yet have to suffer yet-unborn
*Hasret çeken gönül benim mi olsun?*     trials, yet-unlived torments?

---

23. "*Yazıklar olsun*" has shades of meaning in English somewhere between "a pity" and "a shame" (attached to a dative noun to indicate "shame on *x*" or "pity *x*"). The translator has to choose an appropriate shade depending on context. Here, clearly, the singer is calling for pity on himself, but wants to shame those who "make a slave of the slave" and "make other people cry but themselves laugh."

(*"meyan"* section)
| | |
|---|---|
| *Ben ne yaptım kader sana* | Fate [*kader*], what have I done to you? |
| *Mahkum ettin beni bana* | You have imprisoned me in myself |
| *Her nefeste bin sitem var* | A thousand torments with every breath |
| *Şikayetim Yaradana* | I complain to the Creator (x 2) |

("chorus" section)
| | |
|---|---|
| *Şaşıran senmi yoksa benmiyim bilemedim* | Is it you or me who is surprised? |
| *Öyle bir dert verdinki kendime gelemedim* | You have made me suffer so much I am distraught |
| *Çıkmaz bir sokaktayım yolumu bulamadım* | I am stuck on a no-through road, I can't find my way |
| *Of . . .* | (Sigh . . .) |

("opening" section of second verse)
| | |
|---|---|
| *Ben mi yarattım, ben mi yarattım* | Is it I who has created it [the world], is it I? |
| *Derdi ıstırabı, ben mi yarattım* | Its pain, its suffering, is it I who created it? |
| *Günah zevk olmuşsa, vefa yorulmuşsa* | Sin turned into pleasure, faithfulness worn out, |
| *Düzen bozulmuşsa ben mi yarattım* | The order of things in ruins, is it I who created it? |

(The *"zemin," "meyan,"* and "chorus" are then repeated with the same words)

Musically speaking, the song is unsettled. The various different musical elements and processes in play have not yet gelled into an idiom that would later be perceived as unified and recognizably Gencebay's own. Recognition of this unsettled quality was expressed rather negatively in early reviews. For example, a 1976 review in *Hey* (the most significant Turkish popular music journal of the day) praised the instrumental sound, the rhythmic novelty, and the skills of the musicians, but found the voice "weak."[24] The re-

---

24. *Hey,* published from 1970 to 1985, was edited first by Doğan Şener and later by Hulusi Tunca. It was Turkey's major pop music journal, had a huge readership in the 1970s, and was a venue for serious discussion, criticism, and argument. Its vigorous support for popular music lobbying organizations (FISAN, MESAM, etc.) had a tangible effect on Turkish broadcasting policy. *Hey* kept Turkish readers abreast of developments in America and Europe, reporting regularly on music com-

viewer contended that the song, as a consequence, strained for effect.[25] The reviewer for *Ses* agreed. The song was refreshingly "different" (*değişik*) in this reviewer's opinion, but its "vocal delivery" (*şarkının söylenişi*) of the song was "not so successful" (*aynı başarıya ulaşmamakta*).[26]

To put these points another way, the reviewers seemed to detect a misfit between voice and song. *Hey*'s reviewer felt that the weakness of the voice must have "compelled" (*zorlanmış olması*) the singer to be more "attentive" (*dikkatlı*) to "words and music"—that is, to the construction of the song. Two different aesthetics are evoked here, one vocally oriented (the song as a vehicle for a powerful voice), the other structurally oriented (the song as an inventive play of words, melody, and instrumental arrangement). *Hey*'s reviewer evidently felt that the song seemed to want to keep both aesthetics in play without really settling on either, and that this was a problem. Looked at in a more positive light, as Gencebay fans do, one might also say that "Batsın bu dünya" makes a virtue of this misfit.

The detailed analysis on the following pages draws attention to three different aspects of the song. The first concerns tensions between instrumental and vocal elements, the second concerns the relationship between modal and tonal processes, and the third concerns the dialogue between instrumental sounds. I want to show how that which reviewers considered "ill-fitting" and poorly conceived might equally be considered in terms of the emergence of a new popular aesthetic, coherent on its own terms.

First, there is a tension in the song between instrumental and vocal elements. The song is conspicuous from the outset for its long and ornate instrumental introduction. This begins with a spiky sequence on the electric

---

petitions across the continent. Its main rival was the *Milliyet* supplement, *Ses*, which claimed much less for itself as a vehicle for critique and discussion. *Blue Jean*, *Müzik Dergisi*, and *Müzik Magazin* (see also Dilmener 2003, pp. 337–38 for a brief history) were essentially music industry organs, enjoying brief lives in the late 1980s. The somewhat more scholarly *Müzük* and *Çalıntı* appeared equally briefly in the 1990s. *Hey* had no real rival or successor.

25. "The first thing that comes to mind is that the vocal weakness causes the artist to take extra care about the music and the words [*Sesin güçlü olmayışı, sanatçıyı müzik ve sözler yönünden daha dikkatli zorlanmış olması akla gelen ilk neden*]." *Hey* 6 (3), 28 June 1976. The anonymous reviewer did, however, award the record three out of four stars.

26. One might note that many highly popular voices at the time had a muffled and withdrawn character. Ferdi Tayfur and Müslüm Gürses immediately spring to mind. To use the terms of an early review of Gürses, who appeared on the scene late in the 1970s, these singers were deemed "mediocre" (*vasat*) in technical terms, or as "lacking in color" (*rengini yitirmiş*). The sparkling vocal pyrotechnics of İbrahim Tatlıses, another "folksy" *arabesk* singer, are those of a slightly younger generation. It is tempting to connect the "mediocrity" of these voices with the political turmoil of the time. Plain voices, hinting at veiled meanings and emotions, would have appealed to many for whom getting by was a matter of keeping thoughts and feelings to themselves.

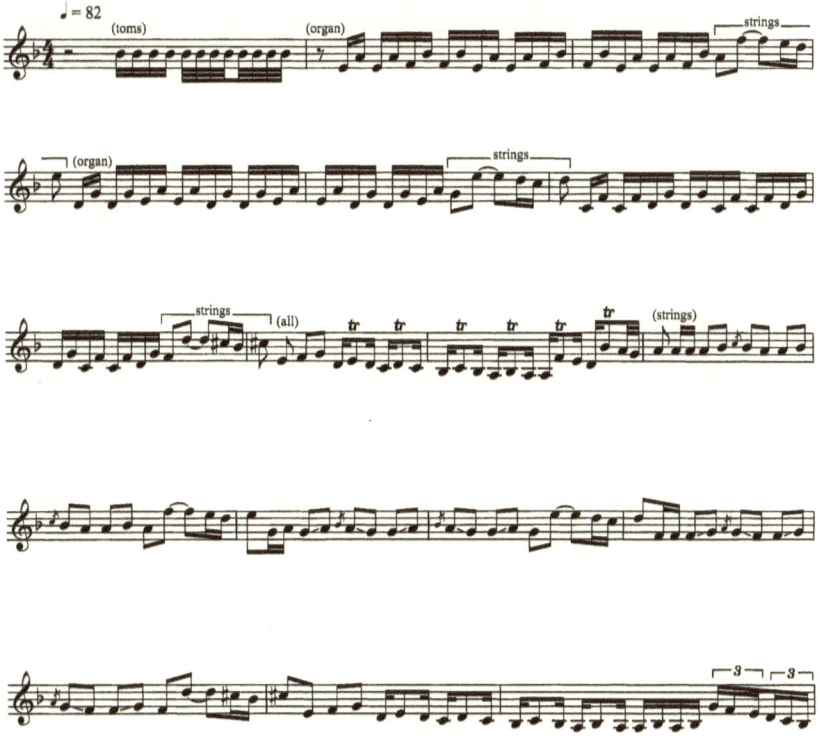

**3a.** Orhan Gencebay's "Batsın bu dünya," instrumental introduction.

organ, with a rock-like feel, echoed by *arabesk*-style (unison, ornamented) strings (music example 3a). This is interrupted by a smoldering vocalization accompanied by flamenco guitar and *elektrosaz* (section 1; see music example 3b).

There is an uneasy relationship between these two elements in the introduction. The instrumental passage at the very beginning suggests a song in a Western pop or rock idiom—modern, upbeat, and cosmopolitan. The opening vocalization, though, wrenches the listener back to the expressive world of *arabesk:* a pained and emotional voice expressing solitary torment. Here and elsewhere, the voice "interrupts" and occasionally even silences other musical elements. The "chorus," for example, ends abruptly. The expected last line is cut off by a long solo vocal sigh of measureless frustration and exhaustion, expressed in the word *of* (see end of music example 3f).

Secondly, the song is a hybrid of modal and tonal processes. The term "modal process" refers in this context to musical production conceived in terms of traditional *makam*-based melody types (whether in urban or rural

3b. Orhan Gencebay's "Batsın bu dünya," opening section. Transcribed up a minor third from the recorded version. The *elektrosaz* notation indicates the two-comma flat according to the conventions of Turkish folk music transcription.

practice; there is a certain overlap). "Tonal process" refers in this context to musical production conceived in terms of a grammar of chords or harmonic progressions. The hybridization of these two processes in "Batsın bu dünya" is typical of Gencebay's later music. Subsequent practice made for a smoother synthesis and a degree of familiarity with listeners. But at this early stage, the rough edges still show.

Gencebay himself described the song's modal process as involving two *makam*-s: *uşşak* "on top of" *nihavent* (Özbek 1991, p. 282). In fact, this is hard to figure out. Such an interpretation would require the song to come to a close on the fifth degree of the *nihavent* and not its "tonic," which would be unusual to say the least. It is perhaps more usefully understood, at least if we insist (as Gencebay does) on using *makam* vocabulary, as a song in *muhayyerkürdi makamı*. It was probably a momentary slip of Gencebay's tongue to mention *nihavent*.[27] Gencebay himself describes many of his songs as being in

---

27. The mistake is comprehensible if one conjectures a momentary muddling of *nihavent* and *muhayyerkürdi*. The tonal structure of both is similar. *Nihavent*'s lower pentachord is G–A–B five comma flat–C–D (a transposition of the *buselik* pentachord from A to G). *Muhayyerkürdi*'s lower tetrachord

*muhayyerkürdi,* so this seems likely both from the point of view of art music theory and in also terms of his later compositional habits.[28]

Textbook art music theory (see, for instance, Yılmaz 1977) presents this *makam* as a mixture of *muhayyer* and *kürdi*—in other words as what is called a "combinatory" *(birleştirilmiş) makam. Muhayyer* is a "descending" *(inici) makam,* in other words, one in which melodies should start high and end low. It comprises a lower *hüseyni* pentachord (an *uşşak* tetrachord with an added whole tone) and an *uşşak* tetrachord above it. The pivotal note between the two is E (called in art music theory *hüseyni;* theoretically this is the *güçlü,* which I will translate here, risking confusion with Western art music theory, as the "dominant"). In theory, *muhayyerkürdi* "mixes" *muhayyer* with *kürdi*—which is to say that in practice, sections of *muhayyer* and *kürdi* alternate, with *kürdi* predominating at final cadences. Many intermediate phrases thus come to rest either on E (the "dominant" of *muhayyer*) or, particularly at approaching cadences, on D (the "dominant" of *kürdi*). A further prescription for *muhayyerkürdi* is the elaboration of, and cadencing on, a *çargah* pentachord on the upper F. These prescriptions are all laid out in music example 3c.

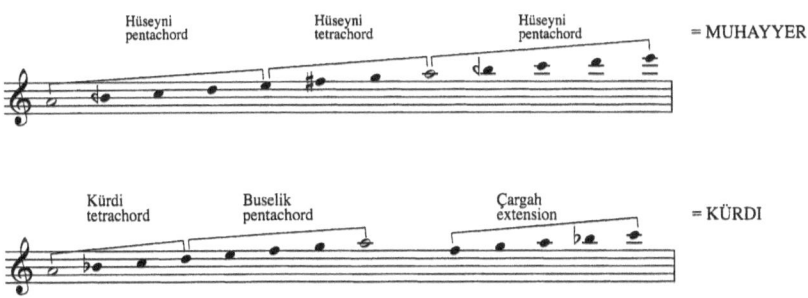

**3c.** *Muhayyerkürdi makamı*

---

(at cadences like *kürdi*) is A–B five comma flat–C–D. *Nihavent,* then, is the same, tonally speaking, with an extra whole tone at the bottom. Özbek is not a music specialist, and İletişim, her publishers, had not published much if anything in the way of music books before, so the mistake—if indeed it is a mistake—would certainly be understandable. *Kürdilihicazkar* is another theoretical possibility, though the *uşşak* move in the *meyan* is less comprehensible if, at least, we insist on understanding it in conventional art-music terms.

28. In addition to Gencebay's *muhayyerkürdi, uşşak makamı* is often used, as is *nihavent. Hicaz* occurs with lesser frequency. *Rast, segah* and *hüzzam* are rare. I would hazard the following generalization, based on a survey of the entire recorded repertoire: 60 percent are in *muhayyerkürdi,* 15 percent in *hicaz,* 15 percent in *uşşak,* and 10 percent in either *segah* or *hüzzam.* See Signell for an English-language characterization of these *makam*-s. The proportions outlined here seem to have remained consistent throughout his recording career.

In conversation with me, Gencebay demonstrated *muhayyerkürdi* in a slightly different way, one that might appropriately be described as a folk musician's take on the classical (urban) construction. He simply played a descending octave pitch set (A–G–F–E–D–C–B flat–A). Running down the scale again, he introduced first E flats and then D flats to demonstrate alternative approaches to cadences. While the E flat is congruent with various cadential patterns in textbook art music theorizations of *muhayyerkürdi*, the D flat makes less sense. In folk music terms, though, D flat–C–B flat–A descents are very characteristic of cadential patterns in the western Anatolian genre *bozlak*, which is characterized by vocal improvisation, virtuosic saz playing, and fate-obsessed texts.[29] So in modal terms, Gencebay's hybridized *muhayyerkürdi* allows him to move between urban and rural idioms.

It also permits hybridization with Western tonal procedures. This hybridization is, in a sense, a possibility latent within the art music formulation. The descending *kürdi* D–C–B five comma flat–A cadence in art-music *muhayyerkürdi* enables a Phrygian chord progression, one which Peter Manuel describes as the bedrock of popular "Mediterranean" harmony (Manuel 1986). It allows both E minor and D minor chords (when the melody settles on the "dominants" of *muhayyer* and *kürdi*, E and D respectively) to play a tonal role in relation to an A major/minor "tonic." It also allows for a move to what might be described as "relative major" (i.e., F major, when the melody, as *muhayyerkürdi* permits, cadences using the *çargah* pentachord on the upper F). Such realizations of the tonal possibilities of *muhayyerkürdi* are theoretically limited if one observes textbook rules. In presenting *muhayyer* simply as a descending scale and avoiding its articulation in terms of the pentachords and tetrachords as art music theory demands, Gencebay maintains the widest possible range of tonal possibilities. In short, Gencebay's *muhayyerkürdi* allows his music to be composed and heard, simultaneously, as folk music, as urban art music, and in terms of Western (or, in Manuel's terms, "Mediterranean") tonality (see music example 3d).

"Batsın bu dünya" is the first of Gencebay's songs in which these three elements are consistently in play. As we have already seen, the first section (introduction) plays with the *kürdi* tetrachord in the voice and repetitions of a basic Phrygian progression (A major–B flat major–A major) on the guitar

---

29. Throughout the 1980s Neşet Ertaş was the most popular singer and saz player in this genre. Though he lived in Germany and was not often to be seen or heard in Turkey during those years, he was very widely admired across the musical spectrum. He has enjoyed a major comeback in recent years.

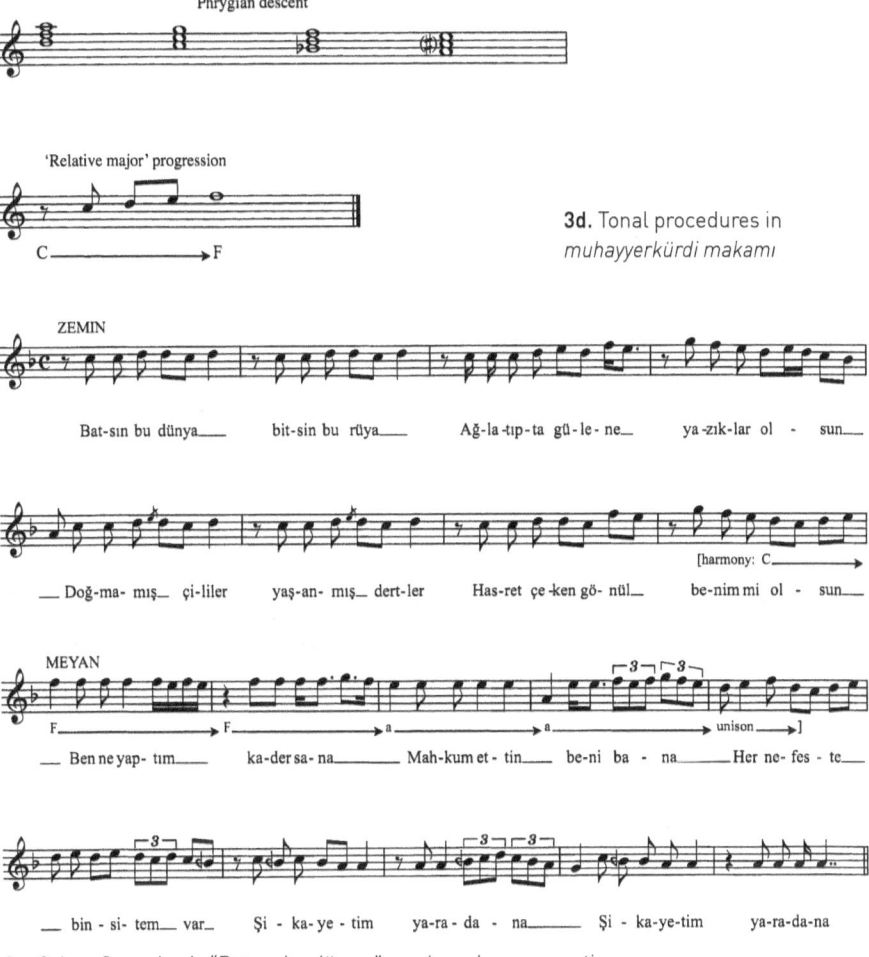

**3e.** Orhan Gencebay's "Batsın bu dünya," *zemin* and *meyan* sections

(see music example 3b). The second section (the *zemin*) of "Batsın bu dünya" has a consistently harmonic feel in ascent, marked by repeated C major–D minor progressions at the beginning and clearly marked C major–F major progression at the end. The third section (the *meyan*) begins on a sustained F major chord followed by an equally clearly articulated A minor chord, and has thereafter a consistently modal feel in descent. The modal feel is emphasized by a pronounced use of the *uşşak* tetrachord (marking the word "complaint"). So a harmonic logic pushes the *zemin* up the scale, and a modal logic pushes the *meyan* down (music example 3e).

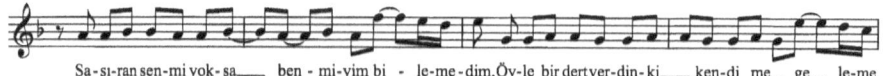

**3f.** Orhan Gencebay's "Batsın bu dünya," chorus section

To conclude this brief account of Gencebay's modal and tonal hybridization, the "chorus" reprises the ensemble theme of the introduction in a clearly articulated, sequentially descending *muhayyerkürdi*. The final solo vocal sigh, "*Of*," descends by an octave and sixth. Another *makam* (*hicaz*) is touched on at the top of this vocal phrase, emphasizing the contrast with what has gone before, and underlining its interruptive nature. This would be unusual in a classical performance of *muhayyerkürdi*, but would not be out of place in folk music practice, particularly the genre known as *bozlak*. Here again, expressive effects are derived from the unsettled relationship between *makam* procedures, Western tonality, and folk improvisatory practices.

The most conspicuous feature of the introduction is a complex dialogue of instrumental sounds. The introduction to the film version of the song makes this dialogue more obvious than it is in the 45 rpm version transcribed above, partly because it is emphasized by the visual narrative and partly because it is compressed, no doubt to help move the action in the film. Music and visuals are closely connected; rapid changes in musical affect align with changing camera angles and backdrops, or with the tense exchange of glances between the two main characters. The opening moments show Seher looking anxiously, left to right, across the viewer's field of vision. Orhan, remember, has taken pity on his waiflike and suicidal wife. But now he is confronted by further crushing indignities. His boss's son and his friends continue to harass Seher and terrorize the villagers with their motorbikes. Orhan broods on the injustice of the situation and on his own helplessness.[30] Seher's anxious glance is linked with ascending repetitions of the opening motif, played heavily by the full orchestra:

---

30. A later version of this scene, which seems to have been shot as a kind of video single with a different actress, makes this violence explicit: Orhan is first seen holding a gun.

**3g.** Seher's anxious glance

This is abruptly silenced by a piercing string motif that is played in loose and heavily ornamented unison:

**3h.** Orhan walking

In the film version, the camera angle cuts between the faces of Orhan and Seher every two measures. Orhan already has been briefly glimpsed walking around a field and puffing on a cigarette, clearly lost in dark thoughts. As a result of this alternating pattern of shots, the first sounds of the string motif coincide with a shot of Orhan, and the second iteration of that motif coincides with a brief cut back to Seher. From this point on, however, we see less and less of Seher. The flamenco guitar breaks in, extending the opening motif with repeated Phrygian (A major–B flat major) chords, *rasgueado* technique, and virtuosic scales. As we hear the first words of the vocal ("Pity . . .") we see the singer silhouetted against crashing sea and sunset, looking right to left (and thus mirroring Seher) as he sings. From then on, visually speaking, we are in the singer's world, watching him ponder his dismal options as he works on his boat and drinks alone in a bar.

The 45 rpm single version is a little different. It starts, as we have seen, with the ensemble version of the opening motif (see, again, music example 3a). The string interruption (music example 3h) is omitted, and the flamenco guitar's contribution is reduced to a few brief chords. An extra element is included, though: a brief *elektrosaz* commentary as the vocal begins (see again music example 3b). The *elektrosaz* dialogues with the vocal using the *uşşak* tetrachord, which sits uneasily with the continuing *kürdi* tetrachord of the vocal introduction and the still resonating Phrygian progressions of the guitar. In this context the *elektrosaz* seems to come from an entirely different sound world.

In both of these introductions to "Batsın bu dünya," instrumental sounds are opposed in a scheme of binary oppositions: Western-style rock ensemble versus *arabesk*-style unison strings, modern and cosmopolitan flamenco guitar versus "traditional" *elektrosaz*. Gencebay suggests that for him this binary opposition of timbres unites in a higher-level synthesis, a "totality" of emotional life. As he put it to me in conversation: "It's like this. In life you've got everything. Birth, death. Crying, laughing. Happiness, unhappiness. Joy, tears. I mean everything. There's a polarization [*kutupsallık*]. These are the main outlines [*ana hatları*] of our lives. That's what we've got in my compositions. Sometimes mainly tears. Sometimes mainly laughter. It depends on what I'm trying to do in a particular composition. But generally, everything [emotionally speaking] in life exists in my music."

This explanation neglects a significant musical fact: that there is an unsettled *temporal* relationship between these polarized (i.e., binary) elements of signification. Western/cosmopolitan instruments introduce a theme but they are interrupted, as by the *arabesk*-style strings in the introduction to the film version of the song, or almost literally undermined, as by the *elektrosaz* in the introduction to the 45 rpm version. There is indeed a polarization, a binary logic. But it is an unstable one, constantly interrupted by its second element, its "supplement" in Derridean terms: an "East" signified here by heavily ornamented, heterophonic unison strings, a sobbing solo vocal, and the *elektrosaz*'s dissonant interpolations. For fans Gencebay may be right, but only up to a point. His music may well contain "everything, emotionally speaking." But its instrumental significations are not so simply synthesized or unified. Its identity as *arabesk,* for fans, is defined by its interruptive elements, which have anguish at their core.

"Batsın bu dünya" is the focus of nostalgia today because it is an old song with recognizably forward-looking qualities, but also because in it the hybrid elements of Gencebay's style (rural, urban, and Western), though consistent, have not yet settled. Put simply, the song has resisted interpretative closure, particularly in the terms Gencebay himself offers, and it has continued to pose questions. The public nature of these questions and their place in the broader discursive formations surrounding *arabesk* will concern us next.

## Gencebay and the Intellectuals

Prime Minister Turgut Özal's political party, the Anavatan Partisi (ANAP, or Motherland Party),[31] co-opted *arabesk* in the mid-1980s in moves consonant with Özal's promotion of a laissez-faire economy and the dismantling of the state's patrimonial role. The managers of the Turkish state at that time sought a more proactive role in the Middle East and Central Asia, which necessitated public symbolic statements stressing the Ottoman past and the significance of the Ottoman state as a European Muslim power. Under its ANAP mayor, Bedrettin Dalan, Istanbul increasingly became a powerful symbol of a golden era. Dalan focused heavily on restoring the mosques and other Ottoman monuments in the old city, and he broke with republican tradition by naming new public constructions after Ottoman sultans rather than after Atatürk. The promotion of Islam as a public virtue that accompanied this process antagonized the secular left, for whom *arabesk*'s visibility was yet more worrying evidence of this new "hegemony of the periphery."[32] The Özal period was often referred to by its detractors as one of "*arabesk* politics," indicating a certain cynical populism and cultural traditionalism.

A ministerial aide wrote of the need to reverse the TRT's ban on *arabesk* in an article published in *Cumhuriyet*[33] on 12 October 1988. This was followed by an officially sponsored music conference in Istanbul in February 1989 at which the possibility of a new *arabesk* was to be aired. The *arabesk* the TRT intended to endorse was to lack the elements that had most offended critics of the old *arabesk*: its pessimism, sentimentality, and *acı* (pain: a vocal index of poverty, oppression, and the hopeless problems of the Turkish southeast). "Painless *arabesk*" was launched, with all due seriousness, by an aging *arabesk* star, Hakkı Bulut, and light music composer Esin Engin. Needless to say, *arabesk* without *acı* was of little interest to fans and Hakkı Bulut's well-meaning efforts sank without a trace. TRT programmers dug in their

---

31. The Anavatan Partisi (Motherland Party) was established and led by Turgut Özal in 1983, the immediate aftermath of the military regime. In many ways it continued the liberal politics of the Demokrat Parti of the 1950s, though with a distinctly neoliberal program and ethos. It limped through the 1990s in various manifestations, participating both in government and in opposition in various coalitions and alliances. It still exists today, but is no longer the giant it was in the 1980s.

32. I borrow the phrase "hegemony of the periphery," with thanks, from conversation with sociologist Bahattin Akşit.

33. *Cumhuriyet*, one of the few daily papers at that moment to sustain the attention of the Turkish intelligentsia across the political spectrum, was then still the voice of republican officialdom, though this role was waning and the paper was slowly assuming its current role as a bastion of secularist criticism of the Islamist political establishment.

heels and remained resolute in their hostility to any *arabesk,* with or without the pain—though their attempts to stem the commercial tide (as they saw it) were already being undermined by the deregulated satellite channels. *Arabesk* stars were courted by ANAP politicians and invited to perform at ANAP rallies, and their songs were used to promote pro-ANAP slogans.

This co-optation was a matter of significant dismay to critics from the left. The response of writers such as Murat Belge, Meral Özbek, Nilüfer Göle, Nedim Karakayalı, and others to this move, as published in the left-leaning popular intellectual journals of the moment such as *İstanbul, Birikim,* and *Toplum ve Bilim,* constituted a strategy of counter-representation.[34] This project was marked by a thinly veiled nostalgia. The potentially oppositional qualities of *arabesk*—qualities that could be discerned in the veiled social critique of films and songs such as "Batsın bu dünya," for example—had been, in their view, appropriated and neutered. *Arabesk,* many felt at this moment, was beginning to change. The lugubrious melancholy of Gencebay's early songs with their solitary protagonists, slow pace, dark orchestrations, and twisting, unsettled, melodic lines had been replaced in the late 1980s—quite independently of Hakkı Bulut's "painless *arabesk*"—by the up-tempo, cheerful songs of İbrahim Tatlıses and Emrah, with their rattling *darbuka*-s, sprightly violin lines, and invocations of dance and the good life.

Meral Özbek's remarkable study, *Popüler kültür ve Orhan Gencebay arabeski* (Popular culture and Orhan Gencebay's *arabesk*; Özbek 1991) was a product of this moment. Özbek was one of the first commentators to engage *arabesk*'s most conspicuous representative in dialogue and to record and analyze his responses in detail. British New Left cultural theory replaced the critical apparatus of Frankfurt-school Marxism, in which mass culture (*kitle kültürü*) was seen as false consciousness and diversion. The extensive use of the Gramscian theory of Raymond Williams and Stuart Hall (much of it making its appearance in Turkey for the very first time in this book), allowed Özbek to see *arabesk* not simply as a message speaking the unmediated experience of the working classes, but as a contested cultural field. Its messages would inevitably be contradictory, in Özbek's view, since "it is a field both of resistance and coercion" ("*hem direnme, hem de bir boyun eğme alanıdır*"; Özbek 1991, p. 27). The contradictions to which it gave voice were not simply between traditional and modern, rural and urban, but between capitalist rationality and a more progressive "sharing rationality" ("*paylaşımcı rasyonalite*"; Özbek 1991, p. 54).

---

34. Note, by way of particularly thoughtful and theory-informed examples, Belge 1990 and Karakayalı 1995. Murat Belge's early essays of *arabesk* can be found in Belge 1983b.

After setting out her theoretical premises in detail, Özbek combs through Orhan Gencebay's life story, songs, and films for evidence that the themes of emotion, love, and fate are vehicles of popular cultural utopian thinking. Gencebay, who rightly perceived the crumbling of thinking-class opposition to *arabesk* as the perfect moment for him to intervene in and shape public discourse on the genre, accommodated Özbek's searching questions and clearly enjoyed the spirit of serious and respectful inquiry she brought to the interviews. But he often disagreed with her.

There are two areas of Gencebay's resistance to Özbek's questioning that strike me as being particularly significant. First, he disputed the "political" significance of his early classic, "Batsın bu dünya," and, in the process, attempted to qualify the extent to which all of his music might be considered "political." Second, he was reluctant to consider ways in which his music had changed over the years. There are various reasons why well-known musicians, architects of their own place in the cultural scheme of things, have difficulty thinking and talking about the ways in which they have changed or responded to complex social and political forces. But I would argue that Gencebay's reluctance to historicize his own music was connected to the attention he was receiving from the radical intelligentsia in the 1990s. The Turkish intelligentsia's belief that Gencebay was worth taking seriously lay in the conviction that his music had a quality of latent political critique (and thus a kind of authenticity) in the 1970s—a quality at least incipiently socialist, which it then lost in the 1980s as he and other popular musicians appeared to slide to the right. Understandably, Gencebay resisted interpretations that implied that his later work was somehow inauthentic and implicated in the political status quo of the Özal years.

"Batsın bu dünya" stood, in Özbek's argument, for many of the earlier songs with their forcefully masochistic qualities, their palpable hatred of the love object, and their obsessive focus on the humiliation and hurt of the protagonist. A discussion of "Batsın bu dünya," closely argued by both parties, fills more than seventeen pages of Özbek's book (Özbek 1991, pp. 219–36). Gencebay comes close to conceding that the film, together with its title song, makes a political reading almost inescapable. Vedat Yıldırımboğa, a musician involved in the conversation at this point, is particularly concerned that the song, sung at the tipping point of the entire narrative, projects hopelessness and ultimately sanctions an honor killing.

In response, Gencebay turns to the song's opening words and tries to explain. Orhan is trapped. The man who provided him with a living and acted like a father towards him has deceived him, but Orhan is obliged to do his bidding. There is nothing to be done. But why, asks Yıldırımboğa, is there "nowhere to complain?" Gencebay points out that Orhan is helpless, and that he tries to extract himself from his depressed and angry state by putting them into words. This is the nature of his "struggle against negativity" (*olumsuzluklara karşı*) (Özbek 1991, p. 224). And yet, Yıldırımboğa points out, Orhan has choices he doesn't take. He doesn't run away. He doesn't go to the police. Out of sheer machismo (*delikanlılık*) he concludes that the only thing he can do to preserve his honor (*gurur,* in this context) is to kill his persecutor. If this had been an American film, Yıldırımboğa continues, things would have worked out differently. Some reporter would have come along, and the story of the rich man's son would have been exposed in the papers.

Gencebay mulls this over, politely, but clearly thinks the question is absurd. "If it had been an American film . . . well, I suppose that's one way of thinking about it. . . ." He wraps up his own thoughts on the subject, probably feeling the moment has come to impose himself on a conversation that is slipping away from him. The film, in the final analysis, is not about "*muhalefet*" (oppositionality, resistance). Neither does it endorse fatalism or despair. It is, by contrast, about the demands of love (*aşk*), decency (*dürüstlük*), and sensitivity (*hassasiyet*) in an inherently unjust world.

One senses here a significant parting of the ways. Özbek maintains her view that Gencebay's notion of love and sensitivity are inherently "political" by considering "Batsın bu dünya" a moment of change. In later songs, in her analysis, Gencebay imagines a dialogue with the beloved rather than a complaint. This dialogical lyrical stance, implying closure and a reconciliation of desire and the social order, was part of a broader accommodation with the conservative drift of Turkish politics. For Özbek the masochism and self-absorption of "Batsın bu dünya," by contrast, led Gencebay's listeners inescapably to a political understanding of the song. This is necessarily a nostalgic understanding of Gencebay, and one he equally necessarily rejects.

### An Affectionate Modernism

In such contexts Gencebay has talked back from a space labeled "East" by a disciplinary space claimed as "West" by Turkey's political and cultural elites. But the subaltern never simply "speaks," as postcolonial theory has shown (Spivak 1996). Subaltern strategies of enunciation, to use Bhabha's terms, are performative, evasive, and thoroughly entangled with the dominant discourse (Bhabha 2004). So how has Gencebay "talked back," more generally? What are the broader discursive parameters of these kinds of conversation? How successful has he been in shaping a broader public counter-discourse?

I had a chance to ponder these questions after a leisurely interview with Gencebay in his office in Levent in 1995. What follows in this section, both in the text and in the footnotes, derives largely from my written transcription of that interview. What he had to say on that occasion often echoed statements published elsewhere. Such statements have a certain consistency and discursive integrity. Gencebay, as I discovered, is a sophisticated and experienced interviewee. This kind of consistency is the case when, I will argue here, he is appropriating the basic suppositions of the dominant discourse to justify his own music. Other aspects of his self-representations are more elusive. This is particularly the case when he is talking about love. At stake here is a critical venture: an effort to ground Turkish modernity in intimate and affectionate terms (an artistic project that one might describe as a "modernism").

Gencebay's main strategy in interviews, including mine, has been to distance himself from the term *arabesk* and all it implies (at least to the intelligentsia) in the way of alien cultural influence, reaction, emotional excess, disordered urbanism and political violence. He has consistently rejected the term in describing his own music. With me he used the cumbrous circumlocution, "the free styles of composition they call *arabesk*" ("*Arabesk diye serbest çalışmalar*").³⁵ Gencebay grants that the term *arabesk* is currently in circulation, but says that careful distinctions and discriminations need to be maintained. He says that Suat Sayın, in particular, may have copied Egyptian film music and justified the label, but that he himself never did so.³⁶ For

---

35. This circumlocution seems to have been devised to both refer to and distance Gencebay from the notion of "free/independent" (*özgün*) music, a guitar-based popular music then attached to such names as Sümer Ezgü and Ahmet Kaya. The specific reasons for this distancing were to become clear, though Gencebay's broader point is that certain taxonomies created false separations and obscured common practices. *Özgün*, though popular at the time, was nothing "different" in his view. The genre has since disappeared without a trace.

36. Gencebay's frame of reference in these comments is narrow, but his point is made clearly and articulately. Egyptian film made its impact in Turkey in the late 1920s. A number of distinguished Turkish cinema directors and musicians worked in the Arab cinema industry and the musical world that revolved around it, notably film director Vedat Örfi Bengü, music entrepreneur Artaki Candan Terziyan, and bandleader Haydar Tatlıyay. They were just one vector of Arab musical influence in Turkey in the early republican years. Yılmaz Öztuna claims that some 130 Egyptian films circulated in Turkey until they were eventually banned in 1949 (Öztuna 1969, p. 341). Singers such as Münir Nurettin Selçuk (see chapter 5) made films that were either direct translations or adaptations—such as *Aşkın Gözyaşları*, from Mohammed Abd al-Wahhab's early classic *Dumu'a al-Hubb* (The tears of love; 1935)—or films closely modeled on the Egyptian film-musical format—such as *Kahveci Güzeli* (1939) and *Allahın Cenneti* (1941), both directed by Muhsin Ertuğrul. Distinguished and popular composers such as Sadettin Kaynak (see chapter 1, note 53) provided the music, which in Gencebay's opinion was inspired by Arab style, but still decidedly their own work. By contrast, Gencebay implies that Suat Sayın, a short generation later, simply copied Arab music. Singers such as Müzeyyen Sennar, Zeki Müren, and Gencebay himself maintained this tradition into the late 1970s. The term

Gencebay, in the final analysis *arabesk* has to be understood as "a shared music culture in Turkey . . .a sense of freedom (*serbestlik*), autonomy [*özgürlük*], a recognition of everyday life [*günlük hayat tanımak*], of such ways of knowing the world. . . . It has these kinds of broad meanings."

A second move Gencebay makes in interviews is to question the TRT's role as guardian of Turkish national culture, in order to imply that its vociferous critiques of *arabesk* were illegitimate and to suggest that his own efforts to craft a modern national music were more authentic. When we met, his views on the subject were trenchant. In state media circles, as he put it, "there are definite rules and intense control (*denetim*). This control, in my view, inhibits development. It inhibits human development and social development." In Gencebay's view, Turkey had fared badly at the hands of its cultural apparatchiks, especially in comparison to its neighbors. The Egyptians, for example, were to be admired for their nondogmatic approach to the collection and preservation of their own music. Modernist cultural policy in Egypt managed to be simultaneously forward-looking, popular, and historically and ethnically inclusive, in Gencebay's opinion.[37]

Gencebay qualifies *arabesk* not as "foreign" but as a form of indigenous

---

*arabesk,* as Gencebay suggests, builds on a long twentieth-century history of circulation, borrowing, appropriation, and ethnic marking of musical difference, in which careful distinctions must be made between people who simply adapt Arab music, people who compose or sing in direct imitation of Arab styles, and people who happen to be described as "Arab-influenced" simply because they depart from classical codes and conventions. Gencebay was always, however, accused of copying by rivals. In 1973, Selahattin Cesur rejected the description of his own latest record as *arabesk,* and accused Gencebay of copying "Sen hayatsın ben ömür" from the latest LP by "the Arab artist Matar," whose identity is unclear to me (Akyıldız 1973, p. 46). The accusation inadvertently reveals Cesur's deep and detailed knowledge of Arab musical culture.

37. Gencebay: "As far as developing a variety of instruments is concerned, right now I use all of the rhythm instruments in Turkish art music. Before me, this wasn't the case. It was the case in Egypt, though. You're wondering what Egypt has got to do with it. There's a connection, of course. In Ottoman times it used to be a—what do you call it—a province. In the Ottoman period, all these instruments were played in the palace school, the Enderun. There was the *bendir* family, the cymbal family, all sorts of percussion instruments. . . . In the republican period, right up until very recently, you would never see these instruments on TRT. They just didn't get used. Because I understood the importance of rhythm, I treated rhythm seriously, really prioritized it [*ön plana aldım*]. One of the differences between what I do and classical performance lies here. But the Arabs were also doing what I'm doing; they were doing it in Egypt. But most of these instruments used in Egypt, most of the education in them was done by the Ottomans. In other words, they got it from the Ottomans. Even Egyptians admit to this. They'll say: our art music is basically Turkish music, Ottoman music. But Egypt has an advantage. They just . . . take their own culture more seriously than we do. They attach more importance to it, they develop it, they have just done better with it [*daha iyi bir yerlere kadar ulaştı*]. . . ." For a succinct but authoritative account of cultural politics and musical modernization in Egypt in the twentieth century, see Castelo-Branco 2002.

cosmopolitanism.[38] He is always quick to mention that his first musical studies were in Western music, not in Turkish art or folk music. He suggests to his Western-oriented critics that he knows Western music better than they do,[39] and makes much of his own fascination with other musics. Gencebay is particularly interested in the sitar, the sound of which is to be heard in his recordings from the mid-1970s to the present. Indian music is an important point of reference partly because of the popularity in Turkey of Indian films in the 1950s[40] but also because of the trade in musical instruments along the hippie trail between Istanbul and Kathmandu in the 1970s.[41]

---

38. Gencebay understands his own cosmopolitanism as being personal and circumstantial rather than programmatic. As he put it: "Right from the beginning I used folk music, I used art music. I used *oriyental* [belly dance music]. I used mysticism [*tasavvuf*]. I was influenced by Western music. But in the final analysis . . . I have tried to use my own personality, my own self [*kimliğimi*]. And by personality I mean the particularities, the differences peculiar to every person, every artist. There's nothing objectionable about this. If they can be used well, I always reckoned something good could be made of them. . . ."

39. As if to prove the point, Gencebay wrote a lighthearted "Nihavent üvertür" for the end of his *Yalnız değilsin* CD of 1995. In this, a baroque *moto perpetuo* on the violins and motoric continuo bass give way to long solo flourishes on the *elektosaz* and *kanun*, and then to a more conventionally recognizable *arabesk*-style tune played by the unison orchestra with an up-tempo *arabesk* rhythm. The piece is humorous, but it underscores an important component of Gencebay's self-presentation: that his eclecticism is based on a deeply internalized grasp of Western art music and the universalism (*evrensellik*) with which it is associated. In his own words, to me: "I started out, aged six, on the mandolin. The mandolin is a Western instrument, as you know. It used to be played in schools in Turkey; I learned it before I went to school. My teacher in this was Emin Tarakçı; Meral Özbek has written about it in her book. He was a violinist and an opera singer. But he had emigrated from Russia to Samsun. He was one of those Russian Turks—Crimean Turks, I mean. He was a graduate of the Russian conservatory system, I mean, a graduate of the Western music conservatory system. I learned the basic rules of music from him. I learned notes at the age of six, and in a month I could do *şifre* [*chifre*, i.e., notation for chords], and I could sing by sight from notation. We used to do a lot of *bono* [solfege exercises]. I worked on the violin after that. But in my heart of hearts, while I loved all this, I was more inclined to folk music. I really wanted to play *bağlama* [saz]. I began playing *bağlama* at age seven. Along with the *bağlama* and all its regional styles, I started work on the *tanbur*. That's how I got to know Turkish art music. After that, I did a bit of jazz. Basically, I concentrated most on folk music and Turkish art music. But Western music was kind of the foundation [*temel*]."

40. *Avare* was a hit in the late 1950s, and was still remembered in the 1990s. See chapter 2, note 34, on *Avare* and Hindi film music in Zeki Müren's repertoire.

41. Gencebay: "I really used to love the sitar. I try and enjoy the music of the whole world. The sitar is just a beautiful instrument. I had a friend bring one back from India. Ravi Shankar has got a teach-yourself method. I had that brought over as well. I wanted to study it [the instrument], just because it was beautiful, basically. It's an interesting instrument. You look at it, and it's got chromatic stuff going on, it's got a chordal system [*akort sistemi*]. . . . Interesting, very interesting. Not one diatonic sound on it; all chromatic. You play it differently. It's got a metal plectrum! (laughs) I don't have any claims to be a sitar player. I kind of figured it out at a basic level but didn't work hard on it. I just wanted to get to know about it. I could also see a lot of similarities between Indian ragas and Turkish *makam*-s. I had learned this from the method beforehand. I could see the resemblances." Short sitar riffs are to be heard for the first time on Gencebay's mid-1970s "Uğrunda bir ölmek kaldı," a song with a mellow, resigned tone set to a cha-cha-cha/rumba rhythm, with an instrumental introduction

Third, Gencebay is well aware of the ways in which his intellectual critics have disparaged *arabesk* in the past, and he challenges or subverts these characterizations. For critics, *arabesk* is about warped development (*çarpık geliştirme*), uncontrolled rural-urban migration, and the culture of the *dolmuş*, the informal transport system. Gencebay either moves the topic swiftly away from what he regards as sociological clichés,[42] or refutes those clichés on empirical grounds.[43] Another critical cliché had it that *arabesk* was fatalistic and masochistic, encouraging a passivity that had no place in a modernizing republic. The accusation of fatalism was linked, for many critics, with *arabesk*'s complicity in religious reaction (*irtica*) and the Islamization of the Turkish public sphere. Gencebay does not deny religious elements in his music, but locates them in an indigenous "humanism" (*hümanizm*) that might yet, if it were better understood, bring together a country which at that moment was obviously divided.[44] At the time of our discussion,

---

featuring flamenco guitar. Gencebay's most extended use of the sitar is to be found on his 1978 recording, *Aşkı ben yaratmadım*, on the song "Zaman akıp gider," in which the opening melody is played in full by a solo sitar accompanied by tabla. The sitar disappeared in later recordings but the tabla can still be heard, for example, on "Ben kendim bir alemim" on his 2004 CD *Yürekten olsun*.

42. Gencebay: "According to sociologists, *arabesk* is a story about people migrating from the villages to the cities. I have never considered *arabesk* in this light. As a musician, I see this music as music. The heart of the issue, in my view, is in the music."

43. Gencebay is fond of facts and figures. For example, he quoted statistics from research conducted in the early 1980s showing that *dolmuş* drivers actually listened to a variety of music, and not just *arabesk*. Not only is it wrong to call his music *arabesk*, he argues, but it is also wrong to call *arabesk* "*dolmuş* music."

44. Gencebay responded to the criticism linking *arabesk* and fatalism with a subtle point in an interview with Meral Özbek in 1987, which is worth translating and repeating here: "The beloved about whom our *aşık* poets talk may or may not be an actual loved one. The beloved is a friend, a companion, someone you get angry with. I mean, everything sounds as though it is addressed to an actual beloved, but it's not all for or about the beloved. It's about the whole of life, the effects of events.... You've got this in Aşık Summani, in Mevlana, in Yunus. The beloved is a fellow sufferer, someone you can talk to, like Fate [*Felek*], kind of. There's no such thing as fate. But fate is a mode of address [*hitab*], for the purposes of poetic release [*şairi deşarj*], like something existing in front of one, with whom one can converse" (Özbek 1991, p. 189).

In another interview, with me on the subject of "Sende haklısın," a song on *Akma gozlerin* sonically indexing Mevlevi spirituality through the prominent use of the *ney*, Gencebay added: "You have to see that [song] more from a humanist perspective [i.e., less as an endorsement of fatalism]. There's a Nasrettin Hoca story. The story inspired me. Someone comes to the Hoca with a problem [involving somebody else], and puts it to him. 'You're right,' says the Hoca. Someone else comes along and says, 'It's not like that. This is the way it was,' saying the exact opposite of the first person. The Hoca says, 'You're right, too ["*Sen de haklısın*"].' A third person comes along and says, 'Hoca, you've told both of them they are right. Is that the way to arrive at the truth of the matter?' The Hoca thinks for a moment, turns to him, and says, 'You know, you're right.' (Much laughter.) The story inspired me. The Hoca here sees things from a humanist perspective, valuing the people [more than the issues]. It's more about humanism than mysticism. It's better to start by assuming people consider themselves to be in the right than to search for injustices. I'm not putting this well. But

Sunni-Alevi[45] conflicts were raging in Ümraniye and neighboring *gecekondu* districts, and were a topic of considerable public anxiety.

So Gencebay's counter-narrative is based on his claims that currents of experimentalism and quests for modernity in Turkish popular music have been persistently misunderstood, that national institutions such as the TRT are *not* the sole arbiters of the modern in Turkish music, that cosmopolitanism has deep roots in Turkish musical culture and should be seen as a progressive force, and finally that *arabesk* cannot simply be understood in terms of the officially led populist religiosity of 1980s but draws instead on deeper and more "humane" roots. Many of the presuppositions of Gencebay's critics are reproduced in this discourse: that musical "progress" is desirable, that all good citizens strive towards "modernity," that leadership is required, that copying neighbors is problematic, and that religion still might be an integrative element in Turkish national culture. We might describe Gencebay's language as an appropriation of the dominant discourse of Turkish modernity from below.

In other ways, though, Gencebay has made efforts to sidestep this language and forge another. One of the spaces in which has done this consistently has been in his spoken pronouncements on love. His rambling and earnest disquisitions on the subject are a feature of almost every published interview. Consider, for instance, this exchange from the mid-1970s. A journalist had simply asked him "what he had to say about love [*aşk*]." Genecebay, who had just been discussing his modest drinking habits in a lighthearted way, suddenly became serious.

> The person who loves is sensitive [*duygusal*]. Because s/he is set in motion by his/her feelings, his/her actions are out of control. Something you can't make somebody do by force of arms, you can make them do with love. There's no way of measuring love. It changes from person to person. Just as love can place a crown on somebody's head, it can bring an end to their life. For the lover, love is the beginning and end of everything. Its joy, its pain, its anxiety, its fate, its everything. The lover might find him/herself in various crises. But somebody who hasn't suffered [*dert çekmeyen*] doesn't know the value of happiness [*neşe*]. In my opinion,

---

'Sende haklısın' was written from a humanist perspective, and there are a good number like this. I wouldn't really describe it as religious [*buna da din mefhumu yok, da*]."

45. Alevi are a significant minority (by some accounts up to one-fifth of the population), being Anatolian Shia, revering Ali and the Prophet's family as rightful heirs to the Caliphate. Turkish cultural practices are quite distinct from those of neighboring countries. In Istanbul in particular, many Alevi are Kurdish. See Shankland 2003.

love means loving without expectations. For the lover, getting a response from the beloved should be a surprise. To go on about one's own love, and to expect the same from the opposite side, that's not love (Akyıldız 1977, pp. 18–19).

The journalist quickly picked up on the political undercurrents of Gencebay's reply. Instead of leaving matters there as others later would have done, he opted for the direct approach, immediately asking Gencebay to expound on his "political views." Gencebay brushed him off politely but firmly. "In my opinion, it's not regimes that are important, but their managers [*Bence rejimler değil, yöneticiler önemlidir*]".

The dark political clouds of the moment hovered over these words. Bloody clashes between right and left were already more or less daily events. "Force of arms," suffering, and crisis were very much on the horizon. "Expectations" of all kinds were indeed to be put on hold after the military coup. The journalist's question about "political views" was natural and instinctive, bearing in mind the serious countercultural tenor of *Hey* in those days, as was Gencebay's necessarily evasive response. Gencebay had nothing to gain by aligning himself with one side or the other, and a lot to lose. Little was to change: his conversations with Meral Özbek ten years later would essentially repeat this position out of habit.

It was, though, a contradictory position. The length and convoluted nature of these kinds of exchanges are signs, one might say, of the discursive pressure of a fundamental contradiction: Gencebay's efforts to appear "nonpolitical" push him inexorably in the direction of politics. In declaring love to be a superior way of "making people do things" in comparison to the "force of arms," he clearly states his opposition to the right-left polarization of the country, and to the looming threat of a military coup. In referring to lovers as being "out of control," he evokes citizens in the grip of a crisis of political emotions. In declaring his preference for "managers" rather than "regimes," he anticipates the emerging neo-liberal "solution."[46] The

---

46. The speed with which Gencebay struck up friendly relations with the new political managers surprised nobody. The cover of *Müzik Magazin* 2(7), 25 January 1988, shows him standing next to a smiling Özal, with a banner headline: "Prime Ministerial Support for *Arabesk* . . . [*Arabesk Başbakan Desteği*. . .]." Note also a long and interesting footnote in Özbek's book (1991, p. 121): "One can provide a good example, once again in Orhan Gencebay's own words, of the transition from the personal to the political from the point of view of *arabesk*. Orhan Gencebay gave this as one of his reasons for considering President Özal a democratically minded man as follows: 'A man who would give his daughter [in marriage] to a *davul* [a lowly folk instrument, often played by Roma] player is in my eyes a democrat (interview with Orhan Gencebay, 6 November 1987). News such as this, the result of an interview with *Söz*, was published with the commentary 'Özal Believes in Love.'"

language of the personal, affectionate, and intimate here is plainly political, collective, and social. Gencebay's attempts to free himself from the grip of this basic contradiction produce a more and more anxious and convoluted discourse on the topic of love.

But, I would argue, there is more to understanding these kinds of pronouncements than exposing their underlying contradictions or searching for coded signs of resistance. Gencebay is also, I would argue, exploring the possibilities of other ways of talking about the responsibilities of the musician in modern Turkish society. The dominant discourse of Turkish modernity articulates these responsibilities as a matter of leadership: turning people Westward, being proactive in modernizing traditional culture, resisting the regressive influence of the commercial market. As we have just seen, Gencebay is often in tune with this discourse and he echoes many of its characteristic turns of phrase as he makes his arguments for *arabesk* and confronts his critics. But another voice can be detected in his comments about love.

Referring to this 1977 interview, though many others could also have served as illustration, one might paraphrase these claims as follows. Society faces a crisis. "Politics," in Gencebay's negative sense, involves violence, unrealistic expectations of others, and a lack of forbearance. For Gencebay, "politics" cannot be the solution. But "love" (broadly understood as relations of affection and reciprocity) most certainly can. As bearers of powerful mystical traditions of love deeply rooted in Turkish society, musicians have a duty as citizens to step forward at a moment of crisis. They, and perhaps they alone, have the capacity to forge new communicative protocols, new and less antagonistic ways of representing the diverse currents that make up society, new ways of mediating social relations. Bureaucratic initiatives to modernize Turkish music have made the task difficult; they have marginalized the true musician-lovers. The struggle must be carried out on two fronts: one discursive (engaging in public discussion to keep minds and hearts open and combat negative elements in the media and the state conservatories), the other practical (the development of a musical style, vernacular yet modern, that might carry this struggle forward). Gencebay seems to be saying that with musicians engaging in this kind of "sly civility" (Bhabha 2004), people in Turkey might yet put its efforts to be modern on a more democratic and *affectionate* footing.

## Conclusion

Though Gencebay is no longer central to Turkish popular music life, he continues to be understood as an exemplary figure of sincerity, decency, and civic virtue. He has responded to his critics intelligently, founded a primary school, dispensed avuncular advice as a panel member on *Popstar*, repeatedly addressed moments of national anxiety with citizenly appeals to mutual affection, and—perhaps most importantly—continued to produce his own music.

This music, as we have seen with reference to "Batsın bu dünya," tells a complex story. The unsettled modal qualities, the "eruptive" vocalizations, and the helter-skelter dialogue of instrumental sounds discussed with reference to this song are consistent elements of his later style. "Batsın bu dünya," the first song to work such performative qualities consistently, resists easy accommodation in terms of the dominant vocabularies for understanding music in Turkey. Furthermore, it resists easy accommodation in terms of the language Gencebay himself provides. Its meanings are still up for grabs, and the matter is no longer entirely in its creator's hands—if it ever was. A recent dance remix of the song by Gencebay himself, for example, provoked howls of protest from fans.[47]

Discussions about public emotionality in the aftermath of the violence of the late 1970s and early 1980s have been tense and contradictory, as we have seen. They have been bound up, as I have tried to show in this chapter, with a nostalgia for the 1970s—in which "Batsın bu dünya" has been central—and with complex patterns in the ongoing circulation and reception of Gencebay's music. This nostalgia, far from being a "monochroming" of historical experience,[48] has kept complex historical and political issues alive. How might the pursuit of modernity be made "Turkish" in ways that do not lead (as so often before) to violence? How might it be made a genuinely popular and democratic proposition? How might it come to involve dialogue and cultural exchange with Turkey's regional neighbors? How might it forge friendliness and community without resorting to a narrow and authoritarian nationalism?

Gencebay has exploited the situation intelligently, both musically and

---

47. See comments appended to a YouTube clip posted in 2006 at http://uk.youtube.com/watch?v=-JF_Xib9c0Y&feature=related. The following comment, from Mithoman, is typical: "*Bu Remixin . . . mina koyim. Mokuma benzemis yaw, Orhan Babayi arkadan mikmisler yoksa nasil kabul edebelirdi bu sova, yoksa iflas'mi var? Yazik olmus adama yaw. . . .*" (Rough translation: "F*ck this remix. Sounds like crap. Did they f*ck Orhan Baba's a**? How did they make him agree to this? Or has he gone bust? Pity the man. . . ." Notice the orthographic adaptation to English-language computer keyboards.) The audience in the YouTube clip seemed to enjoy it greatly, however.

48. I would argue, then, for an understanding of nostalgia in terms that owe more to Boym 2001 than Grainge 2002. For Boym, nostalgia is a tangled, emotionally inflected, and popular political engagement with the past. Grainge, by contrast, sees it as a kind of historical false consciousness, a sanitized version of history that is controlled to a significant degree by media.

in terms of his engagements with the media. This has had important consequences. As the TRT's media hegemony unraveled in the 1980s, the "Gencebay project" (to use Karakayalı's term) publicly maintained musical alternatives grounded in popular practice and popular historical experience. It has enabled conversation between Turkey's elites and popular classes, which were briefly compacted in the 1980s and early 1990s but are now in danger of drifting apart once again. This has been a genuine, if fragile, achievement.

For many, the hyper-liberalism set in motion after the 1980 coup has fundamentally reframed questions of national belonging and the citizenly virtues. As these issues are publicly reframed in the private and domestic sphere, gendered and sexual issues have once again come to the fore. As in Iran, as Najmabadi suggests, "the articulation of homeland as female body has had highly contentious repercussions for women as citizens" (Najmabadi 2005, p. 207). Globalization has raised stark questions about the territorial integrity of the Anatolian heartland (*Anadolu*), a land "full of mothers" (*ana-dolu*). Neoliberalism and the Islamist movement, with their radically different claims on women, have accentuated identity politics, fragmenting the cultural space. The patriarchal state apparatus has been displaced by the market as the taken-for-granted context of making meaning in everyday life. Gencebay's affectionate modernism had by the early 1990s run its course. Pop star Sezen Aksu's "diva turn" on neoliberal citizenship and national belonging concerns us next.

# 4

# Why Cry?
# Sezen Aksu's Diva Citizenship

One summer evening in 1995, viewers who had switched on TRT 1[1] to watch the news found themselves watching a long report about the release of Sezen Aksu's latest CD/cassette: *Işık doğudan yükselir / Ex oriente lux*. Given the usual fare and the TRT's sober style of presentation and analysis, this was a surprise indeed. Aksu introduced her new project, responded to questions, and sang live.[2] My own memory is of only one song, a plaintive and haunting rendition of an Alevi *deyiş*,[3] "Ne ağlarsın" ("What are

---

1. The Turkish Radio and Television Corporation was still the dominant provider of televised news at the time. The development of a market in private media had not yet produced Turkish CNN and the proliferation of news and current events channels that could be found ten years later. The format and, indeed the content of the evening television news on TRT 1 had changed little over the previous ten years: coverage featured diplomacy and high-level diplomatic visits, progress of major development projects, news from military struggles with the PKK, sports, and weather. Usually there was only one presenter and interviews, to say nothing of musical performances, in the studio were extremely rare.

2. The performance's "liveness" was in many ways its most conspicuous feature, assertively differing from the stilted, staged nature of much TRT folk music performance—a move that will be explored in detail later in this chapter. My use of scare quotes implies (following Auslander 1999) that "liveness" should not necessarily be understood in opposition to "mediation." When considering performances as "live," one is talking about an event whose perceived closeness, embodiment, presence, and intimacy owes more to interpretation than conditions of production.

3. A *deyiş* ("saying") is Alevi spiritual poetry sung by specialist musicians known as *aşık* ("lovers") who usually accompany themselves on the saz, the long-necked folk

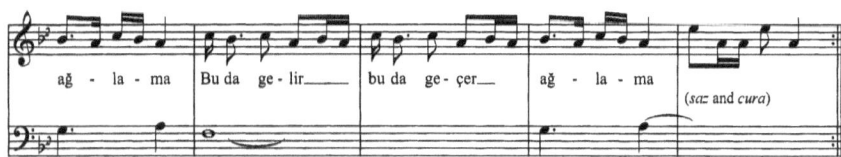

**4a.** Sezen Aksu's recording of Aşık Daimi's "Ne ağlarsın," first verse. The transcription begins thirty seconds into the recorded version. Saz and cura (long-necked folk lutes) are played şelpe—that is, with both hands on the fretboard. The transcription is transposed a major sixth up from the pitch levels on the recording. Key signatures and accidentals follow folk music conventions, here representing B two commas flat and F three commas sharp.

you crying about?"). Accompanied on the program by *bağlama* (a kind of saz) virtuoso Arif Sağ, the song traces a graceful descent in the folk *aşıklama*

---

lute. The song in question was attributed to Kurdish folk poet Aşık Daimi, from Erzincan. A short biography of the singer (in Turkish) can be found at http://www.turkuler.com/ozan/daimi.asp and the TRT's full notation of the song, collected by Mine Yalçın, appears in the notations (*notalar*) section of this same official-sounding site (http://www.turkuler.com/nota/ezgi_590.html). Older listeners know this song in many different versions, including one easily locatable on YouTube, by *arabesk* star İbrahim Tatlıses, dating probably from the early 1980s. On the Alevi in Turkey, see chapter 3, note 42. On their music, see Markoff 1986 and Markoff 1991/92.

style (Markoff 1990/91).⁴ Its melancholy words remind the grieving lover of the thorns around the rose and the suffering of the nightingale. As spring follows winter, these miseries, too, shall pass, if only in death. Why cry?

Words and translation:

| | |
|---|---|
| *Ne ağlarsın benim zülfü siyahım* | Why cry, my beloved with the dark side-locks? |
| *Bu da gelir bu da geçer ağlama* | This too shall pass, don't cry |
| *Göklere erişti feryadım ahım* | My cry reached the skies |
| *Bu da gelir bu da geçer ağlama* | This too shall pass, don't cry |
| | |
| *Bir gülün çevresi dikendir, hardır* | There are thorns around the rose, thorns |
| *Bülbül gül elinden ah ile zardır* | The nightingale cries out because of the rose, with an "ah" |
| *Ne de olsa kışın sonu bahardır* | Whatever happens, with winter's end comes spring |
| *Bu da gelir bu da geçer ağlama* | This too shall pass; don't cry |
| | |
| *Daimiyem her can ermez bu sırra* | I am Daimi; not everybody attains this secret |
| *Eyüp sabır ile gitti Mısır'a* | Eyüp⁵ went to Egypt patiently |
| *Koyun oldum ağladım ardısıra* | I became like a sheep, I wept by and by |
| *Bu da gelir bu da geçer ağlama* | This too shall pass, don't cry |

"Ne ağlarsın" was an instant hit. The CD sold heavily and Aksu's subsequent concert at Rumelihisarı⁶ sold out within days. Demand for the CD

---

4. Erdener 1995 is the most thorough and scholarly account of the traditional (as opposed to urbanized) context of *aşık* singing. Confined mainly to the northeast of the country until relatively recently, this tradition, in its rural as opposed to urbanized form, seems to be going through something of a revival thanks to the municipal sponsorship of urban festivities in popular working-class neighborhoods during, for instance, Ramadan.

5. Eyüp, the common Turkish name for Abu Ayub al-Ansari, was the Prophet Muhammad's standard-bearer. He came to Constantinople with the Arab armies late in the seventh century. He has a large shrine in today's Istanbul, close to the old Byzantine city wall and overlooking the Golden Horn.

6. Rumelihisarı is the large Ottoman-constructed fortress north of the old city on the Bosphorus, built during the siege that resulted in the occupation of the Byzantine city in 1453. In the 1990s it became the major rock and pop concert venue in Istanbul, since it afforded easy access from wealthy suburbs on the European side and was located in close proximity to a major university campus. Most Productions held the franchise until 1999, when it passed to İstanbul Productions, with additional sponsorship from the major media companies Telsim and Kral TV. According to a

was evidently still running high ten years later.[7] The song, selected as official party congress song by the left-of-center Cumhuriyet Halk Partisi (Republican People's Party) that year, continues to be both popular and ubiquitous. In its performance by others, Arif Sağ's opening solo,[8] Aksu's vocal inflections, and Attila Özdemiroğlu's studio arrangement are often faithfully reproduced. Wherever I have heard it played and sung, people listen quietly, seemingly lost in private and melancholy thoughts.

This chapter tells how Aksu's version of this song became an icon of national soulfulness. In part, its iconic status rested on its evocation of a deeply familiar trope: nation imagined as suffering woman. In the Middle East, this trope has a rather distinct history. The political struggles of modernity have been played out over images of women's bodies. "State feminism" (Kandiyoti 1991) in Turkey asserted a desired national modernity in images and narratives that on the one hand evoked women as scientists, aviators, and public intellectuals, and on the other located women in orderly heterosexual narratives of romantic love, companionate marriage, and nuclear family.[9] These assertions played with long-standing and more popular conceptions of Anatolia as *ana-dolu,* "full of mothers" (Delaney 1991): passive, fertile, long-suffering, demanding constant devotion and protection.

---

report in *Hürriyet*, under Most Productions the fortress saw some 471 concerts by some 55 artists or groups. In 1997 the concerts stopped as a result of concerns expressed about the possibility of damage to a historical monument, but they resumed in 1998. For reasons I was never able to determine, they were canceled again in 2006. The only performance that took place in the summer of that year was one of Qur'anic recitation. Rock and pop concerts continued meanwhile at the open-air venues in Harbiye (Açıkhava) and Kuruçesme. See Tuna 1999 for a brief and journalistic history of Rumelihisarı as a rock and pop venue.

7. Seyhan Müzik rereleased it in their Sezen Aksu retrospective in 2005. They bought up the rights to Aksu's recordings at around that time, bringing out the CDs with new covers and extensive booklets containing critical essays by Murat Meriç. Aksu rarely stayed with one company for any length of time. This kind of retrospective repackaging is unusual and presumably reflects Seyhan's efforts to establish the Aksu career as a media event with shape and form unfolding over time—an *oeuvre*, in short. And an attractive package would have inclined people towards their own products rather than toward pirated retrospectives such as Yıldız Müzik's multivolume *Düğünden bügüne Sezen Aksu*, which sells, according to Dilmener, for a mere six new Turkish liras—about half the price of a single non-pirated CD (Dilmener 2006, pp. 45–46).

8. The opening *bağlama* solo involves *şelpe* technique, in which the fingers of the right hand are used instead of a plectrum to strike the string in various ways, including tapping the fret board. Turkish folklorists have various theories about the origins and distribution of this technique, and one, Erol Parlak, has become well known as a proponent. Its current popularity owes a certain amount, I would argue, to the immense popularity of "Ne ağlarsın" and Arif Sağ's introduction to it.

9. On companionate marriage in Ottoman and republican Turkey, see Duben and Behar 1991. On Iran, see Najmabadi 2005—particularly "The Tragedy of Romantic Marriage," pp. 156–80. On Egypt, see in particular Baron 2005. On continuities between the "new Muslim woman" and republican ideals in Turkey, see White 2002.

Aksu's "Ne ağlarsın" also marked something new. Its TRT news performance took place at a particular moment of national anxiety. Recent Islamist success in municipal elections had called the founding principles of the republic, and its constituent bonds of sociality, into question. Communal violence in Istanbul's squatter towns bought hitherto remote struggles between the separatist Partiya Karkerên Kurdistan (Kurdistan Worker's Party, or PKK) and the Turkish army uncomfortably close to home. The first Gulf War had dealt a worrying blow to the Turkish economy.[10] The state seemed to be withdrawing from its familiar and everyday roles.[11] Its performance raised questions that were very much of the moment. There was plenty to talk about right then. At exactly what point had Aksu suddenly become so important? Why were Turkish citizens in such need of distraction? Since when had they become quite so absorbed by the spectacle of their own pain and melancholy?

An early response to the CD was to be found in a review by *Cumhuriyet* art critic Cumhur Canbazoğlu on that paper's culture page (Canbazoğlu 1995). It was published that same weekend—so soon, in fact, that the author hinted that he had not yet actually listened to the CD itself, but had instead drawn most of his conclusions from the TRT news broadcast performance.[12] Canbazoğlu's perceptive comments cue the overarching theoretical concerns of this chapter, which is concerned with the local and regional politics of "world music" (Turino 2000; Regev 2006; Ochoa-Gaultier 2003); cosmopolitanism, nationalism, and feminist critique in the Middle East (Baron 2005; Kandiyoti 1991; Najmabadi 2005; Shissler 2004; Sirman 2000); and emotion and sexuality as neoliberal civility (Berlant 1998). Canbazoğlu was particularly concerned that Turkish listeners should consider the CD *musically*. In his view that could be a problem, given the high degree of hype and

---

10. The flow of oil along the Ceyhan pipeline, which connects Iraq to the Mediterranean ports and refineries around İskenderun, was an early casualty with enormous repercussions at both local and national levels.

11. On the everyday as the site of engagements with neoliberalism in Turkey, see the contributions to Kandiyoti 2002. It is of course difficult to say what the neoliberal state is withdrawing "into"; a common position is to stress its emerging role as a manager of transnational corporate finance (a position I draw, crudely perhaps, from publications such as Balakrishnan 2003, Keyder 1999, Sassen 1998).

12. Canbazoğlu notes that Aksu performed five pieces from the CD (Canbazoğlu 1995). I only remember one, as do others. Canbazoğlu must have been right, in which case "Ne ağlarsın" quickly came to "stand for" the whole performance. It also underlines the extent to which this news broadcast constituted a remarkable departure from the norm. Clearly Aksu's performance would have left little time for other "news."

polemic already surrounding it.¹³ One needed, he suggested, to step back and consider the CD in the broader contexts of Sezen Aksu's career and of Turkish pop music more generally. That would seem to be a good way to proceed here.

### Aksu's Early Career

Sezen Aksu's powerful and ubiquitous position in Turkey is the product of the 12 September 1980 military coup, the intense period of political repression and economic austerity that immediately followed it, and the liberalism of the early Özal years (see chapter 3). This is not to suggest Aksu's political complicity, or that her vocal art should be judged simply as a reflection of those dismal times. It is, though, to argue that the roots of her enormous popularity and significance in Turkey today are to be found in the conditions that prevailed then.

Consider first the timing of her training and professional formation. She came of age, musically speaking, in auspicious circumstances. She was born Sezen Yıldırım in Saraköy, Denizli (western Anatolia) on 13 June 1954.¹⁴ In 1957 her family moved to Izmir, where her father was first a teacher and then an education administrator. After graduating from high school, Aksu attended Izmir University's Agricultural Faculty. Her heart was clearly not in it, and she dropped out before finishing the course. In the meanwhile she continued to attend classes run by Izmir Radio's Artists' Club (*İzmir Radyosu Sanatçılar Derneği*), where she studied voice, piano, art music, theater, and folklore. Her parents struggled against her ambition to be a professional musician, but finally gave in and supported them. Her determination to per-

---

13. Canbazoğlu suggests that sales were low and that people were having difficulty understanding the album. It seems to me to have been far too early to tell, and no precise figures or sources are offered. Ten years later it would be seen in retrospect as a best seller. Sales figures are in any case a very problematic way of talking about popularity in Turkey or elsewhere, since they are controlled by parties who have a vested interest in either exaggerating or minimizing figures, and since they say little about the complex ways in which music circulates, either in copies, in simulacra (such as cell phone jingles), or in performance. The first efforts to establish official figures by MESAM (a music industry organization established primarily to lobby for firmer copyright control) took place in 1990. Dilmener reproduces a list of sales from *Boom* that confirm the kinds of figures I would hear in Unkapanı in candid conversations with producers and small company owners. Aksu's *Sezen Aksu söylüyor*, for instance, had sold 845,000 copies by June 1990. By way of comparison, İbrahim Tatlıses' *İnsanlar* had sold 800,000 while Madonna's *Like a Prayer* had sold 151,000 (Dilmener 2003, p. 349).

14. Biographical information here is derived from an interview with Aksu conducted by Anne Ellingsen and the author on 12 July 1996 in Aksu's apartment in Istanbul, and from her official website, Sezen-aksu.com.

form in some capacity—"in theater, in music, as a dancer (*dansöz*), even"[15]—forced her parents to confront and eventually overcome their natural conservatism; from this point on they were highly supportive of her career.

Her first recording, the 45 rpm single "Haydi şansı"/ "Gel bana," was released in 1975 under the assumed name of Sezen Seley. By all accounts this song, an *aranjman* set to Aksu's own words,[16] did not do too well, even though it was profiled on a TRT New Year's Eve program.[17] In an early article in *Hey*,[18] accompanied by pictures showing a tense and unsmiling young woman, Aksu vented her frustration: "The choice of songs was not right [*isabetli değildi*]. I was afraid I would make mistakes. You want to know what I gained from my first recording? Precisely nothing. Only maybe people were saying, this girl has got some talent. But that's all." (Türk 1976a, p. 24)

A second single, "Kursura bakma," followed in 1976. By then Aksu was married and had left for Canada, where her husband, Ali Engin Aksu, was beginning graduate school. She recalls having given up for all intents and purposes on the idea of a recording career, but she returned to visit Turkey after the second single had been released, only to discover that the single had become a hit and that she was now famous.[19] "Olmaz olsun" appeared in 1976, shortly followed by "Allahaısmarladık" and "Kaybolan yıllar" in 1977. Most of these early singles were bought together that year on her first LP, *Allahaısmarladık*, and in 1978 on her second LP, *Serçe*. Following the charts compiled by *Hey* in these years, one notes not only that these songs were "hits" according to all of the conventional criteria,[20] but also that they had an unusual capacity to stay on the charts for long periods of time. Classic sleepers, their success seemed to puzzle reviewers, who consistently

---

15. Interview with Aksu, 12 July 1996.

16. "*Aranjman*" refers to versions of non-Turkish songs (usually European or American) with Turkish words.

17. Note an article published in *Hey* in November 1984 by İbrahim Ünsu, one of the first to present a history of Aksu. He draws heavily on the recollections of Aysel Gürel, an early lyricist and mentor, and describes her first TRT appearance in the following terms: "Millions of people glued to the television on the night that connected 1974 and 1975 were witnessing the addition of a brand new voice in Turkish popular music. The owner of a voice that mixed an inner sensitivity (*içten bir duygu*) with melancholy (*hüzün*) was singing 'Haydi Şansım' that evening." (Ünsu 1984, p. 26)

18. *Hey* was the major popular music journal of the 1970s. For a brief history, see chapter 3, note 24.

19. Interview with Aksu, 12 July 1996.

20. According to a short article in *Hey* (1 May 1978, p. 25) "Kaybolan yıllar"/ "Neye yarar," for instance, achieved gold. The compilation of charts before the relatively recent days of monitoring, data collection, and relative transparency was inevitably somewhat subjective. As *Hey*'s editor's diligently explain, they were derived from estimates by friends of the editor in music stores across the country of weekly sales figures.

turned in lukewarm and even faintly damning reports. *Hey*'s (anonymous) reviewer, for instance, had this to say: "On *Olmaz olsun*, which occasionally smells of *arabesk* [*yer yer arabesk kokan*], the Girl from Izmir reminds one, to an extraordinary degree, of Gökben.[21] We hope this isn't imitation. The song composition is cute [*sevimli*]. Şanar Yurdatapan's[22] orchestration and Dün, Bugün, Yarın's[23] accompaniment is successful. On the B side there's another one of Sezen Aksu's compositions. The arrangement here is Attila Özdemiroğlu's. What we said about the A side might be said again of this piece." The reviewer, who seems more anxious about the reputation of the music industry stalwarts involved than about that of Aksu herself, gave the single three out of five stars: good (*iyi*) but not excellent (*mükemmel*), and certainly not a masterpiece (*şaheser*).[24]

Nonetheless Aksu was, by the time of the release of *Serçe*, a well-established recording and concert artist. Though still referred to as the "Girl from Izmir" and as the "Little Sparrow" ("*Minik Serçe*," a nickname alluding to her stature and her quirky looks, and possibly also to Edith Piaf),[25] she

---

21. Gökben, a near contemporary of Aksu's, had recorded some major hits in the years immediately before "Olmaz olsun," notably "Şiribom Şiribom" in 1974. She worked with Izmir-born music producer Ali Kocatepe, and with producers, lyricists, and musicians who were connected with Aksu, such as Attila Özdemiroğlu and Aysel Gürel. Comparison was inevitable.

22. Şanar Yurdatapan, born in Susurluk in 1941, was a well-known film and popular music composer and arranger in the 1970s. With Atilla Özdemiroğlu, he ran ŞAT Müzik, a production company that quickly became central to Turkish pop and its struggles with cultural officialdom. He became general secretary of DEMAR, the Democratic Artists' Community, in 1979. He was out of the country during the 1980 coup, and stayed away for some time. He is currently a prominent human rights and freedom of expression activist, working from his office in Üsküdar. He remembers his first meeting with Aksu well. She phoned him out of the blue from Izmir, saying (as he recalled in English), "I believe I have a beautiful voice. I trust my own talent. I want to work with you." Alongside Aksu, Yurdatapan produced many of the major female stars of the 1970s: Füsun Önal, Cici Kızlar, Nilüfer, and his former wife, Melike Demirağ. Interview with Şanar Yurdatapan, 10 September 2008.

23. Dün, Bugün, Yarın broke away from İstanbul Gelişim in the early 1970s; it comprised Şanar Yurdatapan and Attila Özdemiroğlu, two musicians closely associated with Aksu's early career. As Yurdatapan recalled in interview, the principal raison-d'etre of Dün, Bugün, Yarın's was to get the two musicians out of the nightclub world, which was exhausting work for men with families. In addition, Yurdatapan had mainly been involved in İstanbul Gelişim (basically the house band in Bostancı's Lalezar club) as arranger; they had already found a bass player. Dün, Bugün, Yarın quickly expanded its operations and evolved into ŞAT Müzik. See note 23 above, and Dilmener 2003, p. 195.

24. The review is mentioned (though not quoted in its entirety) by Dilmener (Dilmener 2003, p. 242). He also cites poor reviews in *Hey* from as late as 1979.

25. I am grateful to Elizabeth Branch Dyson for pointing out to me that this was Piaf's nickname, too. The Piaf reference may well have been its source, though I believe that most people in Turkey would now be unaware of it.

had moved to Istanbul and had cosmetic surgery.²⁶ She had steadily climbed up the ranks of *Hey*'s "Music Oscars" year by year and was now regularly gracing the covers of both *Hey* and *Ses*. Her transfer from the Hop label to Kent made news for the huge sums of money involved.²⁷ She toured the provincial cities on a two-month tour involving a number of other up-and-coming singers.²⁸ She had a spot at the Izmir Fair, and had made a film.²⁹ She had an identifiable vocal style and was also known as a composer and lyricist. Sufficiently secure in her recording career, and recently married a second time, she now publicly declared her readiness to quit the concert stage.³⁰ A chapter in a rather conventional story of Turkish media success seemed to be coming to a close.

This biographical narrative does little to explain the dominant position

---

26. A short and anonymous article in *Hey* (8 May 1978, p. 26), "Sezen Aksu nihayet ev sahibi oldu" (Sezen Aksu becomes a homeowner at last), reports on significantly changed circumstances. For three years Aksu had been living with Melike Demirağ, a musician friend in Istanbul, but she was now living with her fiancé, Üstün Doruk, in their own house. This suggests that she moved to Istanbul around 1975. The article also reports on cosmetic surgery done on her ears and nose. She had been called *kepçe* on account of her ears, she claimed. Such candid declarations of insecurity and anxiety about her appearance played an important role in inspiring her popularity.

27. Note a short, anonymously written article in *Hey* (14 November 1977, p. 14), "Sezen Aksu yılın transferini yaptı" (Sezen Aksu made the transfer of the year). Aksu's transfer fee for moving from Hop to Kent was reputedly 150,000 Turkish liras. These and other "*astronomik rakamlar*" (astronomical figures), whether accurate or not, suggest a new climate of competition over the big stars, a category that now definitively included Aksu.

28. Amongst others the SAT–TUR Anatolian tour included Kartal Kaan, Ercan Turgut, Melike Demirağ, Timur Arda, and Ali Çetin. It set out in February, returning in April after performing in no less than fifty provincial capitals. *Hey* reported regularly on the tour's progress (see, for instance, *Hey* 4 April 1977, p. 15). Aksu would later report on the tour as a major learning experience. "On the first days my knees would be shaking with nerves. Now I can even dance on stage" (Ünver 1977, p. 10).

29. The film *Minik serçe* was made in 1978, with the first advertisements and reviews appearing in *Hey* in February 1979. It was directed by Atıf Yılmaz, with script by Deniz Türkali and music by Hürşit Yenigün. In addition to Aksu it starred Bulut Aras, Hulusi Kentmen, Bilge Zobu, Hüseyin Kutman, and Tunca Yönder. Aksu sang eight songs. The film was favorably reviewed by Giovanni Scognamillo in *Hey* 19 February 1979, p. 38. On Aksu's debut at the Izmir Fair in 1977, see Ünver 1977.

30. *Hey* 8 May 1978, p. 26, "Sezen Aksu nihayet ev sahibi oldu" (Sezen Aksu becomes a home owner at last), mentioned above, also reports that Aksu was considering giving up stage performances in three years' time. Another note of dissatisfaction with the life of the touring musician was struck in her passing comment that she would prefer to have her own orchestra, and not simply sing with house orchestras or bands, as was the custom at live events. These are statements about status and musical control. Orhan Gencebay, readers will recall, stopped performing live very early in his career (see chapter 3). Aksu, however, never did quit the stage. In the summer of 2006 all of the major rock and pop festivals and concert programs (Kuruçesme, Harbiye Açıkhava Tiyatrosu, and Bodrum) either opened or concluded with a Sezen Aksu concert.

Aksu came to assume in the drastically changed circumstances of the early 1980s. One needs to consider the pre-1980 period a little more systemically to understand how these later transformations came about. In the first instance, Aksu's appearance coincided with a moment of energetic cosmopolitanism. *Hey*'s charts and "Oscars" suggest a buoyant, eclectic, and well-educated musical public, not only in Istanbul but in the provincial cities too. Its articles, reports, and reviews kept Turkish readers well informed about American and European pop. It reported on local and international competitions, usually with a keen eye on Turkish representation. Developments not only at the Sanremo festival and at Eurovision but also at song festivals in Split, Alexandria, Athens, and Barcelona were keenly followed and editorialized. Turkish media politics, as well as issues concerning cassette piracy and labor rights in the music industry, were discussed with some sophistication. A long series of articles, usually published on the last pages of what was by then a lengthy publication, was devoted to techniques of orchestration and song arrangement. *Hey*'s editorial team certainly played a significant role in the development of this cosmopolitan popular music public in the 1970s. But it also reflected an independently existing world of consumption, performance, experimentation, and adaptation, all very much oriented to the outside world.

Pop and rock in Turkey in the 1960s were dominated by two complementary though antagonistic tendencies. One group of singers, comprising Erol Büyükburç ("the Turkish Elvis"), Ajda Pekkan, and Fecri Eyuboğlu in particular, developed a tradition of rendering non-Turkish popular styles for Turkish audiences, often in Turkish but also in popular foreign languages.[31] Büyükburç, as his moniker suggests, represented the (translated) rock and roll moment. Pekkan specialized in Turkish versions of *chanson* and *canzone*, making something of a name for herself as a recording star in France and Italy in the process.

So-called "Anatolian pop" or "Anatolian rock" ("*Anadolu pop*" / "*Anadolu rock*") reacted against this. Cem Karaca (1945–2004) was a key figure, working with a series of bands closely associated with the movement, notably Apaşlar (1969), Kardaşlar (1969–72), Moğollar (1971–74), and Dervişan (1974–78). In pursuit of an Anatolian version of Western rock, conceived as an alternative to Büyükburç and Pekkan, Karaca and others found ways of

---

31. The practice goes back at least to the Turkish versionizing of tango and foxtrots. The first Turkish tango is generally considered to have been Necip Celal's "Mazi" ("The past"), of 1928. The fashion for tango continued into the 1950s, overlapping with the beginning of Zeki Müren's career (see chapter 2).

bringing together keyboards, guitars, and drum kits with the *yaylı tanbur* (a long-necked bowed art music lute), the *bağlama,* the *kabak kemane* (a smaller bowed folk music lute), and a variety of Anatolian percussion instruments in performances that were predominantly organized around the guitar-based rhythms and textures of Western rock. Though excluded by official media, both Turkish pop and Anatolian rock were well supported by an Istanbul-based recording industry, by prominent competitions organized by national newspapers,[32] by a lively music press, and by public support at concerts in the major cities. Both drew equally on thoroughly internalized and up-to-date knowledge of both American rock and pop (both black and white) and French chanson and related styles.[33] This particular moment of popular musical cosmopolitanism was not to last, but it established enduring points of reference for Aksu in the early 1980s.

Aksu's musical formation also took place at a moment in which popular musicians were coming to think of themselves as politically positioned intellectuals and as professionals—in other words, as serious public figures. Anatolian rock took on a radical cast towards the end of the 1970s. Cem Karaca and Dervişan's 1978 song "1 Mayis" ("1 May") marked perhaps the most conspicuous moment of left-internationalist political identification amongst the Anatolian rockers, their most conspicuous moment of opposition to the state, and their slow drift into self-imposed exile, mostly in western Europe. Many, such as Karaca, were the products of foreign-language schools and literary family scenes;[34] their lyrics had marked literary aspirations.[35]

In the less overtly politicized world of Turkish pop, attitudes were more cautious and pragmatic but nonetheless increasingly articulate and critical

---

32. Hürriyet's "Altın mikrofon" (golden microphone) competition, which ran between 1965 and 1968, played a crucial role in the development of Turkish (and particularly "Anatolian") rock and pop. See http://www.milliyet.com.tr/2002/10/24/sanat/san18.html for a brief review of the competition, as well as DMC/Dost Müzik's archival CD, *Altın mikrofon müzikte değisim yılları ansiklopedisi, 56 unutulmaz eser 1965–1966–1967–1968,* released in 2002.

33. The Sanremo competition in Italy was keenly followed in Turkey during the 1970s, and frequently reported on in *Hey*; it continues to be commented on by critics (see, for instance, Dilmener 2006, p. 7). *Hey*'s annual "Oskars" regularly celebrated Adriano Celentano, Rafaela Carra, Julio Iglesias, Peppino di Capri, and many others. Enrico Macias's brief partnership with Ajda Pekkan in the mid-1970s made him into a household name in Turkey, and his 1976 hit "Melissa" made Melissa a popular girl's name there. Cem Karaca told me in interview (with Anne Ellingsen, 1996) that Gilbert Becaud had been a formative influence. Dorsay writes at length about the influence of Jacques Brel (2003, p. 215–17) The *chanson/canzone* tradition has been an enduring point of reference in the world of Turkish popular music.

34. Cem Karaca's mother, Toto Karaca, was, for example, a well-known actress. The family ran a theater in Beyoğlu.

35. Karaca set to music and sang a number of Nazım Hikmet and Orhan Veli songs throughout his career, for example.

of the state. Doğan Şener's editorials in *Hey* relentlessly criticized the TRT for the incoherence and ineptitude of the *Denetim Kurulu* (review board),[36] which to many seemed to systematically exclude anything of truly popular interest and significance. Many of Aksu's close associates at the time were highly visible spokesmen for recording company interests. Their involvement in these highly publicized rows with the TRT may have been parochial and professionally self-interested, but their arguments were invariably expressed, or at least mediated by music journalists, in terms of broader questions about the state of the nation.[37]

The mid- to late 1970s also provided Aksu with prominent female role models whose significant achievements and mistakes might be contemplated and learned from. Chief amongst these was Ajda Pekkan. Born in 1946, Pekkan had begun with her sister Semiramis as a *gazino* singer specializing in chanson-style songs, many of which were composed or arranged by Fecri Eyuboğlu. She graduated to film,[38] and thence to a remarkable recording and concert career that blossomed in Europe with a series of collaborations with

---

36. A short note in *Hey* suggests that the board was established in 1972 ("TRT'de köklü bir reform yapılıyor," *Hey* 16 August 1972, p. 3); subsequent reports indicate convulsive transformations, the establishment of advisory groups for popular music, and efforts to co-opt critics—partly, one suspects, as a result of *Hey*'s prominent campaigns against it. Its avowed purpose was to maintain public broadcasting standards in folk, classical, and "light" (*hafif*) music, and to maintain a space of public music-making that was separate from the commercial market. In practice, the *Denetim*'s main role was that of determining the authenticity of compositions, which would be rejected if they were suspected to be *aranjman* of either European or Arab originals. *Hey*'s editors relentlessly attacked the board's inconsistent attitude to popular culture and the popular music market, their handling of Turkey's entries to the Eurovision contest, and their plain incompetence.

37. Attila Özdemiroğlu and Şanar Yurdatapan, for instance—the two musicians associated with Dün, Bügün, Yarın and with Aksu throughout her career—led a boycott of the TRT in January 1973, during which music companies refused TRT access to their recordings by exercising their copyright (the rights to strike and collective bargaining having been suspended after the 1971 coup). Their slogan, "*Az yasak, çok teşvik*" (fewer bans, more incentives), directed attention to the fact that, it was claimed, only 21 songs had been passed by the board in two months while 204 had been turned down. The campaign seemed to have some effect. Though the TRT initially declared that as a state institution, they had no obligation to answer to anybody, they subsequently announced the formation of a Müzik Danışma Kurulu (Music Information Board; see "Sanatçılar denetim kurulunda anlayış bekliyor," *Hey* 10 January 1973, pp. 8–9) as a means of mediating such issues. Two years later they had recruited Yurdatapan, but strikes and boycotts of this nature continued to haunt the organization throughout the 1970s. Interview with Şanar Yurdatapan, September 2008.

38. I have never seen an Ajda Pekkan film, but evidently there were a number of them; see, for instance, the Wikipedia article under her name. People I know who have seen these films inform me that they are very bad. Dilmener reports getting his hands on a copy of *Harun Reşid'in gözdesi* (Harun Reşit's sweetheart) and instantly realizing why Pekkan (who he says was "incompetent and rather overweight" in that film) was both quick and right to give up acting and concentrate on music (Dilmener 2006, p. 88).

Enrico Macias and major hits in France.[39] She represented Turkey at the 1980 Eurovision Song Contest in The Hague, having been an obvious candidate to do so (appropriately "modern"- and "European"-looking women were regularly chosen to represent Turkey in that competition). As it happened, "Petr'Oil"—a curious song, evidently chosen for complicated reasons—did badly.[40] Pekkan's career suffered after this, but a slow process of nostalgic recuperation in the mid-1990s subsequently reversed her fortunes.

If Ajda Pekkan represented pop internationalism, and with it a Euro-American ideal of beauty and sexiness, she was counterbalanced by others whose music showed their art or folk music roots and whose femininity was more obviously and self-consciously "Turkish," such as Nükhet Duru, Seyyal Taner, Yeliz, Gökben, and Neşe Karaböçek.[41] The marketing of female stars relied heavily, then as now, on the production of a highly sexualized visual image, mostly for male audiences. But it also increasingly relied on locating female stars in sentimental film narratives. Film director Atıf Yılmaz was already prominent in the market for melodrama,[42] and Aksu eventually made a film with him. *Minik serçe* (1979) was an obvious vehicle of self-promotion, modeled on Kris Kristofferson and Barbra Streisand's *A Star Is Born*. But Aksu's acting skills were noted by critics and the film was well received.[43] Aksu's bold gender politics of the 1980s would have been a hard, if not impossible, act to maintain had she not been able to bounce off Pekkan's brash cosmopolitanism on the one hand and the "Turkish" femininity represented by Duru and Taner on the other.

---

39. Her collaboration with Macias involved a major concert at the Paris Olympia in 1975, the release of a live concert LP with Macias (*La fête a l'Olympia*) the next year, and appearances with Macias on French TV. *Pour lui* came out in 1978.

40. See Dorsay 2003, 302–5, and Dilmener 2003, 267–77, on "Petr'Oil" and other Turkish Eurovision entries.

41. Note Büker 2002 on the earlier shift from (blonde) Cahide Sonku to (dark) Türkan Şoray as icons of beauty in Turkish popular cinema. The relationship between Ajda Pekkan and Sezen Aksu might be understood in similar terms, I suggest.

42. For a critical retrospective of Yılmaz's (1925–2006) films, see a collection of short articles in *Altyazı*, June 2006, pp. 66–71, "Biz Atıf Yılmaz'ı çok sevdik." His reputation as a woman-friendly director rests on films such as *Adı Vasfiye* (1985), which featured Müjde Ar in the title role, and sympathetic portrayals of women's struggles in traditional and small-town settings. Yılmaz's films involved all of the major actors and actresses of his day, as well as musicians such as Attila Özdemiroğlu.

43. The major Turkish film critic Giovanni Scognamillo reviewed the film for *Hey* (Scogamillo 1979, p. 38). Though finding it somewhat derivative, he had strong words of praise for the acting. Of Aksu he had this to say: "Of course she occasionally plays herself in the dramatic setup, and behaves as she herself would. But, apart from this, she succeeds in bringing a sense of dimension, a certain spirit to [the character of] Hülya. It's far from being a game of tics, affectations, and artificiality."

Finally, one might also consider the fortunate circumstance of Aksu's birth, childhood, and education in Izmir, a provincial but nonetheless large and musically vital city with its TRT station and its International Fair. Conflicts with her parents over her choice of career—later much discussed by Aksu—may have had a sharper edge in the provincial city than would have been the case in Istanbul, and this in turn may have contributed to the insistent focus on matters of shame and female sexuality one notices in her later music. The Izmir Radio station established an Artists' Club (*Sanatçılar Derneği*) where local students could take classes. Aksu, who attended classes there, remembers an eclectic, creative place with a strong amateur ethos. She remembers her piano teacher suddenly quitting to run a pastry shop, for instance.[44] The Artists' Club was evidently neither torn apart by ideological disputes nor run according to tenets of ideological purism, as many such organizations in Istanbul undoubtedly were during this period.[45] A young singer could learn folk, classical, and Western repertoire, could develop skills in acting, dancing, and various musical instruments, and could mix with other students and professionals in an unselfconsciously productive and collaborative environment. Aksu's ability to move between musical styles, her consistent use of her literary and dramatic skills, and her apparently effortless professional savoir faire owed much to her musical upbringing in Izmir.[46]

### Aksu and the Coup: *Firuze, Sen Ağlama*, and *Git*

The timing and location of Aksu's early career success were fortunate indeed. This observation extends to the period following the 12 September 1980 coup. That coup and its aftermath can hardly be called fortunate for anybody, except perhaps those who orchestrated it and continue to evade justice. It may also have ushered in a period of relative security, for which many of my friends on my first trips to Turkey during those years were

---

44. Interview with Aksu, 12 July 1996.

45. Music societies, referred to either as *dernek* or *cemiyet*, had been an important feature of Turkish social life since early republican times. By the 1950s they loomed so large in the musical landscape that many singers would claim to find them somewhat constricting and controlling (note, for instance, an interview with Mualla Mukadder in *Resimli Radyo Dünyası* 15 (1950), 26–33 ("Musiki aleminde yeni parlayan bir yıldız"). On the *dernek*-s as social institutions in Istanbul in the 1980s, see Stokes 1992a. At that time they were certainly driven by rather clearly articulated political and ideological concerns.

46. Many of the same things could be said about Orhan Gencebay's upbringing in Samsun, a city that also boasted a well-established music festival, a cosmopolitan musical life, and a strong sense of itself as a major provincial capital. This observation would extend to the ambitious provincial's irrepressible urge to conquer the big city. See chapter 3.

clearly grateful and relieved. But it marked a period of political repression, censorship, "disappearances" on a Latin American scale, economic hardship, and a powerful sense of international isolation.[47]

As far as popular music—a small issue in the broader pattern of things—was concerned, the coup was a calamity. Popular histories of the musical moment pass over it in silence (Dilmener 2003; Dorsay 2003). It was undoubtedly a moment of stagnation. I remember being struck, as a backpacking visitor to the country during the coup years, by the prohibitive expense of foreign cassettes and, intriguingly for me, by the existence of a generation of students who seemed to have very little knowledge of, or even much interest in, American or European pop. Public musical life was dominated by the TRT, locked as it was into its struggles with *arabesk,* and the monumentalization of Turkish folk and classical music. To me the "light music" (*hafif müziği*) programs offered on Turkish radio seemed to be a previous generation's elevator music at best, and an almost comical effort to divert Turkish youth from the Euro-American pop and rock of the 1970s. *Arabesk*—dominated then by Orhan Gencebay, Ferdi Tayfur, Müslüm Gürses, and the young İbrahim Tatlises—was the only musical field that seemed to have any life in it, though it still struck me forcibly at that particular moment as an exhausted and depressed music for an exhausted and depressed people.

There is no question, though, that the timing of the coup was fortunate for Aksu. It dispersed or silenced her potential rivals. It oriented the music market toward musicians who looked and sounded local. It put a high premium on melancholy and introspection. It created a middle class, frustrated by the heavy hand of the TRT and street-level hegemony of *arabesk,* that was hungry for signs of cultural distinction. Aksu had the musical experience, contacts, ambition, and well-honed professional mind required to define and exploit this situation.

The coup years seem to have been a period of quiet consolidation and exploration for Aksu. She married again in 1981 and had a son. She launched a popular musical review in 1982, the archly named "*Sezen Aksu Aile Gazi-*

---

47. For many, the coup produced the more enduring patterns of violence that plague the country today. See, in particular, Keyder 2004, who argues that the "deep state" continued to operate, to the detriment of a properly civil political culture, long after the transition to civilian government. "The civilian governments that subsequently entered office, beginning with Turgut Özal's election victory in 1983, essentially concerned themselves with economic policy and the management of the debt. Meanwhile, the State Security Courts served as unabashed organs of the 'deep state': their jurisdiction extended to everything political, ranging from human rights to anything that the state construed as separatist propaganda, within which rubric even singing a song in Kurdish could qualify" (Keyder 2004).

*nosu*" (roughly, "Sezen Aksu's family show").[48] She wrote for journals and magazines. She was involved in somewhat unsuccessful efforts to rejuvenate Turkish contributions to the Eurovision song contest.[49] Three cassette (later CD) projects that emerged from the coup years, though, established a distinctly new and highly influential sound. These were *Firuze* (1982), *Sen ağlama* ("Don't you cry," 1984) and *Git* ("Go," 1986), the first products of her career-defining partnership with Onno Tunç and the lyricist Aysel Gürel. Turkish critic Naim Dilmener's apt assessment of *Sen ağlama* is applicable to all three, and worth quoting in full:

> [*Sen ağlama*] . . . translated the feelings of everyone whose heads had been messed up by the government that had come to power with its promise of prosperity [*bolluk vaadi*] after the military regime. Feelings of uncertainty and indecision that had enveloped the entire country were transferred to song by Onno Tunç, Sezen Aksu, and Aysel Gürel in an utterly well-wrought [*usta*], utterly canny [*işbilir*] manner. Everybody now knew where to find the slogan they were after. This album provided the market with an extraordinarily successful formula. Our idea of music had to be done, of course, "crying, sentimentally, emotionally, intimately" ["*ağlayarak, dertlenerek, içlenerek, yakınarak*"], but in a somewhat more veiled [*örtük*], less self-lacerating manner [*göz çıkarmadan*]. This was the formula the market, unbeknown to itself, was after (Dilmener 2003, pp. 310–11).

Musically speaking, these albums were striking for three reasons, which one can associate respectively with the three personalities involved. First, they involved a new studio sound and a new style of arrangement. This can be detected on Onno Tunç's contributions to *Firuze* (specifically, "Ayrılıklar bitmez," "Bazen," and "Bir zamanlar deli gönlüm") and on the two subsequent albums on which his arrangements and studio work predominate. Tunç, born Onno Tunçboyacıyan in 1949, was a noted bassist, bandleader,

---

48. This was the first of several musicals, including *Bin yıl önce, bin yıl sonra*. It ran for twenty days in Istanbul's Şan Müzikholü after opening on 14 February 1985, and costarred the well-known comic actors İlyas Salman, Savaş Dinçel, and Sevil Üstekin, with music provided by the Onno Tunç Orkestrası. An article in *Hey*, 25 February 1985, pp. 10–11 ("Uçtu uçtu, Sezen uçtu") provides a detailed account of the sketches and the music program, which bought together most of the best-known songs of the three albums under discussion here.

49. Aksu regularly competed in the Turkish finals, though she was rarely selected. In 1985 she competed with Neco and Nükhet Duru, for instance, with "Küçük bir aşk Masalı." I am grateful to Meliz Sirman (personal communication) for pointing out that although Onno Tunç was often to be seen on the podium as conductor, his compositions and Aksu's songs were rarely selected.

and producer. His musical life started in the Armenian Church. This, together with a later immersion in jazz, funk, and soul, wrought a meticulous studio style and deft hand in matters of harmonic conception, arrangement, and orchestration. From *Sen ağlama* up to his untimely death shortly before the release of *Işık doğudan yükselir*, he, his orchestra,[50] and Aksu worked more or less exclusively with one another.

Tunç's style remains instantly recognizable. Consider, by way of detail, his instrumental introductions. These alternate solo or ensemble instrumentation with the conventional violin chorus in question and answer phrases. They can always be heard and understood in terms of monophonic *makam* conventions. But they also involved subtle shadings of harmony and voice leading,[51] as well as characteristic choices of instruments. The opening instrumental theme of "Sen ağlama," for instance, starts with a quirky ensemble sound. Here the main instrumental theme is initially stated by accordion and bouzouki, accompanied by quiet, syncopated brass chords and closely microphoned snare drum. For such moments Tunç would typically choose "ethnic" instruments, usually Anatolian, Balkan, or Greek in origin, or instruments associated with the street and everyday life (accordion, *zurna*, and so forth). He would also play with acoustic space.[52] Instruments are often heard unusually close, unusually distant, or in some combination of the two.[53] A certain quietness and intimacy always prevails, as it does at

---

50. The Onno Tunç Orchestra that accompanied Aksu early in the 1980s in her regular concerts at the Bebek Park Gazinosu comprised Turhan Yükselir and Fahir Atakoğlu on keyboards, Harun Koçal on bass, Halis Bütünley on percussion, Berk Yenal on guitar, Cengiz Teoman on drums, and Onno Tunç leading from the piano. See *Hey* 5 November 1984. Tunç died in a private plane flying between Bursa and Yalova on 14 January 1996.

51. The opening theme of *Sen ağlama* has a strong *kürdi* or *kürdilihicazkar* tonality. A flourish on the harp introduces a repeat, performed conventionally enough by the full string chorus; halfway through, however, a quiet trumpet counterpoint is set against it. At this point the harmonic vocabulary suddenly moves far beyond the rather mechanical triadic handlings of *kürdi*-based *makam* material that prevail in much Mediterranean popular music. Its spare and sustained ninths derive from the harmonic and voice-leading universe of jazz. More specifically, they evoke the big band sound and accompanying urban landscapes with which Turkish listeners would have been familiar from American television serials of the late 1970s and early 1980s, like *Dallas* and *Kojak*. On "Mediterranean harmony" and *kürdi*-based progressions in particular, see Manuel 1986; see also chapter 3 for a related discussion of Gencebay's use of *muhayyerkürdi*. In interview, Aksu mentioned that she and Tunç had decided at an early stage to work with, and stick with, "the tempered system" (i.e., Euro-American intonational norms) rather than the *makam* system. Amongst many other things, *Işık doğudan yükselir* marked a reversal of this decision.

52. I borrow the idea of acoustic space from Allan Moore, who is interested in how one might use notions of space (left versus right, close versus near) to reconfigure and expand the notion of the musical "text" in rock. See Moore 1993.

53. The use of two *zurna*-s at the opening of Aksu's *Işık doğudan yükselir* is a good example. These are outdoor instruments, traditionally played at deafening volume and used for dancing. Here, how-

the opening of "Sen ağlama." Tunç's musical contribution to the post-1980 Aksu sound was decisive.

Aysel Gürel's mentorship was also strong, although it slowly declined as Aksu began to write her own lyrics. Aksu's inclination towards lyrics with a self-consciously literary quality, oriented towards female spaces of longing and desire, owes much to Gürel, though. "Firuze," with words by Gürel, depicts a female protagonist weeping at passing years and fading beauty. The dense and rich language, the melancholic and fatalistic themes, the gendering of anxiety, suffering, and pain (*telaş, hüzün, acı*), the acknowledgement of female desire and erotic imagination ("*bazen volkan gibi/bazen bir deli rüzgar gibi*"; "sometimes like a volcano, sometimes like a mad wind"), and its insistent address of an individual woman ("*sen, Firuze . . . ağla ağla Firuze*"; "you, Firuze . . . cry, cry, Firuze") strike an intimate note significantly absent in the pre-1980 work. Gürel's contribution to the lyrics of these three important recordings, then, also marked an important turning point.

Finally, these recordings mark a transformation in Aksu's voice. The heroic chanson diva sound of the later 1970s still prevails in "Firuze," but in "Sen ağlama" it is restricted to the sing-along chorus. In the verses, from the opening line onwards, the voice is quiet, close, intimate. The microphone, as handled by Aksu, registers a body, a vocal apparatus—a "grain," to employ Barthes's well-known term (Barthes 1977). It indexes the presence of a fellow human being rather than a star on a stage. Careworn sighs and breaks are crafted onto emotionally and poetically prominent words: for instance, the opening "A"s of "*Ağlama gözbebeğim sana kıyamam*" ("Don't cry, my love; I can't destroy you") in the second line of the chorus and the "*Al yüreğim senin olsun*" ("Take my heart, let it be yours") that follows. This change in Aksu's vocal style is, obviously enough, connected to the transformations above. Tunç's preference for intimately experienced, dense instrumental timbres was conceived in relation to a similar kind of female voice. Gürel's self-consciously literary and emotional lyrics both enabled and responded to the possibility of this kind of vocal treatment.

The transformation of Aksu's vocal style had broader dimensions. The increasingly emotional quality of her vocal performance was much discussed in the music press, in the general context of the promotion of these albums and in the discursive definition of "the new Aksu." Aksu herself seems to have been keen to draw a line under the past. *Hey* announced an "Interview between 'Little Sparrow' Sezen Aksu and the Little Sparrow" on its front

---

ever, they are heard quietly as though from a great distance, with foreground elements (particularly voice) providing aural "perspective."

cover on 19 April 1982. Inside, the "new" (i.e., older) Sezen Aksu was indeed interviewed by the young Sezen Aksu. The older Aksu reflected on a moment of maturity, a taking stock of her career and her art: "It was popular tastes [*halkın beğenileri*] that turned me into the Sezen Aksu you see before you today. More correctly, it was 'Sezen Aksu's Family Show' that dragged me here. Today I look on the art world with a very different eye" (*Hey* 19 April 1982).

In short, she told her younger self, she has now become a professional. Previously she had followed, or was "dragged." Now she was in control and doing the dragging. Previously she had been serving an apprenticeship. Now she was working with the top professionals in her field: Atilla Özdemiroglu, Onno Tunç, Mehmet Duru, Melih Kibar, Aysel Gürel, Çiğdem Talu. A complicated and much imitated new hairstyle marked the moment (see Dilmener 2003, p. 323).

Others participated in this retrospective making of the new Aksu. Gürel, for her part, located Aksu's new vocal intimacy in a more deeply rooted quality of melancholy, one by which she had always been struck. Recalling in 1984 the first time she met Aksu, Gürel claimed, "It was the best voice I have heard, and remains so to this day. She could interpret each of the songs she sang at the same high level of quality. One could hear in it a great deal of the accumulation of sadness [*hüzün*] in her life. You'll notice it has great swirling clouds of emotionality in it [*buram buram duygusallık var içinde farkındaysınız*] (Ünsü 1984, p. 27). The remarketing of Aksu involved the publicizing of a new kind of vocal intimacy, a new kind of melancholy. As Gürel's quote suggests, this was to be understood by fans as the property of a *life*, with its complex accumulation of sadness and experience, and not simply as the whirling of cogs in the music industry machine.

The market was, however, undergoing significant technological and organizational changes. *Hey*'s charts in the early 1980s reflect the complexity of this market and the pressures on it. Separate charts were compiled for "local" (*yerli*) and "foreign" (*yabancı*) recordings. In the late 1970s the category of "local" was subdivided into pop, classical, and folk. There was sufficient productivity in these various categories to make such distinctions meaningful. This was no longer necessary in the depressed conditions of the early 1980s. *Yerli* constituted one category, subdivided into *Türk sanat müziği, arabesk, halk,* and *Türk pop.*" Another new category had been added, a sign of its times: *diskoteklerin gözdeleri* (disco favorites).[54] Charts in the early

---

54. On the fashionable discos and nightclubs of the 1980s, particularly the famous "Stüdyo 54" in Etiler, see Dilmener 2003, p. 318, and Ahıska and Yenal 2006, pp. 230–33.

1980s were, however, divided by media format into 45 rpm singles, 33 rpm long-plays, and "legal cassettes." They also included a separate chart for recordings by official TRT artists, and a nostalgia chart (*anılarımızdaki sesler*) had been added—subdivided, interestingly, into "five years ago" and "ten years ago." These categories reflected what was by now the nearly complete dominance of legal and pirated cassette production,[55] the significant role of the TRT as gatekeeper and an arbiter of taste, and a somewhat melancholy sense that the past, musically speaking, was preferable to the present.

These chart categories also suggest a disorganized space, subject to a variety of different pressures, that can hardly be described as a "market," at least as conceived by liberal economists. A variety of forces—independent record companies, officialdom, and cassette pirates—interacted in a struggle for dominance, or at least influence. The three Aksu recordings discussed above coincided with significant efforts by the independent recording companies to organize, lobby government in opposition to cassette piracy (and by extension *arabesk*), and lobby the TRT in opposition to its ideological stranglehold on the circulation of music in the country. Aksu and her professional circle were prominently involved in the formation of such groups.[56] Their highly public activities and interventions in public discussions produced a string of limited successes, if not decisive victories.

The introduction of CD technology (noted in *Hey* on 15 October 1984; see also Dilmener 2003, p. 313) strengthened their position considerably. CD production involved capital outlay that the pirates, at that stage at least, could not get their hands on. It provided a means of distinction for middle-class consumers; locally produced CDs were initially about twice the price of locally produced cassettes. The shift to CDs also made possible practices of musical and aesthetic distinction. If the cassette market and the predominant conditions of working-class reception (e.g., noisy public spaces, public transport) favored a strongly focused melody line, the reception of CDs in

---

55. Özbek 1991, p. 123, posits Plaksan, which started in 1976, as the first Turkish cassette company, followed by Sabra (known later as Raks) in 1978. Early in the 1980s, these were joined by Teletrans, Uzelli, Nora, and Bantsan, and LPs quickly disappeared. By 1987, Turkey boasted an annual cassette production capacity of 78 million, with some 40 to 50 million cassettes produced legally each year. It is more or less impossible to estimate the number of pirate cassettes produced, but if one were to add them to the nation's yearly total, that number would probably just about double.

56. Fikir ve Sanat Eserlerlerinden Doğan Hakları Koruma Sirketi (FİSAM), founded in 1978 with the support of Paris-based SACEM by Halit Kemal, would have been the first of these groups (see *Hey* 29 May 1978, p. 3); Musiki Eseri Sahipleri Meslek Birliği (MESAM), founded in 1987, which is a member of CISAC, the Paris-based international copyright organization, has been the most enduring (Dilmener 2003, p. 348).

middle-class (private and domestic) contexts favored textured instrumental sounds, acoustic depth, and polyphony.[57] In other words CD technology, with its industry-wide reverberations in Turkey, was crucial to Aksu's post-*Firuze* vocal style.

## Light from the East: Forbearance

The 1995 CD *Işık doğudan yükselir / Ex oriente lux* was widely understood as a radically new departure on Aksu's part. Even in arguing for more of a long-term view, critics such as Canbazoğlu suggested considering it only in the light of her most recent prior CDs, in particular the similarly quiet and folksy *Deli kızın türküsü* (1993). The discussion thus far suggests the need for a broader perspective. *Işık doğudan yükselir*'s place in a continuous process of musical change and market positioning is immediately obvious. The intimate and folksy tone that prevails here can be seen in terms of a slower evolution since the days of *Firuze* and *Sen Ağlama*. Media hype suggested a new moment of maturity (Aksu had just turned forty), and a new moment of world-weary emotionality (Tunç had just been killed in a airplane accident), but this again can be seen in terms of the development of Aksu's public persona since the early 1980s.

What was new, though, was the overt feminism of the CD project.[58] *Işık doğudan Yükselir* is organized as a narrative focusing on and connecting moments in the lives of Anatolian women. It starts with an instrumental introduction, apparently based on themes suggested by Aksu but pulled together by Tunç shortly before he died. It involves a twenty-two-piece orchestra and a wordless chorus, with a striking solo by Sertab Erener, then still known as an Aksu student and not yet as the Eurovision star of 2004. A quiet bolero-like rhythm builds up to a huge climax. It makes for an unusual opening; I

---

57. As Manuel remarks of the new *ghazal* in north India, which were adapted by producers to more sophisticated sound reproduction on cassette players and domestic sites of consumption at the time. Hindi film music, by contrast, circulated by radio; production values focused on voice and the string choruses, which were suitable to low-fidelity sound reproduction and more public sites of consumption. See Manuel 1993.

58. This was directly connected with Aksu's involvement with the "Saturday Mothers," a movement organized and inspired by women on the Argentine model to protest the "disappearances" of the coup years. See *Aktüel* 11–17 July 1996 (cover, gift cassette and various articles) and Canbazoğlu's report in the culture pages of *Cumhuriyet* (Canbazoğlu 1996), including a discussion of rival weekly publication *Nokta*'s claim that Aksu was simply using the movement for the purposes of publicity. "Anatolianism" also took a feminist twist in Yıldız Kenter's production of Güngör Dilmen's *Ben anadolu*, which was a massive theatrical hit in Istanbul immediately before Aksu's album release. I am grateful to Ciğdem Balım for pointing this out to me.

still have difficulty thinking of precedents or points of reference.[59] Its rhetorical purpose seems to be to declare that what follows is not just a collection of songs but a *project*, an overarching narrative—something to be understood as a whole.

What follows might be interpreted as a feminist *bildungsroman*. The song "Davet" (Invitation) describes inadmissible erotic longings. Carefree days are wistfully remembered in "Son sardunyalar" (The last geraniums) and "Alaturka." The mood suddenly changes with the pensive "Yaktılar Halim'imi" (They killed my Halim), which alludes to a feud and a young love crushed by village society. "Rakkas" (Dancer) evokes the careless cruelty of the male gaze. "Onu alma, beni al" (Don't take her, take me), an ironically up-tempo number, describes the anxieties of the wedding market. The soul-destroying demands of motherhood in a strange household are evoked in "Ben annemi isterim" (I want my mother). A woman's-eye view prevails as a woman's emotional and erotic experience unfolds in the CD's narrative.

The remaining songs have lyrics by Anatolian folk poets and mystics (Aşık Daimi, Mevlana Celalettin Rumi, and Yunus Emre). Though the gendered narrative suddenly seems to run dry, one can easily consider the sudden metaphysical turn as a reminder of Anatolian traditions of poetic fatalism, the resources which have enabled women to put up with their lot in life. I put this to Aksu in an interview. As it happened, she strongly disagreed. Her reply is worth quoting in full:

> But it isn't about passive forbearance [*tekevvül*]. "Bu da gelir" [the Aşık Daimi song that featured on the TRT news broadcast] is about accumulated experience [*bir birikimle ilgili*]. Anatolia was the very last society in which men came to dominate women. Women have struggled against this for centuries. I mean it's about accumulated experience, that song. I don't think it's about accepting the way things are. I mean Anatolian women look as though they are dominated by men, but power [*hakimiyet*] in each household is actually held by women. There's a kind of silent agreement. The family unit looks as though it is run by men, but we can actually

---

59. The opening of Yavuz Top's *Deyişler 1*, which came out in 1985, strikes me as a possible precedent. It was loosely based on an Alevi *deyiş*, "Ötme bülbül," but arranged for an orchestra of folk musical instruments and chorus, in a sparse contrapuntal and harmonic idiom. The final climax was built on an ostinato figure and an *uzun hava* vocalization by İzzet Altınmeşe. This provided a model for various experiments in the folk music world early in the 1980s (including Arif Sağ's *bağlama* concerto and many of the cassettes recorded by the Muhabbet ensemble; see Markoff 1991/92). Though these did not circulate widely outside professional folk music and serious amateur circles, they were noted by many in various musical worlds as an attempt to "do something modern with" the Anatolian folk musical legacy and generally think outside of the TRT's box.

see the dominant traces [*dominant izleri*] of that older women-run society in each and every Turkish family. Even in my house, if my husband asked for a *börek* [pastry], he'd get a slap really fast [*zıpla zıpla döverim ben*] (laughs)! You can't just ignore that past. Look, we're the granddaughters of those Anatolian mothers who carried ammunition on their backs during the war of independence. I mean, unlikely though it may appear on the surface, the Turkish woman—the Anatolian woman, I mean—has little to be sorry about.

It was only later that I came across an interview with Aksu in *Aktüel*, probably recorded only a few days before I had spoken with her myself. *Aktüel*'s journalist had also come to the conclusion that the song expressed fatalism. This fatalism seemed to the journalist to be in tension with Aksu's widely publicized support for the "Saturday Mothers," who throughout that summer had been protesting on behalf of the "disappeared" of the 12 September coup in front of the Galatasaray Lycée in Taksim. *Aktüel*'s journalist asked, "Didn't you once say: 'Why cry, my dark locked one/This too shall pass, don't cry'? Is it really the case that 'this too shall pass?'" Aksu's response conveyed the anxiety she had expressed to me about what she viewed as negative meanings that seemed to be sticking to the song:

> There's nothing there, really, about "this too shall pass." The meaning here has nothing to do with passive forbearance [*tevekkül*], in my view. On the contrary, it's about an accumulation of experience. Anatolia was one of the last places in which the dominance of women was replaced by the dominance of men. Mothers and women protested this development for thousands of years. In various parts of Anatolia one can see traces of this resistance still alive today. In our society we have habits of thinking of motherhood as sacred. In our Anatolia, the homeland of mothers, it's great that the stones that the republic's mothers threw into murky waters should increasingly be turning into the new building blocks of our republic (Aksu 1996, p. 24).

Aksu, obviously enough, had drawn on a prepared response when I asked a predictable question. But clearly I had not been alone in thinking of the last songs on *Işık doğudan yükselir* as a continuation of the feminist narrative delineated by its opening songs. Aksu was walking a thin and ambiguous line between espousing traditional virtues of passive forbearance and celebrating a *birikim*—a progressive, forward-looking accumulation of gendered experience. The obvious authorial anxiety that hovers over these exchanges was

**Figure 4a.** Sezen Aksu. Photograph by Necati Sönmez

clearly a response to the accrual of popular meanings to this song (particularly that of "fatalism") that she disliked and seemed unable to control. This feminist narrative was emphatically yoked to a narrative about a nation made by women. Aksu connected the struggles of women at the foundation of the republic with the current struggles of women (particularly the "Saturday Mothers") for justice and political accountability. She was saying that the nation had been built not on women's passivity and forbearance, but on their resistance—their refusal to accept the status quo.

### Light from the East: "Mozaikistan"; or, "What Mosaic, You Bastard?"

The terms in which Aksu represented the nation in *Işık Doğudan Yükselir* were also strikingly new. As we have seen, this significantly involved understanding the nation in terms of gendered defiance. Another striking element was the insistent metaphorization of the nation as a mosaic. This metaphor has a long history of use both in Turkey, as a means of talking about multiculturalism and ethnic diversity, an in Western orientalist scholarship, as a means of representing the Middle East.[60] These two usages, though clearly linked genealogically, need to be distinguished politically in Turkey. Orientalist scholarship favored the mosaic metaphor as a means of depicting a society that was resisting history and modernity. In Turkey it tended to be employed from the 1980s on by leftists seeking a benign way of representing multiculturalism, thinking of parts in relation to the whole, and advocating a relaxation of draconian laws restricting the public use of Kurdish and other Anatolian languages. Leftists who were anxious that the metaphor ignored or downplayed centuries of interactions and exchange between Anatolian ethnic groups, and who were concerned about its kinship with Orientalist representations, could at least take solace in the fact that the far right in Turkey absolutely *hated* the metaphor, which for them implied the recognition of ethnic diversity. Alparslan Türkeş, founder of the fascistic Milliyetçi Hareket Partisi,[61] was, the story goes, dozing during a live debate on Mehmet Ali Birand's *Çapraz Ateş* television program that very year. He woke up to hear someone describing Turkey as a mosaic. His response—a snarling "What mosaic, you bastard?" (*Ne mozaiği ulan?*)—initiated a broad public debate about the appropriateness of this metaphor.[62]

The metaphor so worrying to the nationalist right was an insistent drumbeat on *Işık doğudan yükselir / Ex oriente lux*. The CD's cover, designed by Mehmet Koyunoğlu, depicted Aksu's face in the manner of the Roman mosaics of Antakya.[63] This same image dominated the page on which the CD was reviewed in *Cumhuriyet*. The Anatolian mosaic pieces are clearly identified in producer Üstün Barışta's liner notes: Turks and Kurds, Byzantines and Ionians, Armenians and Hittites, northern Mesopotamians and Romans, Sun-

---

60. For a critique of the mosaic metaphor and its relationship to orientalism and functionalist theorizing, see Eickelman 1989, pp. 48–53.

61. The Milliyetçi Hareket Partisi (Nationalist Action Party), which has, under various names, followed the leadership of Alparslan Türkeş since the mid-1960s. After Türkeş died in 1997, leadership devolved onto Devlet Bahçeli, who continues to lead it at the time of writing. It made significant gains in the 2007 elections.

62. The expression continues to be evoked in most public discussions of Kurdish and other "minority" language issues today, as a quick Google search on the expression will reveal. See, for instance, Türker Alkan in *Radikal* 2 August 2006, http://www.radikal.com.tr/haber.php?haberno =194576, accessed 21 August 2009. Türkeş reputedly added: "It's marble, marble! [*mermer, mermer*]" (i.e., white and solid)—a clever twist on the classical imagery deployed by his opponents.

63. A picture can be found on Aksu's official website (www.sezen-aksu.com), under "*diskografi*."

nis and Shiites, Laz and Zeybek-s, whirling dervishes and Bektaşi-s, dancers and court musicians. The songs allude, through style, instrumentation, and poetry, to diverse regional and spiritual repertoires. "Davet" is in this allusive sense "Greek," its vocal line reminiscent of rembetika and featuring a bouzouki. "Son sardunyalar" hints at the Italian presence in Anatolia with accordion and mandolin. "Alaturka" features an urban art music *fasıl* ensemble. "Yaktılar Halim'imi," "Ne ağlarsın," and "Var, git, turnam" are central Anatolian folk songs with prominent use of *bağlama* (long-necked folk lute). "Rakkas" suggests Egyptian-style dance music. "Yeniliğe dogru" and "La ilahe illallah" suggest Mevlevi sufi tradition, with prominent *ney* (end-blown flute), especially in the former. "Ben annemi isterim" starts with a field recording of a Black Sea lament and continues as a traditional Black Sea folk song, with *kemençe* (fiddle).[64] Though each of these songs dialogues with Aksu's previously established pop style in complex and playful ways, "authentic" and appropriate instruments and tonalities[65] are used consistently and conspicuously.

It was Aksu and Barışta's claim to be representing the nation (presenting "a musical anthology of Turkey") that attracted particular critical attention—not simply because it seemed ambitious and overblown, but also because many saw it as a challenge to the TRT, if not an outright usurpation of its role. This was a matter of anxiety to many at this particular moment. The liberal managers of the state seemed to be more invested in promoting private media than in preserving the TRT. The incursion of Polygram, Sony, Warner Brothers, and other giant media multinationals was well underway; their Turkish media industry partners, with Aksu often acting as spokesperson, had been jockeying for a place in the emerging order. The TRT looked like a spent force, a relic of an era long past. Many were worried about how accountable the new media hegemony would be to national interests.

*Işık doğudan yükselir / Ex oriente lux* focused these anxieties. Aksu seemed

---

64. My friend Ersin Baykal, a TRT instrumentalist, played the Black Sea *kemençe* on the album. At the time, he had a visitor from his native Ordu—an older village woman who had a reputation as a ritual lament (*ağıt*) singer, and was much in demand at local weddings (at which laments for the bride are sung) and funerals. When Baykal mentioned this to Aksu, she immediately asked whether the woman would consider coming to the studio and singing on this track. The woman obliged, performing her wedding lament in a state of bemusement. She is duly credited in the liner notes as "a Black Sea mother."

65. The album marked a break with the immediate past in Aksu's use of the modal structures of art and folk music. Prior to this, she and Onno Tunç had decided to stick to diatonic scales. Interview with Aksu, 12 July 1996.

to pour oil on the fire with her publicly dismissive attitudes towards the TRT's folk music tradition, and with an increasingly open embrace of issues of ethnicity. In an interview with Anne Ellingsen and me in 1996, she was brusque on the subject of the TRT:

> What they do is really primitive [*çok ilkel*]. And what I'm about is producing something new [*yeniden üretim söz konusu*]. Something richer, something more colorful, something with a broader perspective, something all the people in the world can get something out of. I mean, our music is monophonic; monophonic music contains within it very deep modal resources [lit. "it contains a deep modal treasury"]. If only it were to be pushed in the direction of polyphony. . . . There's really no point in perpetuating this primitive approach, there's no meaning in it. It's just folklore. . . . I just want to develop this [i.e., what I am doing] as best I can. Even when I'm old, there'll still be much to do. Those coming after me will continue. But I believe that one day we'll get a sound really appropriate to us, to Anatolia, properly grounded [*bir gün buraya cok has, çok özel . . . Anadolu'ya çok has bir ses yerleşik bir hale gelecek*)]. I mean it'll develop its own real language at last. These kinds of efforts [i.e., this CD] are perhaps just the first step; I believe they'll keep on developing, for ever, really, despite Refah[66] and their crowd.

Despite its grammatical informality, the language Aksu uses here—with its references to polyphony, development, and so forth—has an official ring to it. It implies that the mantle of responsibility for preserving, protecting, and most importantly *developing* Anatolian folk music culture now of necessity passes from the state to private citizens like Aksu. This claim struck many, like Cambazoğlu, as hyperbolic, and struck others as worrying. If the assertion was, broadly speaking, true, could somebody like Aksu be trusted with the task? And for who exactly was she claiming to speak?

In a country whose map has had such iconic status as a symbol of historical achievement and political unity, the publicity surrounding *Işık doğudan yükselir* and Aksu's subsequent CDs struck other worrying notes. In *Düğün ve cenaze*, which followed in 1996, the liner notes speak of the "small patch of land possessing the most noble and powerful melodies of love and

---

66. Refah was the Islamist party that followed Fazilet and preceded the currently dominant Adalet ve Kalkınma Partisi (also known as the AK Partisi). See White 2002 for an ethnography and history of this political movement.

pain, which reach the people today in sobs and plaintive cries" [*günlük insanına çığlık çığlığa ulaşmakta*]. But the "small patch of land" in question is emphatically not "Turkey" but "Anatolia."⁶⁷ Rather than representing "the feeling of Turkish history," Aksu's voice speaks of "the feeling of Anatolian history." The "emotional treasury" represented in Aksu's vocal art is likewise that of not "Turkey" but "Anatolia." The voice that represents it, according to the CD blurb, is "Aegean," a further complication. Aksu's vocal style possesses "a powerful Mediterranean sensibility [*duyarlılığı*]." Much of this rhetoric is familiar and comforting to nationalist ears. Aksu's publicists are able to play with "Anatolía" (the Greek word meaning "Land of the sunrise") as the Turkish expression "*ana-dolu*," "full of mothers" (Delaney 1991)—imagined here as a site of emotional identification, the addressee of "sobs and plaintive cries." The claim to an Aegean and Mediterranean identity accompanies a long-standing nationalist assertion that Turkey's historical destination is the West, not the East.⁶⁸

But it would also have been striking to many that Aksu and her publicists were systematically avoiding the words "Turkey" and "Turks." Those terms were, as it were, under erasure. Thus, in the interview quote cited above, her final verbal crossing out of "*Türk kadını*" (Turkish woman) and replacement of it with "*Anadolu kadını*" (Anatolian woman) was typical of the moment. "Anatolia" discursively enables the idea of the mosaic, a mosaic of identifiable and namable "cultures" and "historical accumulations" (Turkish, Kurdish, Armenian, and so forth) that could be represented as separate, but "emotionally interwoven." "Turkey," at least at that point, did not.

*Işık doğudan yükselir* avoided direct musical references to Kurdish or Armenian music, however,⁶⁹ and all the songs were sung in Turkish. Until the

---

67. Readers unfamiliar with the map of Turkey should know that the larger proportion of the country—east of the Bosphorus, the Sea of Marmara, the Dardanelles, and the Aegean Sea—is known as Anatolia. The smaller part of Turkey—about 24,000 square kilometers—lies in continental Europe, bordering Greece and Bulgaria, and is known as Thrace (Trakya). So quite apart from the fact that in Aksu's usage the term "Anatolia" implies ancient civilizations rather than the modern nation-state, the modern term "Turkey" refers to a geographical space that comprises both Anatolia *and* Thrace.

68. See in particular Özer 2003 and Fritschkopf 2003 for parallels between Turkey and Egypt. In both places it would seem that the middle classes have been involved in the construction of a musical Mediterranean as a means of identifying themselves with cosmopolitan currents into which they can plausibly insert themselves while also distancing themselves from some uncomfortably dominant forms of political identification with Islam and Middle Eastern neighbors.

69. It is certainly the case here, as elsewhere in Turkish popular music making, that a great deal of Kurdish and Armenian song is passed off as "Turkish," with newly composed Turkish words. Or, to put it another way, while a great deal of Anatolian folk song existed in multiple languages; the

mid-1990s, Kurdish-language popular and folk music had had a checkered career in Turkey, to say the least. Özal had tried to liberalize media restrictions, but with limited success and no successors. Kurdish cassette companies, and a number of Kurdish singers, exploited loopholes in existing legislation and pushed boundaries with varying degrees of energy and success. Liberalization and European Union pressure on Turkish state policies regarding minority language issues provoked a backlash. Confined to universities and Türkü bars, singing in Kurdish raised few eyebrows.[70] But at that particular moment, noted political singers such as Ahmet Kaya seemed provocative and aggressive when they insisted on using the language at large concert venues. Its use was, after all, banned in public contexts in Turkey until 2002; to insist on speaking Kurdish in public not only marginalized non-Kurdish speakers (who may well have been fans), but also flouted the law.

Soon after *Işık doğudan yükselir*, however, Aksu was herself singing in Kurdish, and was central to a broad public debate about minority languages and the state. A concert tour of Turkey and the major northwest European capitals brought together a 174-member orchestra and chorus comprising the choir of the Feriköy Vatanart Armenian Church in Istanbul, the Los Pasaros Sephardic Jewish Music Ensemble, the Oniro Greek Music Ensemble, and the Diyarbakır (Kurdish) City Council Children's Choir, along with the Dersaadet Chamber Ensemble and the Izmir State Opera and Ballet. The concert tour simply went under the name of "Türkiye Şarkıları" (Songs of Turkey). The musicians involved sang in Armenian, Greek, Ladino, and Kurdish. Aksu herself sang one song ("Buke") in Kurdish, along with the Diyarbakır children's choir. Aksu herself is not Kurdish and does not speak the language, so cynics, unsurprisingly, found plenty to scoff about.[71] Oth-

---

Turkish forms and adaptations of these songs were the only ones to enjoy a public life throughout most of the twentieth century. Early in the first decade of the twenty-first century, Kardeş Türküler developed a tremendous reputation in Istanbul reanimating the multilingual performance environment of Anatolian folk song. As regards Aksu's repertory, a great deal of Armenian music found its way to public ears through Onno Tunç. For instance, "Ah kavaklar," on *Sezen Aksu 88*, was once identified to me as an Armenian folk song. In interview Aksu said that she also believed that to be the case.

70. The Boğaziçi University Folklor Klübü led the way in the 1990s, giving birth to Kardeş Türküler. Though it is far from immune to criticism and threats from right-wing nationalists, the fact that its activities are located in and identified with an elite university has enabled it to enjoy a certain license.

71. Faruk Bildirici, a columnist for *Tempo* magazine, pointed out that those currently cheering Aksu's efforts on behalf of the Kurds would probably include people who, only a few years before, had bayed for the blood of the more overtly politicized singer Ahmet Kaya. When Bildirici's article was published, Kaya had recently died, somewhat unexpectedly. The irony of two singers doing es-

ers, however, were full of praise, seeing the concert as an exercise in national integration and a showcase of Turkish liberalism and tolerance, likely to reassure European observers concerned about Turkey's EU admissibility.[72] This possibility must have struck the Turkish Ministry of Culture, which sponsored the tour, heavily. The return of the term "Türkiye" is to be noted here—a further indication that the mosaic metaphor was well on its way to being officialized.

If Aksu succeeded in initiating broad and civil debate about the place of minority languages in the national "mosaic," she did so because she chose her battles carefully, could rely on popular support, and now had the endorsement of the state. The underlying challenge constituted by *Işık doğudan yükselir* was, though, a stark one. Aksu implied that the TRT, and by extension the state itself, was no longer meeting its responsibilities as the guardian of national culture, which she claimed now fell to the private citizen and the market. The TRT and other state agencies responded cleverly. It was hard to deny that they were no longer leading the nation musically. Aksu's project was then to be comprehensively co-opted—both preemptively, by making it the subject of a TRT news broadcast, and prospectively, by the TRT giving its blessing in advance to subsequent reincarnations of the musical mosaic metaphor.

### Light from the East: Anatolian Cosmopolitesse

To many, *Işık doğudan yükselir* seemed to have been designed with non-Turkish listeners in mind. Its representation of Anatolia as exotic and mystical reminded Turkish critics of recent ventures in Islamic mysticism by Robert Plant, Jimmy Page, and Jethro Tull's Ian Anderson. "World music" and *"etno-müzik"* seemed to be all the rage. In 1992 Aksu's "Hadi bakalım" had done well as a CD single in Germany, and there were grounds for thinking that she could capitalize on this with a CD more explicitly geared for the world music market (Canbazoğlu 1995). A fantasy of an appropriately *modern* Turkish music taking its rightful place on the world stage hovered over the discussion. Though a national exercise, it was also clearly understood as an exercise in a certain kind of cosmopolitanism. But critics had their doubts. On the one hand, *Işık doğudan yükselir* didn't seem quite authentic enough to

---

sentially the same thing and eliciting such different public reactions struck many people strongly at the time. See Bildirici 2002.

72. Ozan Ceyhun's report on the Brussels concert of 3 November 2002 for AB Haber is framed in exactly these terms. See www.abhaber.com/ozan/ozan_yorum41.htm

be marketed as an ethnomusicological recording. On the other hand, it was too local to be marketed outside Turkey as a hybrid, pop-oriented "world beat." The idea might play well to a home audience, but would it actually sell abroad? Or would it fall between two stools?

Such anxieties were not quickly to be allayed. Indeed, subsequent developments saw Aksu apparently pushing further in the quest for a transregional audience, and styling herself as a musical cosmopolitan with the help of various allies. Her next CD was a collaboration with Goran Bregovic, *Düğün ve cenaze* (Wedding and funeral), released in 1996. It drew upon the music on Bregovic's album of the same name, and his soundtracks to Emir Kusturica's films *In the Time of the Gypsies* and *Underground*, both of which were well known in Turkey. It resonated with complex Turkish responses to the Yugoslav wars, in which leftists saw the ethnic fragmentation of a formerly unified socialist state and Islamists saw fellow Muslims under siege. Though the lyrics developed the feminist themes of *Işık doğudan yükselir / Ex oriente lux* and the studio work reproduced the intimate acoustic textures of that earlier work, the sound world of *Düğün ve cenaze* was Balkan. A Serbian-Macedonian brass band both accompanied Aksu's voice and provided a narrative figure—a little like the brass band in Kusturica's film, which ducks for cover in gun fights, runs through the streets with the heroes in helter-skelter chases, and pops up out of nowhere during sex scenes. The cover of the CD showed Bregovic and Aksu entwined, with the brass band blurred and dimly visible in the background. Such bands were briefly in vogue in Turkey during the early 1990s, and the Macedonian Kocani Orchestra accompanied Aksu on subsequent tours.[73]

Aksu also recorded and toured with prominent Greek vocalist Haris Alexiou in the immediate aftermath of the Marmara-region earthquake in 2000, again with strong support from the Turkish Ministry of Culture. This was a significant moment of Greek-Turkish détente following decades of political tension over territorial rights in the Aegean. Greek aid to the stricken areas of Gölcük and Yalova was conspicuous and highly appreciated across Turkey. Alexiou and Aksu provided the official soundtrack. The singers were well matched. Like Aksu, Alexiou was closely associated with the Greek popular music intelligentsia (George Dalaras, Manos Loizos, Thanos Mikroutsikos, and others). Also like Aksu, she embraced local and traditional genres at moments of political crisis, and cultivated a reputation as a public and critical voice. She was slightly older than Aksu, with a reputation

---

73. See Stokes 2007b for a fuller account of the Bregovic-Aksu collaboration, and of *Düğün ve cenaze*.

in Turkey that stemmed from an earlier moment of appreciation for Greek popular music.[74] It is probably true to say, though, that the popularity both Alexiou and Bregovic enjoy in Turkey today owes much to their association with Aksu.[75]

Aksu, Alexiou, and Bregovic testify to the emergence in the 1990s of a Balkan music cosmopolitanism (Buchanan 2007). Bregovic and Alexiou constitute two particular variants: the former exilic, the other firmly rooted in a national home. This cosmopolitanism is clearly connected not only to fashions in world music in the 1990s, but also with the eastward expansion of the European Union[76] and broader anxieties about east-west integration across the continent. Europe was undergoing significant changes and Aksu, Bregovic, and Alexiou gave these changes significant shape and feeling. Aksu's musical cosmopolitanism, though, was from the outset very much oriented to domestic markets and national preoccupations. Cosmopolitanism sells, but it has to do so in local terms and in national markets.[77]

How did this cosmopolitanism work in *Işık doğudan yükselir / Ex oriente lux*? In the first instance, the CD articulated what one might describe as an "internal cosmopolitanism"—one recognizing Anatolia's ethnic diversity and its history extending far back beyond the Turkish nation itself. This, as has already been noted, challenged the nationalist myth of the nation united by ethnicity and language and rooted in the Turkic migrations from central Asia. The metaphor's potentially centrifugal qualities are mitigated by a variety of interlinked centripetal gestures, some formal, some thematic, which bring everything back to the nation-state. This implies a new kind of citizenly gaze which relates the viewer to the mosaic's diverse components as a consumer and an aesthete, enjoying a taste of Black Sea here, a taste of an Alevi *deyiş* there, from a certain position of exteriority: as a viewer of the mosaic rather than as a piece of the mosaic itself. Politically understood, all

---

74. Various of Alexiou's songs were, for instance, covered in the 1980s by the group Yeni Türkü.

75. In the summer of 2006 both singers gave concerts to large crowds at the Açıkhava Tiyatrosu in Harbiye, which was the largest open-air venue in central Istanbul at the time.

76. In this regard one would note the dominance of Eastern and formerly Soviet-dominated Central Europe in the Eurovision Song contest, those regions having produced a string of winners since the fall of the Berlin Wall in 1989.

77. On musical nationalism and cosmopolitanism, see Turino 2000 and Regev 2006. Turino argues for a view of cosmopolitanism and nationalism as being coeval and co-constituting. In Zimbabwe, musical nationalism is the product of cultural elites who know other nationalisms; their necessarily cosmopolitan outlook is configured in the musical nationalisms they establish. Musical cosmopolitanism, on the other hand, always has a local point of reference, though this is increasingly conceived in a "global" and relational space. Regev makes a similar point in a different way. "Ethnic" pop-rock inscribes local musical values on a global space; it is a cosmopolitanism made from within the national framework (Regev 2006, p. 567).

of these rhetorical gestures might be considered as means of controlling the highly unstable image of the mosaic, returning it to the service of a nation newly imagined.

Aksu's subsequent and more conventionally cosmopolitan musical ventures, her collaborations with Bregovic and Alexiou, could be seen as extensions of this "internal cosmopolitanism." In her cosmopolite world, a citizen capable of recognizing the nation's ethnic and historical diversity was a citizen capable of understanding others and relating to them in a civilized and democratic way. In the imaginative world of *Işık doğudan yükselir,* as we have already noted, Anatolian women were advantageously positioned in this regard. A nation in tune with such citizenly virtues would press its governments to act accordingly with its neighbors. This was not difficult to imagine at the time; successive Turkish governments were inspired by a certain sense of mission during the Yugoslav wars and in the aftermath of the regime changes across Eastern Europe and Central Asia. Aksu's cosmopolitanism was not entirely incompatible with their efforts to project Turkey as a regional leader and civilizing force.

Finally, the Anatolian cosmopolitesse of *Işık doğudan yükselir* articulated a new and stark claim: that the destination, and therefore the arbiter, of national culture was the international marketplace. Aksu's often dismissive comments about the TRT echoed what was in effect being said by *Işık doğudan yükselir* that the state's broadcasting company was no longer up to the task of preserving and developing national culture. As the state withdrew, or simply atrophied, new agencies were making themselves felt. Aksu's public stance implied that the individual artist, as citizen and bearer of national culture, was obliged to respond. There were of course counterarguments, as immediate critical reactions suggested. It was too early to pronounce the TRT dead, for instance. The world music market might turn Turkish music into meaningless exoticism. And anyway, would *Işık doğudan yükselir* compete successfully in that market? It seemed too riddled with contradictions to do so (Canbazoğlu 1995).

As a serious effort to establish Turkish folk music on the world music scene, *Işık doğudan yükselir / Ex oriente lux* can hardly be judged to have been a success. My efforts to locate a CD to replace the cassette bought in 1995 and chewed up by my automobile cassette player in 1997 were quite systematic and spanned both Europe and America. *Işık doğudan yükselir* was, I discovered, really rather hard to find outside Turkey in the days before Amazon.com. It was only after the significant global successes of former Aksu students and protégées—notably Tarkan, after "Şımarık" of 1999 (an Aksu song), and Sertap Erener, after her 2004 Eurovision success—that Aksu attained a significant following outside Turkey. This, at least, is the impression one gets from the proliferation of non-Turkish language Aksu websites since approximately 2004. The global and cosmopolitan claims surrounding *Işık doğudan yükselir* may well have been somewhat ill-judged attempt to find a "world music" audience for Aksu. But they were also, as I hope to have shown here, a consequential intervention in a public discussion within Turkey about the future of the national project in a world dominated by markets rather than by the state. The next section explores some of the more diffuse ways in which Aksu's vocal art has both shaped and inhabited Turkish neoliberalism in more recent years.

## Popolemik

During the summer of 2006, "*popolemik*" ("ass-polemic") raged in the pages of the popular press. Who was wearing g-strings (and maybe shouldn't)? Who had had cosmetic surgery? Who had had their cellulite airbrushed out of publicity pictures? What did men prefer? Who would next turn on the paparazzi—or on their publicists, as singer Yeşim Salkım did—with an angry "Are you selling my ass or my voice? [*Popo mu ses mi satıyorsun*]?"[78] Sezen Aksu, having been snapped by photographers clambering onto her yacht that summer, remonstrated with journalists at her summer season concert in Bodrum:

> Please stop following me around on my yacht snapping pictures of my ass. Look, I'll pose for you and you can take a picture of me now. I've got no objection while singing. But when you follow me around on my yacht you really get on my nerves. It means I can't swim. For goodness sake, what on earth is the use of a picture of my ass? If it were to be of value to the country [I would let you take a picture of it], willingly [*Memlekete bir faydası olacaksa seve seve*]; I'd even draw eyes and a moustache on it" (Bel 2006, p. 2).

The comment made front-page news in several newspapers. "Ass polemics" abated somewhat. Whether Aksu's comments were responsible or not,

---

78. According to Bel 2006, the "debate" had started when veteran singer and dancer Sibel Can was seen in a g-string (*tanga*). At issue was the question of whether this constituted appropriate clothing for older women. Most of those interviewed on the subject—including Ebru Gündeş, Emel Sayın, Yeşim Salkım—expressed deep disquiet, though Salkım's thoughts about changing attitudes towards the sexuality of older married women and mothers in Turkey echo some aspects of Aksu's gender politics.

they struck a characteristically witty and world-weary note. The new female citizen should have no qualms about sexual display, she seemed to be implying, if one can establish its value for the nation. Her concluding joke hinted that, in this national context, female sexual display may involve a rather potent kind of agency (signified by "eyes" and a "moustache") rather than objecthood and passivity in a male gaze.

That August, shortly after Aksu's comments, I set off with my family for a short vacation near Bodrum. After nearly twenty-five years of travel to and frequent residence in Turkey, I had yet to visit this Aegean resort town. I had been put off, I suppose, by its place in a Turkish bourgeois fantasy of leisure, status, and conspicuous consumption—one that I often found controlling and claustrophobic. But we had friends to visit there. I had Zeki Müren's museum to visit there (see chapter 2). I badly needed a rest after teaching all summer in Istanbul. And I also had a growing sense that I was failing to understand something about the new middle-class Turkey, and Sezen Aksu's place in its imagination, simply by virtue of never having been to Bodrum. I "needed" to visit the place.

So it was that I found myself picking my way across Yahşi beach one morning, initially in search of windsurfing equipment for hire, but increasingly immersed in other thoughts. Walking from one end of the beach to the other, I passed a number of self-contained resort enclaves: British, French, Russian, Czech, on which—with the partial exception of the British—tourist couples sunbathed in deep silence. The central "Turkish" stretch of beach, where we were staying, was by contrast densely packed, noisy, and oriented towards restaurants, bars, shops, barbers, and *dolmuş* (shared taxi) stations ferrying people to and from the town. Here one heard various mixtures of Turkish, Kurdish, German, and Dutch, it being vacation time for *gastarbeiter*[79] too. Music was constantly audible, recorded or live. A warm and friendly atmosphere prevailed. Children mingled, tables were shared for drinks and meals, *tavla* (backgammon) boards and *nargile*s (water pipes), and cushions spilled over the pavement. Boundary markers set up to distinguish the small hotels and apartment complexes were casually disregarded.

Men were in a minority, at least in the central section of the beach. Our own friends' summer routine seemed quite typical. Men would often leave on business, on trips to home villages, or to keep an eye on projects and

---

79. *Gastarbeiter* is the term often still given to Turks and others working in Germany and elsewhere in Western Europe on schemes designed to recruit cheap labor in the 1960s and 1970s without giving them citizenship. Many of these people are now citizens, so that the term, while current and common, is no longer accurate. Since Germany's reunification, many have become unemployed, so that the term is now doubly problematic.

properties elsewhere. Women and children would stay in Bodrum, often in apartments rented for the entire summer season or on long-term plans with hotels. It struck me at first as a space designed by men to sequester women: a middle-class harem. Male sexuality was assiduously kept at bay by all concerned. Women there expressed concern about the very few bars on that strip that seemed to be oriented to drinking, dancing, and flirting, and the nightclubs of nearby Gumbet (a resort notoriously dominated by "the English"[80]) and central Bodrum were spoken of with great distaste. Women's bodies were, however, conspicuously on display. This display took place not only on the beach but also in the broader and highly public process of preparing for it. Advertisements for dieting pills and plans early in the summer preyed on women's anxieties about size and shape with brutal directness. Cosmetic surgery continued to be a major growth industry.[81] The press served up a relentless diet of *popolemik*-s as a prelude to the summer months.

Upon later reflection, my characterization of Yahşi as a middle-class harem seemed wrong. The display of female bodies on Yahşi beach struck me as a public ritual of middle-class modernity: of bodies as projects of discipline and control, as assertions of agency and desire, as spaces of technological intervention and development. To wear a bikini, diet furiously, and work up a suntan was to embody and engender Turkishness in a peculiarly modern way. The young women of Yahşi beach were descendents of their sisters in the early republican beauty pageants described by Holly Shissler (2004): young women who were not simply representations of the modern state, but its citizens and agents. But the women on Yahşi beach inhabit a peculiarly late-modern moral and civic universe, deprived of many of the early-modernist certainties of their early republican sisters and haunted by deep anxieties. An Islamist movement, claiming to be both modern and Turkish on very different grounds, continues to censure and threaten these vacationing women. The nightclubs and topless sunbathers at the "European" ends of the beach suggest problematic consequences and a growing sense of the incompatibility of "Turkish" and "European" ways of desiring

---

80. I think "the English" usually meant rowdy working-class Europeans rather than the English per se. On my brief visit, Gumbet actually seemed more Dutch than English. English vacationers on Turkey's Aegean and Mediterranean coasts generally had a poor reputation.

81. Over the course of ten years the cosmetic surgeries running along the main street between Levent and Etiler have significantly increased in number, as have the pharmacies and beauty salons. These are not only shop fronts and technical laboratories of the embodied and gendered modernity that is at issue in this section, but also sites of complex cosmopolitan imaginings and desires, as Ossman suggests of beauty salons in Cairo, Casablanca, and Paris (Ossman 2002).

modernity. Haves and have-nots in Turkey in 2006 could be neatly defined in terms of who could and could not afford a vacation. For the middling middle-classes represented here, the dividing line was sharp, merciless, and always threatening.[82]

My stroll across the beach in search of windsurfing equipment also bought another thing home to me. From one end of the beach to the other—from each radio, each bar, each restaurant—one would hear the sound of Sezen Aksu's voice. Until that moment I had not realized the extent of her popularity in Turkey. Local bars often had live singers playing oud and guitar, but Aksu's repertoire, or that of her students, predominated in those places as well. Aksu's releases are evidently carefully timed so that each summer's pleasures, romances, and flirtations can be associated with an Aksu hit, and coincide with this period of conspicuous consumption. Her songs lend themselves well to Bodrum's hectic nightlife, but also to the more family-oriented and sedentary habits of listening at Yahşi. Aksi's summer tours these days invariably begin or end in the Aegean region with large concerts in Çeşme and Bodrum, where historic forts have been converted into major rock and pop venues. These concerts attract large crowds, often being advertised in the streets of Istanbul up to a month in advance.[83]

Aksu's voice, you will recall, is both biographically and aesthetically associated with the Aegean. Immediately after *Işık doğudan yükselir / Ex oriente lux*, these associations seemed to be more and more intensely promoted by her publicists. Her collaborations with Bregovic and Alexiou would, after all, have needed some grounding—some local point of geographical and emotional reference. The liner notes to her 1996 collaboration with Bregovic, *Düğün ve cenaze*, were particularly explicit in this regard:

---

82. By way of anecdote, the cab driver who took us from Boğaziçi to the airport had much to say about the emergence of the vacation as a diacritic of class. Once, nobody went on vacation. An occasional evening's walk down to the beach at Florya (within the city, on the Sea of Marmara) was just about all they did. Now, however, vacations seemed to be obligatory for those who could afford it. The cab driver himself—a young man in his twenties, I would guess, and a new father—was obliged to work extra hours in a Coca-Cola bottling plant during the summer months (when employees were unable to take leave, he said), and spend what little extra time he had driving the cab at night to make ends meet. "I wish I could go on vacation," he said at one point. Vacations had come to define both the good life (available to people like me), and those excluded from it (like him).

83. *Vatan Magazin* noted that Aksu's concert in the Antik Tiyatrosu in Bodrum, at which she made the comments that appear at the beginning of this section, attracted an audience of three thousand and caused a traffic gridlock in the city that lasted two hours (*Vatan Mazagin* 30 July 2006, p. 2).

Sezen Aksu is an Aegean vocalist. Music, which has done most to support the unity of the human spirit [*ruh*], was first systematized 2,500 years ago in the Aegean region. The important thing to say about Sezen Aksu's voice and style is that alongside the main feeling [*duygu*; i.e., love, sensitivity] supplied by her songs, there is another important feeling: the feeling of Anatolian history, the emotional treasury [*duygu hazinesi*] of a small patch of land possessing the most noble and powerful melodies of love and pain, which reach the people of today in sobs and plaintive cries, in the Ionian Sezen's voice. Only these two dimensions [i.e., love and Anatolian history] cannot be fully separated from one another. In this world of ours, in which even love has been commodified, we should feel free to wander about a bit in the depths of Sezen's voice, we should be able to touch the feelings revealed by the historical developments connected with that soil. In the final analysis, with her honesty and goodness-nourishing voice, with a style possessed of a powerful Mediterranean sensibility [*duyarlılığı*], and this time with Balkan colors [*Balkan renkleriyle*] added to our own cultural mosaic, she invites us, all of us, to love.

There is a connection between the intimate and eroticized fantasy of the Aegean, the display of female bodies, and the omnipresence of Aksu's voice on the beaches of Bodrum. The performance of sexuality and gender in Aksu's vocal art is intimately related to the kinds of bourgeois self-fashioning on display in the summer months around Bodrum: its pleasures, its intimacies, its anxieties. Women rather than men occupy center stage as desiring, narrating, consuming, and self-constituting agents of Turkish modernity. This performance also involves distinct notions of civility that have been powerful and broadly shared precisely because they have sidestepped predictable terms of debate, and because they have been located in a mass-mediated universe of feeling, affect, and sensitivity.

Fatih Akın's 2006 film *Crossing the Bridge*, is a celebration of Istanbul and its popular music. At the end, Sezen Aksu sings a melancholy ballad many viewers would have remembered from the 1980s. The camera is, unusually in this hectic film, contemplative. It focuses almost exclusively on the singer's face throughout the song. Through windows behind the musicians in the background, we can occasionally see the Bosphorus twinkling in late afternoon sunlight. The song "İstanbul hatırası" (Memory of Istanbul) depicts a woman looking at a picture and recalling a lover from earlier in life. The performance is interspersed with old photographs of Istanbul's slum neighborhoods, working people, and dark cityscapes.[84] Aksu looks directly at the camera as the song ends, holding its gaze for what seems like an eternity. Finally she smiles and turns away. The film ends: music and sunset on the Bosphorus.

It is a striking moment, suggesting a culmination, a completion of Turkish rock and pop history. But it also reflects shifting terrain. Aksu, however beloved and however much a figure of the moment, begins to seem like a figure in history, receding into the distance as we watch. This is, after all, a film about Istanbul and its music—not about the Aegean, and not about Anatolia. The shift in place is significant. Istanbul's role as a site of national intimacy has, since the earliest days of the republic, been an ambiguous one. Love for the city and its music seems to be reemerging as the ground for new configurations of civic and national virtue, though—as we will see in the next chapter.

84. They are Ara Güler's well-known pictures, icons of nostalgia for the 1950s and 1960s. Ara Güler was a Turkish photojournalist of enormous renown for his work in *Time, Life, Paris-Match, Newsweek,* and other such journals. His photographs of Istanbul are included prominently in Orhan Pamuk's Istanbul memoir (Pamuk 2005). Clips of the Sezen Aksu song and still images from this moment in *Crossing the Bridge* are, at the time of writing, easy to locate on various websites officially associated with the film.

# 5

## Three Versions of "Beloved Istanbul"

A new figure of intimacy made an appearance in Turkish popular culture in the mid-1990s: a melancholic wanderer contemplating the cityscape. As we shall see, this figure has a long literary pedigree.[1] It is also now an architectural feature of the city. A few years ago the Istanbul Metropolitan Municipality installed benches at well-known beauty spots that were designed in the shape of open books and displayed poems about the city. For instance, the Aşiyan museum—formerly the home of Ottoman poet Tevfik Fikret—was close to my office space at Boğaziçi University, where I spent the summer of 2006 teaching, and from which one could get a wonderful view of the northern stretches of the Bosphorus. The Metropolitan Municipality had just installed three such benches there.[2] For many people, I expect, this was just another example of the municipality's relentless self-promotion.[3] Its logo was al-

---

1. We should also note the resurgence of this figure in recent "high-concept" literature and film, notably Orhan Pamuk's *İstanbul: Memories and the City* (2005), in which he plays the role of melancholic wanderer, reprising the role of the male protagonist in *Kara kitab* (1990) and other novels. Other examples include Nuri Bilge Ceyhan's film *Uzak* (2002) and Fatih Akın's *Duvara karşı / Gegen die Wand*.

2. The poems displayed on the benches were Yahya Kemal's "Bir tepeden," Ahmet Hamdi Tanpınar's "Bir gün İcadiye'de," and Ümit Yaşan Oğuzcan's "Üstüme varma İstanbul!"

3. The Metropolitan Municipality invested heavily in self-publicity, erecting large notice boards in central city locations informing passersby about progress on current projects, and providing a free magazine (the *İstanbul Bülteni*) at all downtown public

**Figure 5a.** Book-benches at the Aşiyan Museum, Istanbul. Photograph by the author.

ways easy to see, while the words of the longer poems could actually be read only with much uncomfortable twisting of the neck. Whether the poems were read or not, these benches had a job to do. Offering a seat to passersby, they connected the Metropolitan Municipality with the long tradition of late Ottoman and early republican verse extolling the city, and they promoted the idea of wandering and enjoying views of the city as new but historically rooted forms of civility and urbanity.

---

transport nodes. This magazine provides an interesting insight to a non-Istanbullian about current managerial preoccupations, or at least about what the managers thought would impress and educate the city's inhabitants. The June 2006 issue, for instance, reported on the "final assault" (*"son hamle"*) on Istanbul's decrepit drinking water, sewage, and water transport infrastructure; progress on various environmental issues (particularly the return of lobsters and sea horses to the waters around the city); Mayor Kadir Topbaş's recent trip to Damascus (to sell the idea that Istanbul was providing regional leadership in city management); celebrations of the 553rd anniversary of the Ottoman conquest (a nod in the direction of conservative Islamists); new plans for parks in downtown areas snarled with traffic; a celebration of summer-blooming trees and flowers; the announcement of new free funeral services, child care facilities, and literacy courses; a profile of *muhtar*-s (the leaders of the smallest unit of city administration) and leaders of *belediye*-s (municipalities administered by the Metropolitan Municipality); upcoming piano recitals; and a Rodin exhibition. It also included a crossword puzzle for bored transit passengers, and information about contracts for upcoming municipal projects. See also Çınar's analysis of the Ankara Metropolitan Municipality and the struggle over public space in the capital (Çınar 2005).

It is, however, the *popular* circulation and refractions of this figure that concern me in this chapter. The Metropolitan Municipality's current efforts to forge new practices of civility and urbanity are being played out on complex, unstable terrain, without an understanding of which these efforts can only partially be grasped. With this in mind, I will focus in this chapter on a particularly significant poem, iconically connected with late Ottoman/early republican melancholy and wandering, that was set to music in the 1950s. I will then describe the reemergence of this musical setting in the 1990s, and two subsequent versions of the song by different people. The poem is Yahya Kemal Beyatlı's famous love lyric to the city, "Aziz İstanbul" ("Beloved Istanbul"). It was set to music by Münir Nurettin Selçuk, possibly in 1956.[4] Selçuk was a composer and art music singer who set many of Yahya Kemal's poems to music during Kemal's own lifetime.[5] In 1996 *arabesk* and classical music singer Bülent Ersoy released a version of the song on a cassette devoted to nostalgia from the middle years of the century, *Alaturka 95*.[6] In 2003 Timur Selçuk, Münir Nurettin's son, released yet another version in a CD called *Babamın şarkıları* (My father's songs).

These competing performances suggest a complex struggle over the figure of the melancholic, contemplative wanderer recruited by the Metropolitan Municipality as exemplary citizen and urbanite. This at least is the

---

4. Timur Selçuk suggested this date to me. Apparently Münir Nurettin Selçuk wrote dates of composition on his sheet music; Timur consulted a photocopy (which I was able to glance at briefly), but failed to find the date. Timur remembers being introduced to Yahya Kemal around this time, however, and associated this composition with that moment. Interview with Timur Selçuk, 12 September 2008.

5. I draw on John O'Connell's work on Münir Nurettin Selçuk (in particular O'Connell 2002 and 2005), a popular biography (Kulin 1996), and many articles in the popular music press of the 1940s and 1950s, such as *Radyo Magazin* and *Resimli Radyo Dünyası*. On Yahya Kemal there is a wide literature. My understanding of him in the context of Ottoman and Turkish poetry is dependent on the various publications of Mehmed Kaplan (see Kaplan 1954 and 1963 in particular) and also owes much to a visit to the Yahya Kemal Institute in Istanbul in the summer of 2006. On the connections between Yahya Kemal's poetry and Münir Nurettin's music, there is very little in the way of published work. I am grateful to Mehmet Güntekin for pointing me in the direction of Bozdağ 1998. A reference to an interesting-sounding article by Yılmaz Öztuna in Cunbur 1994, entitled "Yahya Kemal'ın Aziz İstanbul'u" (*Hayat Tarih Mecmuası* 5, no. 1, 1 February 1969, p. 96) appears to be incorrect. However, Ömürlü 1999, a musical anthology of a large number of settings of Yahya Kemal's poetry, is invaluable.

6. The Bülent Ersoy version was not the first rerecording of this song, though it was easily the most conspicuous, associated as it was with a major *arabesk* star at the height of her popularity and on a major recording label. A TRT recording by art-music singer Nesrin Sipahi, for example, exists from the early 1980s (before the construction of the second Bosphorus bridge); it makes for an interesting comparison with the Ersoy version. See http://uk.youtube.com/watch?v=Euo65sggTZk (accessed 7 January 2009).

principal claim of this chapter. It draws, at the most general level, on a long-standing ethnomusicological interest in music as a means of imagining and inhabiting the densely packed urban spaces of late modernity (Nettl 1978; Erlmann 1999; Allen and Wilken 1998), on theorizations of the circulation of recorded sound (Feld 1996), and on psychoanalytic accounts of the relationship between voice and scene (Silverman 1988 and 1992; Zizek 1996; Chion 1999; Middleton 2006). It also involves more local questions about nostalgia, changing cultural idioms of intimacy in Turkey, and the dramatic transformation of Istanbul in the last half of the twentieth century. Before discussing the poem and the performances in detail, I will need to contextualize these three local issues briefly.

First, the struggle over "Aziz İstanbul" is in part about the place of the Turkish musical past in the modern. Münir Nurettin Selçuk represented an idiom that republican critics had long declared outdated and incompatible with musical modernity. As John O'Connell puts it, *alaturka* deferred to *alafranga,* to use the oppositional terms of debate signifying "Eastern" and "Western" tastes current in the early decades of the twentieth century (O'Connell 2005b). If modernity was by definition Western, there was no room for accommodation between musical modernity and the urban art music tradition, habitually understood by many intellectuals as a complex, tangled relic of an earlier civilization. For them, rural Anatolian folk music provided a much more promising start, being considered simpler, natural, and more authentically Turkish. To sing and compose in the art music tradition was of course to cater to a market and to both popular and educated tastes, but it was also to defy the dominant republican elites, whose pronouncements upon culture carried considerable weight in the 1930s and 1940s, and still do today. Bülent Ersoy's version of "Aziz İstanbul," as we shall see, was an explicit exercise in nostalgia, marked by the date ("95") included in the title of the CD, the sepia-tinted photography on the cover, and the rendering of the liner notes in a flowing italic typeface evocative of the past. Timur Selçuk's version was part of a project explicitly devoted to the restoration of his father's musical heritage. It would be easy and not entirely inappropriate to consider these different forms of nostalgia as products of a local culture industry exploiting the past as a resource in easily digestible, commoditized form.[7] However, this would be to underplay the competing forms of modernity at play, and the competing claims about how the musi-

---

7. Such an approach would be compatible with Paul Grainge's recent characterization of nostalgia in 1990s Hollywood as a process of "monochroming" (Grainge 2003).

cal past connects with the present and with imagined futures—a topic to which we will return.

Second, the controversy over "Aziz İstanbul" is a struggle over changing representations of intimacy. In the poem, the lover's desire for his beloved is imagined in the act of looking at the city. At first glance, the image is simple and stable. A male viewer holds in his gaze a feminized love object which is simultaneously the beloved, the city, and the nation. The gendering and the insistent visualizing of the scene suggest mastery, control, and order. On closer consideration, as we shall see, the scene is complex and unstable. The love object is elusive. The poet himself has his doubts. Extraneous elements (particularly sounds) intrude and trouble the picture. The poet's redoubled efforts to exert his mastery over the scene seem only to compound them. Münir Nurettin Selçuk's musical version amplifies the tensions that tug at Kemal's poem—tensions, I suggest, we might ultimately understand in terms of conflicting currents within the emerging liberal order in mid-century republican Turkey, and a corresponding ambivalence about what Istanbul (the beloved city, maybe, but *not* the capital) might represent. Bülent Ersoy fragments and relocates these tensions in a context within which they have been pushed dramatically to the surface in the then rapidly emerging neoliberal order, one shaped by consumer desires and an ideology of personal freedoms (in the sexual arena as elsewhere). As we shall see, Timur Selçuk attempts to pick up the pieces and reassemble them, putting love for the city—love more generally, once again—at the service of the old modernist state-project.

Third, the controversy is a struggle over Istanbul's rapidly changing cityscape. As mentioned in the last chapter, the adoption of neoliberal programs in Turkey coincided with the Islamist rise to political power, and also with a wholesale reorientation of the Turkish state away from Ankara's bureaucrats and towards Istanbul's mercantile elites (Seufert and Weyland 1994; Robins and Aksoy 1995; Keyder 2004). This involved a relocation of Istanbul in the national imaginary, as well as related symbolic moves of enormous resonance. Thus, when Turgut Özal, the president and architect of Turkey's neoliberal transformation, died in Ankara in 1989, his body was taken to Istanbul and buried in Fatih, in the heart of the Islamist movement's power base—thus reversing the custom established by Atatürk, the founder of the republic, who had died in Istanbul and was buried in Ankara (Seufert and Weyland 1994). Özal's political ally, Istanbul Mayor Bedrettin Dalan, and his Islamist successors since the 1990s (including Recep Tayyıb Erdoğan, who would later become prime minister) devoted vast funds and highly conspicuous energies to reshaping the visual experience of Istanbul—cleaning the Golden Horn,[8] bulldozing inner-city and waterfront *gecekondu* (squatter) developments to create parks, rezoning unsightly and malodorous heavy industry, and illuminating the old city's mosques. These efforts were intended to point up the city's picture-postcard skyline of domes and minarets, revealing the city's—and hence the nation's—Islamic and Ottoman heritage.[9]

Viewers need to be schooled in the new arts of viewing; the mere act of managing built space has never been enough. The city's Islamist managers in the 1990s were highly attentive to the issue. For example, a Metropolitan Municipality *Bülten* from August 1995 contains a cartoon showing a young man looking across the Bosphorus at the old city, the piled-up domes and minarets cartoonishly exaggerated. "Hey brother, why drink? With all of this beauty before you, it's like you're already drunk!" he exclaims. The young man is observing the scene from one of the popular locations from which people view the setting sun (probably Salancak, between Üsküdar

---

8. The Golden Horn, known as the Haliç in Turkish, is the waterway that runs off the Bosphorus and alongside the old part of the city.

9. The city's new managers reconnected with a long-standing tradition of Ottoman city planning. As Zeynep Çelik (1986) has shown, the Ottoman sultans of the mid-nineteenth century were absorbed by Hausmann's Paris, Viviani's Rome, and the Vienna Ringstrasse development of the 1860s, and they established various plans to project their power and ambition onto the built fabric of the imperial capital. Though this tradition of city planning was significantly disrupted by the relocation of the capital to Ankara, it continued in Istanbul, as Çelik notes, up to and including the period of Henri Prost's work in the city between 1936 and 1951 (Çelik 1986, p. 161). This tradition of planning bore the well-known and much-discussed marks of Hausmann's Paris plan, which was designed to facilitate the circulation of commodities and traffic and the penetration of the state: straight streets, grid patterns, bridges, tunnels, and subway systems, and an ancillary visual aesthetic involving sightlines, vistas, and perspectives that were focused on significant buildings, monuments, and clock towers. Repeated efforts were made to clear local human traffic away from waterside areas, not least to please European companies that were dependent on speedy access to and from dock areas. The development of waterside and hilltop parks assumed particular importance following Selver Efendi's Golden Horn park and transport plan of 1869. Planning—on this subject see in particular Gilsenan on north African cities (Gilsenan 1982), Mitchell on Cairo (Mitchell 1988), and Fuller on Italian-colonized Addis Ababa and Tripoli (Fuller 2007)—was a powerful technique of colonial control and discipline across the Middle East. Straight and wide streets literally permitted unprecedented forms of supervision, but were also intended to produce viewing subjects attuned to colonialism's particular "metaphysical effect": a world split between a power to plan and represent and an authentic and indigenous space onto which that power was irresistibly projected. Since Ottoman Turkey was not directly colonized, its city plans could be debated and contested to a degree impossible in the colonized Middle East. Such contests evoked lively distinctions between a (properly pursued) modernity and a (mere) imitation (Çelik 1986, p. 54). But Hausmann's Paris provided a model for those who would claim power over the city and its inhabitants and project that power upon them—a model that still remains powerful.

**Figure 5b.** Municipality anti-alcohol campaign, 1995. "Hey brother, why drink? With all of this beauty before you, it's like you're already drunk!" (*İstanbul Bulteni*, 1 August 1995, p. 30)

and Harem).¹⁰ What makes the view beautiful, at least from the point of view of the *Bülten*'s anonymous cartoonist, is the Ottoman/Islamic profile of the city, the manifestation of a political heritage of which the Refah Partisi and their successors claimed guardianship. While the cartoon overtly accompanied their then aggressive anti-alcohol campaign, the picture's meanings also operated more generally against the background of their pursuit of a simultaneously modern and Islamic Istanbul and of practices of civility appropriate to it.

The observer depicted in this cartoon plays a number of important roles. He affirms not only the splendor of the architectural heritage but also the role of the municipality in making the view possible and pleasurable. In a rather direct sense, he tells people where to go. Not everybody reading the magazine will necessarily know the city that well. Recent research sponsored by the Metropolitan Municipality concerning people's quality of life suggested that quite large numbers of people living in Istanbul had never actually seen the Bosphorus or the old city.¹¹ People seeing the cartoon may be inspired to take a bus to Harem or Üsküdar and spend an afternoon walking around the parks that line the coastal road built in the early 1990s—seeing it in conjunction with an extensive popular literature teaching people how to enjoy the city and its views. The figure in the cartoon also has a disciplinary function. The pleasures of viewing and the new civic virtues are connected and mutually implicated. The three different versions of the song "Aziz İstanbul" can usefully be understood, I suggest, as three different (and competing) ways of considering these connections and implications musically.

This, then, is the context in which Yahya Kemal's famous poem came to enjoy a new lease of life in the 1990s: a context of radical and massive urban transformation; a systematic effort to relocate Istanbul as a (visualized) object of affection in the national imaginary; and efforts by the city's managers to forge new senses of urban belonging and civility. The poem, with its

---

10. At the time of writing, this problem is shortly to be compounded by the completion of the Sarayburnu-Üsküdar tunnel—one that will link the European and Asian shores of the city and turn the entire area into a major traffic intersection. This is a view that will have to be enjoyed, in the future, from a speeding car window. Writing about modern Teheran, Varzi (2006) suggests that the view from cars has important ramifications for the design and political order of contemporary Middle Eastern cities. I would suggest that new kinds of viewing practices shape new kinds of subjects in both Istanbul and Teheran—and for broadly similar reasons, despite differences in political context between the two cities.

11. Research cited in a paper by Ayşe Öncü, "Laying Claim to Istanbul: Competing Narratives of the City's 'Ancient Heritage,'" presented at a University of Chicago symposium entitled "The Cultural Study of the Middle Eastern City," February 24–26 2005. I am grateful to her for allowing me to pass this information on.

famous opening line, *"Sana dün bir tepeden baktım, Aziz İstanbul"* (I looked down on you yesterday from a hilltop, beloved Istanbul) conveniently lent itself to these purposes. It is also, as we shall see in the next section, a complicated and ambiguous poem.

## "Aziz İstanbul": Yahya Kemal's Poem

Yahya Kemal is commonly understood in Turkish literary scholarship as the connecting link between the late Ottoman and early republican periods, whose separation was canonical in the official historiography that prevailed until recent decades. He was born in Skopje in 1884, into the upper echelons of Balkan Ottoman society. He studied in Paris between 1903 and 1912, and spent the war years and the independence struggle in Istanbul, teaching and establishing his reputation as a poet and writer. In 1923 he moved to Ankara to become editor of the *Hakimiyeti Milliye* (an important nationalist publication). Shortly after, he embarked on an administrative career that took him to Urfa, Tekirdağ, and Istanbul as a *milletvekili*, as well as a diplomatic career, during which he served in the Turkish embassies in Warsaw, Madrid, and finally as ambassador to Pakistan. He retired to Istanbul in 1949 and died there in 1958. Though his republican credentials were impeccable, it was the conservative Fetih Foundation (dedicated to commemorating Sultan Fatih Mehmet's conquest of the city in 1453) that oversaw his memorialization, establishing the Yahya Kemal Institute in 1961 and republishing his scattered poems and essays.

It is not difficult to see Yahya Kemal's attraction for religious conservatives. Where the republican modernists celebrated Ankara and its rural Anatolian hinterland, Yahya Kemal was drawn to cosmopolitan Istanbul. Where the republican modernists were drawn to the idea of "culture" adumbrated in Ziya Gökalp's influential *Türkçülüğün esasları* (Gökalp 1923) and understood as the binding elements of the nations of the future, Yahya Kemal was drawn to Gökalp's "civilizations," to the empires of the past and the multilayered marks they left on Istanbul's landscape.[12] His Istanbul poetry drew heavily on the Servet-i Fünun and Fecr-i Ati poets of the Tanzimat and Sec-

---

12. On Gökalp on "civilization" (*medeniyet*, as opposed to *hars* or, roughly, "culture") see Stokes 1992a. Gökalp arguably has overshadowed understandings of the cultural politics of the early republican period, associated as he was with the "winning side." Other early republican modernist intellectuals such as Ahmet Ağaoğlu have fared less well in the historical record, though their rather different concepts of culture, civilization, nation, and modernity were clearly influential. See Shissler 2003 and O'Connell 2005a for an alternative musicological picture, focusing on Mahmut Ragıp Gazimihal's "Mediterraneanism."

ond Constitutional periods, in particular Namık Kemal, Tevfik Fikret, Ahmet Haşim, Cenab Sehabeddin, and Hamdullah Süphi Tanrıöver. Like them he looked to the French symbolists and Parnassians and was absorbed by the task of depicting the city of Istanbul— with its dense social life, rich history, neighborhoods, and scenic views—in all of its varied moods, using dense and highly formal language.[13] Where republican modernist poets looked to rural culture and the urban everyday for direction in poetry, choosing simpler language, syllabic (*heceli*) verse forms, and rural and everyday themes, Yahya Kemal continued to develop the Ottoman prosodic tradition of *vezin* and used a language packed with the rich Arabic and Persian lexicon that the language reformers were bent on purging.[14]

Where the republican modernist poets of his generation used rural folk music to signify the new nation-state's culture, Yahya Kemal was drawn to urban art music, constantly weaving references to in into his poems. He developed a passionate attachment to the music of Tanburi Cemil Bey on his return from Paris, and often declared that he had discovered his love for the *vatan* (the homeland) through Cemil Bey at a time when he could all too easily have got bored of Istanbul and returned to Paris. On these and other grounds he vociferously defended the art music tradition from its detractors, for whom it could never be sufficiently national and modern. He wrote some forty-four poems that directly evoked Turkish art music (Abacı 2000, pp. 45–46). A great many of his poems were set to music by a musician who shared his ambivalent position in the new republic: Münir Nurettin Selçuk. His student and follower, Ahmet Hamdi Tanpınar, developed this fascination for "the old music" a great deal further, sharing Yahya Kemal's love of Cemil Bey and Dede Efendi, and systematically weaving music and musicians into the dense urban landscapes of his poems, novels, and writings on Turkish cities.[15]

"Aziz İstanbul" itself is a brief eight-line lyric in two stanzas, each with an ABAB rhyme scheme, and in a simple and emphatic *vezin* (prosodic) pat-

---

13. On the role of the picturesque in Servet-i Fünun and Fecr-i Ati poetry, see in particular Kaplan's discussion of Cenab Sehabeddin, Tevfik Fikret, Hamdullah Süphi Tanrıöver, Mehmet Akif Ersoy, and Rıza Tevfik Bölükbaşı (Kaplan 1954).

14. Abacı argues that *vezin* (metrical, or "old") and *hece* (syllabic, or "new") are not necessarily to be seen as mutually exclusive principles (Abacı 2000, p. 20). Yahya Kemal sought to reconcile them in a poetry that would be both modern and rooted in the craft of the past. It was the proponents of *heceli* poetry, Abacı suggests, that were responsible for polemicizing the issue.

15. On Tanpınar's views on music, see Abacı 2000 and Kaplan 1963. For his writings on cities, see especially Tanpınar 2003.

tern.¹⁶ Its mood is serene but it registers fleeting ambiguities and anxieties. In the first stanza the poet addresses his memory of a blissful view of the city to the city itself.

| | |
|---|---|
| *Sana dün bir tepeden baktım aziz İstanbul* | I looked down on you yesterday from hilltop, beloved Istanbul |
| *Görmedim gezmediğim sevmediğim hiç bir yer* | I couldn't see one place I had not strolled around, had not loved |
| *Ömrüm oldukça gönül tahtıma keyfince kurul* | Dwell on my heart's throne for as long as I live! |
| *Sade bir semtini sevmek bile bir ömre değer* | Loving just one of your neighborhoods is a life's work.¹⁷ |

Whether to a lover or to a wife, the relationship implied is conjugal, nuclear, affectionate, and long-term, conforming to an ideology of domestic reproduction that began to take shape in the Tanzimat period and settled, at least amongst the middle classes in Istanbul, in the early republic (Duben and Behar 1991). Like many songs of this period, it evokes the memory of a moment of pleasure, either collective (the Bosphorus *alem* parties, for instance)¹⁸ or solitary, hinting that there are moments that transcend words. This genre of lyric poetry and song inhabits something resembling a Wordsworthian poetic universe of "emotion recollected in tranquility." He implores (her) to keep him happy. This, it seems, is likely to be the result: the love of just one neighborhood is "enough to last a lifetime." But a fleeting anxiety is nonetheless registered with the imperative "Dwell on my heart's throne."

---

16. The second *ramal*, represented according to Ottoman and Arabic poetic convention as *fa'ilatun fa'ilatun fa'ilatun fa'ilun* (ᵘ ᵘ - -, ᵘ ᵘ - -, ᵘ ᵘ - -, ᵘ ᵘ -). I am grateful to Bob Dankoff for helping me identify this.

17. There are numerous excellent English translations of this elusively phrased poem. I have attempted my own here in order to explore the meanings most relevant to its various musical settings.

18. The most famous literary celebrants of the Bosphorus *alem* parties were Abdülhak Şinasi Hisar (see in particular Hisar 1978) and Ahmet Rasım, who detail the musical ensembles (the *ince saz* orchestras) maintained by high-ranking Ottoman administrators and officers whose palaces dotted the Bosphorus shores. Thus we learn, through a dense patina of nostalgia, about the concerts, which usually took place in boats on the Bosphorus in the vicinity of Göksu, Kanlıca, Rumelihisarı, Kalender, or Mihrabad (north of the city) and ideally on moonlit nights; about Halim Paşa's famous orchestra; about Sadettin Paşa's forty-eight musical slave girls; about Bestenigar Kalfa, one of these slave girls, who while dying from tuberculosis brought the gathering to tears with a performance of *ağıt* (laments) and *mersiye* (spiritual laments) composed only the night before by Hafız Yusuf Efendi; and about the elaborate social protocols of these occasions (Tura n.d., pp. 5–8). The time period in question is evidently the middle to late nineteenth century.

The poet could be taken as wondering: What if she turns her back on me? What if I get bored of her?

The opening words ("I looked down on you yesterday from a hilltop") make an emphatic deictic move, locating the poet "above" in relation to the beloved city "down there." The act of "looking down" enables the poet to consider the whole in relation to its constituent parts. This sends out a curious message to the city as love object—a message that may be taken as betraying another kind of anxiety about the nature of companionate love. On the one hand he says: "I will be with you as long as I live and never tire of you." On the other: "I can't love you whole but only in parts, since it is only the parts that I can, as it were, master." There is in this sense a suggestion that love of the whole and love of the parts are at some level irreconcilable, or are at least in tension.

Indeed, in a great many related lyrics and songs from this period (see Aksüt 1994, Behar 1997–98), the specific parts of the city repeatedly draw the erotic attention of poet and singer.[19] Sometimes these are simply named, the endless list implying a whole that lies beyond grasp: Rumelihisar, Kuzguncuk, Beylerbeyi, Tarabya, Hünkâr, Emirgân, Yeniköy—"even Sarıyer" (today the most remote northern Bosphorus suburb), as Zeki Duygulu's song "Boğaz'ın incisi Rumelihisar" has it. Sometimes the topographical item is individuated and eroticized by metonymic connection; it is in Bebek that the poet sees his *"yüzü ay güzel"* (his "moon-faced beauty"); from the hilltop the poet imagines the Marmara Sea, the Bosphorus, and the Black Sea as the "three girls" he "makes love to"; it is in Yeniköy that he meets the flirtatious Sarı Zambak. In Ünal Narçın's famous song "Kız sen İstanbul'un neresindensin?" (Girl, which part of Istanbul are you from?), the poet insistently tries to figure out where the beautiful girl comes from, eliminating one neighborhood after another. In such lyrics the whole is not graspable for erotic purposes, but the part is.[20] Two different kinds of love are implied and at play: one romantic, focused on an overwhelming whole, the other fetishistic, focused on a part made to stand for the whole.

Related anxieties haunt the second stanza:

| | |
|---|---|
| *Nice revnaklı şehirler görünür dünyada* | What sparkling cities there are in the world. |

---

19. These are modern versions of Ottoman *şehrengiz* poetry (accounts of the beauties of the neighborhoods and urban amorous escapades), discussed extensively by Andrews and Kalpaklı (Andrews and Kalpaklı 2005).

20. The lover's dilemma, then, is precisely that of Karl Kraus's fetishist. He only wanted the shoe, but had to put up with the whole human being (see Giddens 1992, p. 84).

| | |
|---|---|
| *Lakin efsunlu güzellikleri sensin yaratan* | But it is you who creates enchanting beauty. |
| *Yaşamışdır derim en hoş ve uzun rüyada* | He who has lived long, who dies, who lies with you |
| *Sende çok yıl yaşayan, sende ölen, sende yatan* | Has lived, I say, in the sweetest and longest of dreams. |

The first line evokes the poet's roving eye. We may crave stability in love, it suggests, but it rarely works out that simply. The poet is a man of the world, after all. He has traveled, and seen other cities. The matter seems to be quickly resolved, but the anxiety reverberates. The second couplet invokes a more complex set of concerns. In "Aziz İstanbul" the lover has lived in the "sweetest and longest of dreams" (*en hoş ve uzun rüya*), outside of historical time with its petty calculations and privations. The passing "I say" (*derim*) underlines the gesture, as though this stepping out of time is the lover's ultimate prize. One might perceive a tension in the poem, then, between two different kinds of time, both emotionally inflected. One is an orderly historical progress in which love begins, develops, and reaches maturity and repose after long experience. The other kind of time is a stepping out of time, as if into a dream—a significantly more unstable prospect.

Yahya Kemal and his literary followers[21] were absorbed by the question of time: its richness and dense social textures, its multilayered nature, its complex simultaneities, its reversals of flow, its quickenings and prolongations. Yahya Kemal's lifelong fascination with music, and particularly with the *taksim* (improvisation)-oriented art of Tanburi Cemil Bey, is surely connected to the concern with time. But this interest stands in significant tension with the resolute and secular clock time espoused by the new republic, whose official commitment to the national march of progress went hand-in-hand with efforts to desacralize socially deeply ingrained habits of time-marking.[22] As is well known, the Turkish reformers abolished the Islamic calendar and replaced it with the Julian. Weekends were celebrated on Sundays and not Fridays; secular rather than religious holidays officially

---

21. Specifically novelist and poet Ahmet Hamdi Tanpınar. Like Yahya Kemal, Tanpınar was obsessed by "the old music" and by time, an obsession worked through in his famous trilogy of novels (*Huzur, Saatleri ayarlama enstitüsü,* and *Mahur beste*), and developed in his travel writing (notably *Beş şehir,* Tanpınar 2003) and poetry (see Kaplan 1963 and Abacı 2000). Tanpınar's literary theory in encapsulated in lecture notes written up by students. In them he has relatively little to say on the subject of music, but a great deal to say on the Ottoman and European context of early republican literary endeavor, as well as revealing insights into his literary relationship with Yahya Kemal.

22. Though Anderson (1983) does not specifically mention the Turkish case, it exemplifies one of his most basic contentions extremely well.

punctuated the year. Though Yahya Kemal was no outspoken critic, a great deal of his writing interrogates the dominant narratives concerning history, time, and progress espoused by the new republic.

A highly compressed essay about Istanbul by Yahya Kemal, "Bir bir çalan saatler" (The clocks that strike one by one), emphasizes the point. It seems to have been written as notes towards a longer essay, "Türk İstanbul" (Turkish Istanbul), which was originally given as a talk at the Beyoğlu Halkevi (People's House) in Istanbul on 12 March 1942. Written up in Ottoman script, both essays were first published in 1964 by the Yahya Kemal Institute (Beyatlı 1964). "Bir bir çalan saatler" consists of six loosely articulated sections, each running to four or five short paragraphs. The second of these paragraphs strikingly echoes the language and themes of "Aziz İstanbul." It begins:

"*İstanbul'da çok zaman yaşamış, yaşadıkça birçok semtleri sevmiş, sevdikçe onları, zamânın derinliğine doğru, enine boyuna öğrenmiş bir insan, yaşı ilerledikçe, öğrendiklerile o kadar dolar ki, bu şehrin, sonu gelmez güzellikleri olduğuna inanır.*" (A person who has lived in Istanbul for a long time, and who has in living there loved a number of neighborhoods, and who in loving them has learned fully and in historical depth as they get older, becomes so full with what he/she has learned, that he/she comes to realize that this city possesses unending beauties) (Beyatlı 1964, p. 75).

The title given to the essay by the Institute editors was adopted—appropriately—from what was originally a marginal scribble to its third sectionon Kemal's original manuscript. "Bir bir çalan saatler" orients the reader from the outset to the complex questions of historical time that absorb Kemal in each individual section of the essay. In the first section, the author argues that the conquest of Istanbul by Fatih Sultan Mehmet in 1453 transformed a confederation of tribal *beyliks* into a unified modern nation (*vatan*), consolidating a process of westward expansion that began in 1071 at the battle of Manzikert. In the second section, Yahya Kemal evokes the "artist" (*sanatkar*) surveying the city, entranced by its endless physical beauties—those that "strike the eye"—and its rich history, an "inner" and unseen Istanbul (*deruni bir İstanbul*) requiring an act of historical imagination. In the third section, the author addresses an intimate—"*haydi azizim*" (come, my dear)—in thrall to Marxist materialist ideologies, who fails to grasp the peculiar spirit (*hiss*) of the city. But this failure is not the intimate's fault. Our national literature lags behind others in celebrating nature and the beautiful views on our doorstep, says the author, and we must press ahead with our efforts to forge a properly national history. And what views these are: modern Istanbul is a natural and social historical achievement whose magnitude can be grasped if we try and imagine New York imposed on the environment before our eyes. That, Yahya Kemal argues, is today's equivalent of what the Turks have created in Istanbul.

The fourth section evokes the spiritual atmosphere of Üsküdar (opposite the old city) prior to the assault on the Byzantine city, but reminds the reader that in Üsküdar "spirituality and pleasure" (*zevk ve şevk*) are as one, stuck together "like meat to skin" (*et ve deri gibi birbirine yapışık*). The fifth very briefly asserts that the Bosphorus lies at the heart of the new and singular urban entity the Ottomans created; it is the significant difference between the Byzantine city, for which it constituted a boundary, and the Ottoman city, which enclosed it. The final section again emphasizes the Turkish character of the Ottoman capital. With "mathematical precision [*riyazi bir hesabı varmış gibi*]," Yahya Kemal argues, the built city reached its moment of perfection and attained its distinct profile with the great architect, Sinan, precisely when the Ottomans "completed" their imperial conquests.

Each section of the essay imagines complex time games, inviting the reader to play with temporalities and teleologies. To take just one example: in the first section, the word *imtidad* (extension, prolongation in time) is emphasized. The Ottoman conquest of Istanbul, Yahya Kemal says, was not simply an event that occurred and then receded, carried away by the river of time. It is a memory that the city's inhabitants have built on, day by day, for five hundred years. The event we remember "was" its future—what it allowed us to become, and what it continues to enable us to become. Memory, then, is not simply a matter of looking back, but also one of looking forward. The power (*kudret*) of the event lies in its *imtidad*, its "prolongation"—its being, in important regards, outside of historical time. To a certain degree this can be read as the poet's plea for republican reformers to recognize that the new Turkey, the new national entity, is Istanbul and Islamic history just as much as it is Ankara and the story of the new nation's independence struggle. So the poem "Aziz İstanbul" might also be read as an invitation to consider time as a multidimensional, heterotopic proposition pregnant with possibilities, and not simply as a straight line railroading the nation toward a pre-fabricated modernity. The "longest and sweetest dream" of the final couplet might usefully be understood as a state of *imtidad*, a temporality at odds, both experientially and politically, with the abstract, linear, and secular temporality of the new state.

Yahya Kemal's poem, to conclude the section, encapsulates and develops the preoccupation of the Ottoman Servet-i Fünun and Fecr-i Ati poets with the depiction of Istanbul as observed by a melancholic wanderer, and their gravitation towards densely textured formal language and poetic artifice. The poem is not entirely conservative: it openly, even aggressively, embraces the principle of the nation and its organizing narratives.[23] So for all of its serenity of mood, for all the clarity of its organizing tropes and its linguistic formality, the poem is full of submerged ambiguities and surface anxieties: of impossible love, unstable currents of desire, and a subject stuck in the secular historical time of the nation but wishing himself out of it.

## "Aziz İstanbul": Münir Nurettin Selçuk's Version

Münir Nurettin Selçuk stood somewhat apart from the state's musical reforms, being associated with a genre that, despite the convictions of ideologues such as Ziya Gökalp (see above), was opposed rather half-heartedly and unsystematically. Münir Nurettin was however a reformist, a popular exponent of the view that the urban genre should not be condemned but modernized. According to his Turkish biographers he was "the man who put Turkish music in Western dress" (*Türk musikisine frak giydiren adam*).[24] The allusion to Atatürk is deliberate and explicit; the founder of the republic quite literally "put Turks into Western dress." The promotional photographs of Münir Nurettin show him striking a dandified, Westernized stance, smartly dressed in a variety of suits and hats, often looking at some point above and beyond the photographer, as in many of the more famous portraits of Atatürk to be found in offices and cafes all over the country.

Münir Nurettin Selçuk was a member of a family whose position in the bureaucratic establishment straddled the Ottoman and early republican period. His class background was in many regards exactly that of Yahya Kemal, who was several decades his senior. His father was a high-ranking religious official. Münir Nurettin learned his art at the foremost musical institutions in Istanbul and went to France to further his musical studies in 1926. He worked extensively with the emerging Turkish film industry, making a name for himself singing in some of the very first imitations of the Egyptian

---

23. Ahmet Hamdi Tanpınar was first introduced to me by Meral Özbek in 1996 as a writer who had long been championed by religious conservatives and published by their printing houses but was increasingly being discovered by the left. Ten years later, the question "How are Yahya Kemal and Tanpınar understood politically these days?" would produce a great diversity of answers. A simple breakdown would suggest that those who might identify themselves as the "literary left" more or less unanimously hailed them as historically aware progressives and critics, while others on the left still saw them as tainted.

24. The phrase is taken from Kulin's 1996 book; the illustrations I refer to are also to be found there. Information here derives from the published work of O'Connell (particularly O'Connell 2002, 2003, and 2005a), Kulin 1996, Bozdağ 1998, and various articles in the popular music press.

musicals, which were quickly banned by the new republic. His recordings were the best-selling hits of the day; he was the first Turkish music star in the modern sense. Most conspicuously, it was he who initiated or popularized the practice of standing apart from the seated musicians. Formerly the singer (a mere *hanende*, seated alongside the instrumental *sazende*) had been part of an ensemble. Selçuk was thus directly responsible for introducing a "modern" and hierarchical division of labor into Turkish art music practice.

He also composed a large proportion of the music he recorded, specializing in settings of poetry by republican literati, particularly Yahya Kemal. Many of his most enduringly popular songs—those he sang throughout his concert career, such as "Rindlerin ölümü," "Rintlerin akşamı," "Yeniçeri'ye gazel," and "Endelüste raks"—were composed on Yahya Kemal's poems. He also set a great many works by other poets who are less well known today.[25] Dates of the compositions and recordings (mostly with HMV/Sahibin Sesi) are hard to establish. Many would seem to date from the late 1940s to the 1950s. The details of Münir Nurettin's working relationship with Yahya Kemal has not yet been the subject of much published research.[26] But it is clear that Münir Nurettin was deeply committed to Yahya Kemal's poetry and very much in tune, I would suggest, with the constitutive tensions and contradictions of Yahya Kemal's Ottoman-haunted republican modernism.

Münir Nurettin's "Aziz İstanbul" bears this observation out. It captures the limpidity, lyric compression, and formal grace of the poem. It lasts about three minutes and involves the singer, a female chorus, and a small and un-

---

25. Ömürlü's useful collection of musical settings of Yahya Kemal's poems (1999) provides 17 settings by Münir Nurettin out of a total of 117, and 34 others that are mentioned but not included. This may well represent the total number or something close to it. Though this is a separate topic for discussion, it is striking that many of the poems Münir Nurettin chose had also been chosen, or would later be chosen, by other musicians. Some of his settings were vocal improvisations. He rendered Yahya Kemal's "Aheste çek kürekleri," a depiction of a moonlit Bosphorus from a rowing boat, as a remarkable *gazel* (vocal improvisation), for instance. Where Münir Nurettin's contemporaries gravitated towards the *gazel* as an art of vocal pyrotechnics often for merely conventional expressions of lament and love (see O'Connell 2003), this setting observes the *seyir* rules of its *makam* (*uşşak*) with textbook precision, subtly painting and shading a complex poem whose words are clear throughout. Despite the fact that Münir Nurettin's settings are popular and well known, and despite the fact that Yahya Kemal resented their popularity (see Bozdağ 1998), other well-known musicians, notably Çinuçen Tanrıkorur, set more of Yahya Kemal's poems; Ömürlü (1999) lists nineteen of them. It is also worth noting that Yahya Kemal's poetry attracted severe musical modernists such as Hüseyin Sadettin Arel, as well as sentimental nostalgists such as Münir Nurettin.

26. Bozdağ 1998 is anecdotal and, I believe, unique. He relates, for instance, the well-known comments by Yahya Kemal that Münir Nurettin's song settings had given his poems "wings," and he alludes to rivalry and tension between the two men. He also provides accounts of how Münir Nurettin composed, how he spoke about how he worked, and how he constantly tinkered with his songs.

obtrusive backing orchestra. It is cast in compressed *şarkı* (classical song) form. The first two couplets (*beyt*) constitute a *zemin* and a *zaman*, musically speaking (i.e., two contrasting opening phrases). A shift in pitch introduces the *meyan* in a higher register and the third couplet. The final couplet reprises the musical material of the *zaman*. As an exercise in modality (*makam*), the song follows textbook rules for *zirgüleli hicaz makamı*, with the higher pitched *meyan* effecting a modulation to *hicaz* on the fifth degree of the scale (see Yılmaz 1977). Peculiar care has been taken to render the *vezin* (prosodic) structure of the poetry.[27] For all of the lyric limpidity of Münir Nurettin's setting, there is an academic formalism at work, very much in tune with Yahya Kemals' poetics.[28]

There are two striking musical complications. One relates to a metrical ambiguity. The poetic meter (the second *remel*) has Münir Nurettin casting the opening foot (*failatun*, i.e., short–short–long–long) in an emphatic triple meter.

Sa - na dün bir te - pe - den— bak - tım a - ziz_____ Is - tan - bul

**5a.** "Aziz İstanbul," opening. From Aksüt 1994. An alternative notation can be found at Neyzen.com. Key signature follows notational conventions of Turkish art music for *hicaz makamı*; (♭) indicates four commas flat, (♯) indicates four commas sharp.

This is, however, contradicted by the opening orchestral vamping figure, supposedly based on a lullaby (*ninni*) melody,[29] which is metrically duple rather than triple (despite a 3/4 time signature in most transcriptions). One should note that transcribed versions of this song start with an instrumental version of the opening lines of the *zaman*—in a strong triple meter, in

---

27. There are two particularly important studies of prosody and musical setting in Turkish: Tanrıkorur's recently republished study of 2003 (assembled from articles written in the late 1980s and early 1990s), and Hüseyin Sadettin Arel's 1992 study. Tanrıkorur looks at the correspondence between musical and poetic meter in the Ottoman repertoire (with particular emphasis on nineteenth-century compositions). Arel provides a practical guide in the context of contemporary poetic and musical practice, with reference to Ottoman practices of connecting musical and poetic meter. Tanrıkorur's study shows that the first *remel* would habitually elicit shorter agglutinative patterns (the *usûl* known as *ağır aksak, devri hindi*, and *curcuna*) or longer chains (*müsemmen*) (Tanrıkorur 2003, p. 104). The 3/4 meter Münir Nurettin uses in his setting corresponds, unusually, to Tanrıkorur's simplest notational representation of the opening "*failatün*" figure ($^{u\ u}$ - -).

28. Yahya Kemal was known to be a great admirer of the French Parnassians, for instance.

29. The Neyzen.com version and the Ömürlü (1999) version both label this a *ninni* (lullaby) without saying what exactly it is.

other words. The best-known recording of this song by Münir Nurettin omits this and starts instead with the "lullaby," establishing at the outset a strong duple meter. This is followed by the free-rhythm "call to prayer" (to be discussed shortly); only then do we hear the music that accompanies the first lines of the poem, at which point the triple musical meter / second *remel* poetic meter is established. Given the first measure of the lullaby figure, with its anacrusis, a significant ambiguity hovers over the first iteration of the metrical pattern, which can be heard as being simultaneously in duple and triple meter.

5b. "Aziz İstanbul," "lullaby" figure

If there is a metrical ambiguity at play in the introduction, it is rendered even more ambiguous in performance by the singer's practice of inserting pauses after phrases—a fact that has caused difficulties for later musicians in transcribing the piece.[30] The common habit of prolonging phrases in the *meyan* section,[31] arguably, amplifies the poetic drift of the Yahya Kemal poem. Here the "longest and sweetest dream" discussed above is underlined by the addition of the women's chorus, and also by a free-floating rubato. There is no rhythm section on the recording, meaning that these metrical ambiguities, rubatos, stops, and starts are not grounded in a constantly ticking pulse. In other words one is not in a simple and singular metrical

---

30. The Neyzen.com version, the Ömürlü (1999) version, and the Aksüt (1994) version all differ in significant details, reflecting different hearings of the Münir Nurettin original, and different performance traditions. If we assume the first two are "correct," then Aksüt, for example, misplaces the phrase beginning "*Bir ömre değer,*" hearing the first notes as an anacrusis. Both Neyzen.com and Ömürlü start the phrase at the beginning of the measure.

31. The *meyan* section usually occurs at the third *beyt* or couplet, here corresponding to the beginning of the second verse and the words "*Nice revnaklı şehirler. . . .*" For art-music composers in the mid-twentieth century, it would habitually involve a change in register (moving from lower to higher) and a modal modulation.

world, but—at a structural level—in two (duple and triple). This metrical and structural ambiguity is heightened by a rhythmic flexibility and extensive rubato in performance. The empty temporality of "pure succession" and the temporality of the dream noted above in the Yahya Kemal poem are, one might say, subtly rendered in musical performance.

There is a dramatic new element to the musical setting, though. Where Yahya Kemal presents a view, Münir Nurettin presents a soundscape. After the duple vamp figure, and before the start of the *zemin* of the opening couplet of the song, the singer vocalizes on "ah," tracing the figure of a call to prayer (*ezan*).[32]

**5c.** "Aziz İstanbul," "call to prayer" figure

The end of the phrase is repeated by a chorus of female voices:

**5d.** "Aziz İstanbul," female chorus

32. Bozdağ 1998, a musician and friend of the singer, provides the following account of how the "call to prayer" came to be included. Münir Nurettin invited Bozdağ to come and hear his new composition, promising his wife's *dolma* (stuffed vine leaves). Bozdağ accepted. His story instantly digresses to Münir Nurettin's drinking habits (his liking for *rakı* mixed with milk, and his habit of starting an evening's heavy *rakı* drinking with a glass or two of whisky); Bozdağ himself also comes across as a bit of a drinker. Returning to the point of the anecdote, Bozdağ says that he expressed some reservations about Münir Nurettin's setting of "Aziz İstanbul." Pressed by an irritable Münir Nurettin, he said it lacked the master musician's "signature"—something like the "Olé" he had added to an earlier setting of Yahya Kemal's "Endelüs'te raks." A week or ten days later, Bozdağ was summoned again. This time he heard Münir Nurettin begin the song with the famous *ezan*. Münir Nurettin said he had been thrown into deep thought by Bozdağ's comment, and had found himself wandering around the city wondering where on earth he could add this "signature," and what it would consist of. At that very moment the muezzin of the Teşvikiye mosque—one of the larger mosques close to a neighborhood where many musicians, artists, and literati lived—struck up the noon call to prayer, beautifully intoned, in a well-honed *hicaz*. "And that was how the song was completed!" (Bozdağ 1998, p. 9) I am grateful to Mehmet Güntekin for relating this anecdote to me over a meal in August 2006 (with imitations of the voices of all the personalities involved, suggesting that this was a well-worn story in musician's circles), and also for pointing me in the direction of the written source. See also note 26.

The repetition communicates multiplicity. The viewer is imagined listening to the *ezan* at a distance—hearing not one particular call to prayer but a number, staggered in time, as one often does when the wind is blowing in the right direction, or when one is away from traffic noise or a little distant from the city. The repetition, in other words, effects a deictic move similar to that with which the poem starts: the poet "above," the city (with its mosques) "below." It also locates the event in time. In Istanbul, by convention, prayer is called in a particular *makam* at particular times of day. *Hicaz makamı* usually signifies afternoon prayer (*ikindi*).[33] The call to prayer in Münir Nurettin's version, then, situates both the remembered scene and the poet himself in time and in place.

The repetition also establishes a scene of gendered reciprocity, mirroring the scene of conjugal affection—city as spouse—portrayed in Yahya Kemal's poem. A male voice initiates and a female voice responds. The male voice is a singular voice and the female voice is collective, de-individuated: a neat picture, one might say, of companionate marriage as imagined by late Ottoman and early republican elites. The picture is complicated, though, by the insertion of a lullaby which is part of the soundscape, perhaps, but also sets up a parallel gendered relationship between viewer and viewed: the viewer (as male infant) is being sung to by the city (as mother) and sonically rocked in its cradle. The opening moments of the musical version, which occur before the opening line of poetry and are repeated an octave higher and extended at the very end, present a complicated sonic picture of the city as a space of gendered intimacy. The sonic environment is presented simultaneously and uneasily as distant love object (signified by the *ezan*) and maternal environment (signified by the lullaby).[34] The repetitions of the *ezan* figure perform both a conventional (republican-modern) gendered picture, with men and women's musical roles clearly defined and separated, and a complication of that picture in which those roles overlap and impinge on one another.

Münir Nurettin's performance of the song thus reinforces significant

---

33. See Koçu 1969, p. 20. According to him, early morning (*sabah*) prayer uses *saba* or *dilkeş haveran makamı* for the *ezan*. Noon (*öğle*) is *saba, hicaz,* or *bayati*. Afternoon (*ikindi*) is *hicaz*. Early evening (*akşam*) is either *hicaz* or *rast*. Night (*yatsı*) is *hicaz, rast, bayati,* or *neva*. This leaves plenty of room for variation and maneuver if the muezzin doesn't have much vocal training or confidence in his vocal prowess. *Hicaz,* according to Koçu, could actually signify a number of different times. For musically literate Istanbullians, however, it is most likely to indicate *ikindi,* afternoon prayer.

34. On sound in narrative as maternal sonic environment, see specifically Silverman 1988. She has a specific historical and cultural contexts in mind, of course, but her account of the complex and ambivalent place of sound in film narrative is highly suggestive here. This is not a scene of gendered mastery, but, as she would suggest, something much less stable.

figures and themes of the poem, the poet looking down on the city, the configuration of the poet-city relationship as a husband-wife relationship, and the persistence of memory. Given the close artistic relationship between poet and music, Yahya Kemal's gravitation towards classical music and love of song forms (Abacı 2000), and Münir Nurettin's literary inclinations, this is hardly surprising. The musical version does not simply restate the poem's literary effects, though. The repetition of the wordless "call to prayer" at the end of the song, extended and intensified at the octave (in the male voice), suggests, rather more directly than anything in Yahya Kemal's poetry, memory that cannot be quite so easily filed away. Listeners are left with the "call to prayer" as an object of memory: persistent, not fully assimilated into the musical textures of the song, and somehow intensified by the act of recall. I want to suggest here, though, that Yahya Kemal's poem and Münir Nurettin's song are intimately connected. As we have seen, the song does not simply restate Yahya Kemal's poem in another medium. But as meditations on the constitutive tensions of early Turkish republican modernity, the song and the poem are intimately linked.

### "Aziz İstanbul": Bülent Ersoy's version on *Alaturka 95*

A half-century later, we are in a significantly different world. A latecomer to the golden age of *gazino* culture (see chapter 4), Bülent Ersoy is a product of the cassette culture, *arabesk,* and the satellite television channels of the later 1980s and early 1990s.[35] Ersoy left the country in 1981 to undergo a sex change operation in London; this resulted in a stage ban and years of virtual exile in Germany. The singer has been the subject of a great deal of journalist

---

35. Bülent Ersoy's moment of conspicuous fame came in 1976 and 1977, when she stole headlines for contract deals (75,000 Turkish liras for concert performances in Bursa, according to a note in *Hey* 27 June 1977, and a recording contract that involved a two-million-lira signing deal and a luxury apartment worth 750,000 liras) and was a major hit at the İzmir Fair, performing in the new prestige venue there, the Büyük Efes Oteli. In 1975 the singer performed a concert of art music on Turkish television, and between 1975 and 1977 she released three austerely classical LPs simply called *Konseri* (His/her concert). She gradually withdrew from the performing stage as her gender transformation slowly took place in the later years of that decade. Subsequent recordings, many made in Germany, were unambiguously in the *arabesk* style: *Mahşeri* (1980), *Yüz karası* (1981), *Ak güvercin* (1983), and so forth, through to the *arabesk* classics *Suskun dünyam* (1987) and *Biz ayrılamayız* (1988), many of which were for *arabesk* films. Another *Konseri* in the art-music style was released in 1986; *Alaturka 95* came out in 1995. Both albums were recordings of classical music, but they sounded significantly different: "classical" in the first case, nostalgic in the second. For useful discographic information, see http://www.diskotek.arkaplan.com.tr/catalog (accessed 31 July 2008).

writing, and not a little academic interest.[36] Her sex-change operation is of course striking in a society that is generally conservative in matters of sexuality. But as my discussion of Zeki Müren in chapter 2 will have suggested, it might also be seen in the broader historical context of gendered ambiguity in Middle Eastern musical culture and a pragmatic attitude toward the assignation of sexual and gendered identities in Islam.[37]

In 1986, Turkey's new leaders were already signaling the need for cultural change with reference to Bülent Ersoy and other banned and marginalized artists. It was no secret that Semra Özal, wife of President Turgut Özal, was a great fan, and an amnesty (of sorts) secured Ersoy's return. No particular offense to public sensibilities was likely, and inasmuch as a case was made, it was made on liberal grounds. But Ersoy may well have felt some pressure to prove her worth. If her exile years had been years of *arabesk,* her return to Turkey was marked by recordings in a severely classical style. The earliest recordings in this vein may well have been designed to counter perceptions of Ersoy as "merely" an *arabesk* star, and to justify the artistic amnesty.

*Alaturka 95,* which appeared in 1995, was a typical recording from this moment of Ersoy's career. It comprised well-known classics, accompanied by a large art-music-style orchestra, with *peşrev*-s (instrumental introductions) and long, academic-sounding *taksim* improvisations. It was released by S-Müzik, then the elite *arabesk* division of the recording company Raks. It was, by all accounts, conceived as a gift to the singer's mentor, Muzaffer Özpınar, a composer and *tanbur* (long-necked lute) player who had trained under Mustafa Kona at the Eminönü conservatory.[38] Özpınar's training and tastes are severely classical, despite the fact that he penned many of Ersoy's most enduring popular hits. The cassette did not sell very well, according to

---

36. For what is, I believe, the first English-language discussion of this remarkable singer, see Stokes 1992a. For a detailed comparison of Zeki Müren and Bülent Ersoy, with reference to some of the relevant Turkish literature, see Stokes 2004a. For an excellent English-language study of Ersoy's gender politics, see Altınay 2008.

37. On homosexuality and gender ambiguity in Islam, see, for instance, Murray and Roscoe 1997. On early Islam in particular, see Rowson 1991. For a classic anthropological study elsewhere in the Middle East, broadly supportive of this observation, see Wikan 1977. For interpretations of gender ambiguity in various areas of expressive culture in the Middle East, on which I draw heavily in this book, see for instance Najmabadi 2005, Andrews and Kalpaklı 2005, Swedenburg 2000, and Kandiyoti 1999.

38. He also composed extensively for Zeki Müren. Most of the information in this paragraph draws from an interview with Özpınar in June 1996, conducted by Anne Ellingsen and me at the S-Müzik office in Levent.

S-Müzik manager Sacit Suhabey—about half a million copies, as opposed to the two million they generally expected for each Ersoy recording. However, Özpınar was obviously pleased to be able to present his somewhat notorious former student as a dutiful citizen, prepared to put financial considerations aside and make an occasional contribution to the artistic health of the nation. As far as S-Müzik was concerned, the cassette may not have made as much money as anticipated, but did at least serve to indicate the rapidly growing market for nostalgia.

"Aziz İstanbul" is the first song on the first side of the cassette. The opening notes of its extended introduction are a radical departure from the version recorded by Münir Nurettin Selçuk, and they instantly relocate the song in an entirely different style and different sound world. Ersoy's recording is faithful to later notated versions (specifically those to be found on Neyzen.com), rather than to the old Münir Nurettin recording, which was rereleased by the label Coşkun Plak and was already widely circulating in the late 1980s.[39] So it starts with a descending fourth followed by an instrumental rendition of the first vocal line:

**5e.** "Aziz İstanbul," instrumental rendition of first vocal line

One is instantly struck by the size of the orchestra. A glance at the cassette's liner notes reveals, in an unusual profusion of information, a large orchestra listed by name: seven violins, three violas, a cello, a *tanbur*, a *yaylı tanbur* (bowed long-necked lute), a *kanun* (plucked zither), an oud, a *ney* (end-blown flute), two *darbuka* (goblet drum) and *bendir* (frame drum) players, an electric bass, a piano, and a vocal group. On the recording one hears a harmonic progression: a D minor chord followed by A major chord,[40] after

---

39. I bought the Münir Nurettin CDs in the summer of 1989, having stumbled across them while visiting the Coşkun Plak offices in Unkapanı with my friend İbrahim Can (mentioned at the end of this chapter), who was then one of their signings. The assistant in the office said that upon inheriting the HMV/Sahibin Sesi catalog, they discovered that they now held the rights to these recordings and had just decided to bring them out on CD without having much of an idea what their market would be. The CD market in musical nostalgia was not at that point well understood. The assistant at Coşkun told me that the company had apparently been amazed by how well the CDs had sold.

40. This progression implies not so much a tonic-dominant movement (in D minor, as it were) as a IV–I move within Turkish (and broader Mediterranean) conventions of harmonizing a *hicaz* on A (see Manuel 1986).

which a single-line monophonic texture prevails. In both regards—the size and constitution of the orchestra, and the opening harmonic gesture—the performance declares itself as *arabesk* to anybody familiar with the basic conventions of the genre, and also to more finely tuned minds already familiar with S-Müzik's lavish productions of the immediately preceding years. Ersoy's version of this song strikes an immediate contrast with the one recorded by Münir Nurettin, who rarely harmonized or added counterpoint to his own music despite that being a constant preoccupation of the mid-century musical intelligentsia, and despite his own efforts to portray himself as a modernist. Münir Nurettin also generally preferred a small chamber group behind him, while others in the classical musical world were making efforts to "grow" the art music ensemble to orchestral proportions.[41] In these two ways he was for the most part a traditionalist. In the opening two musical strokes of Ersoy's version, then, the listener is firmly extracted from Münir Nurettin's sound world and located in the *arabesk*-saturated musical textures of popular art music.

The opening instrumental theme is underway in the third measure, and the listener is struck by another distinction: a slowness or even a heaviness of pace. The string articulations are pointed, as in *arabesk,* picking out details that flow swiftly by in the Münir Nurettin recording, such as the staccato triplets of the "lullaby." This slowness of pace is bound up with a significantly different vocal aesthetic. Where Münir Nurettin could shape whole poetic phrases in one breath, Ersoy stops for breath between individual words. It also involves splitting up consonants: *"baktım"* in Münir Nurettin's version becomes *"bak-ı-dım"* in Ersoy's. Individual notes in phrases stand out for particular dramatic treatment: the high C of the *meyan* (on the poetically meaningless final syllable of *"görülür"*), an emphatic glissando on the F–G sharp of the middle syllable of *"dünyada"* that immediately follows. Where Münir Nurettin shapes entire poetic phrases, Ersoy shapes isolated musical elements. Classicists find Ersoy mannered and her emotionality affected, exaggerated. But this is *arabesk*. What is exaggerated, affected, and lacking in literary sensibility in Ersoy's performance for some is, quite simply, "meaningful" (*manalı*) and "significant" (*ifadeli*) for those attuned to the vocal aesthetics of *arabesk*. So we are being asked to listen to something "classical," an act of homage to the art music tradition of the mid-twentieth century. But much of what we are hearing in the performance locates it unambiguously in the world of *arabesk*: affective voice, lavish strings, and a slightly heavy tempo.

---

41. Hüseyin Sadettin Arel, for instance, was heavily invested in the idea of producing a Turkish art-music symphony orchestra. See (for a critical view) Behar 1993, particularly pp. 126–34.

The slowing down of the overall tempo and the focusing on note-level details to ornament and nuance has another important effect: it reduces the metrical ambivalence of the Münir Nurettin recording. It is significantly more difficult to hold both the duple meter of the "lullaby" and the triple meter of the song proper in mind when the song is slowed down. If one is unable to do this, the impact of this rather significant ambiguity is minimized, if noticeable at all. The Ersoy version also has percussionists playing *bendir* and *zilli def* (a large frame drum and tambourine) rather than the *darbuka* common to *arabesk*—a move possibly intended to lend gravitas to the proceedings. These spell out an unambiguous triple meter *usûl* (*düm tek teka*) throughout.

The Münir Nurettin version has no percussion at all. One is therefore obliged, in the Ersoy version, to hear the implied duple of the "lullaby" against the triple meter as a metrical dissonance—in Krebs's terms a "type A" metrical dissonance (Krebs 1987). The supple ambiguity of the Münir Nurettin version, in which duple and triple succeed one another sequentially with the former complicating the latter, disappears. There are other consequences to this "spelling out" of the meter by percussion instruments in Ersoy's version: the flexibility and pauses that were littered throughout the Münir Nurettin version disappear. Where Münir Nurettin pauses for an undefined moment for effect, the orchestra in the Ersoy version simply adds a beat. Thus the rubato in the Münir Nurettin version, that accompanies the "longest and sweetest dream" to specific literary effect, also disappears. In short, the Ersoy version lacks the dreamy quality of the Münir Nurettin version's *meyan* (central section)—a quality that, as we have seen, subtly engages the ambiguities and backward glances of *imtidad* in Yahya Kemal's poetry.

Finally, there is a dramatic addition. The "call to prayer" follows the basic pattern of the Münir Nurettin version but adds a third voice: a muezzin's call to prayer, containing the words, intonation, and vocal techniques heard five times a day from all of the city's mosques. This recurs at the closing repeat in the original song, and a fragment is also heard in the background with the closing orchestral cadence. As the call to prayer is heard in the acoustic background, we hear in the foreground a warm, sensual, and individualized voice instantly recognizable as that of Ersoy, whose sigh on the C sharp of the "call to prayer" figure speaks very much of worldly, present-tense desires and erotic needs. This sigh is instantly locatable in the expressive universe of *arabesk,* but it is entirely unthinkable in that of Münir Nurettin. The call to prayer tails into the female chorus "echo," whose role is similar to that of the female chorus in the Münir Nurettin version, though now it seemingly responds to two voices rather than just one. To add to the complexity, and to the minor scandal associated with the recording (see below), it became known rather quickly that Ersoy had sung this muezzin part herself. The use of studio multitracking to "split" her voice in two thus has a technological aspect which further locates it in the sound world of *arabesk* while distancing it from that of the mid-century concert stage and the "live" aesthetics of Münir Nurettin's vocal style.

The Ersoy performance transforms "Aziz İstanbul" significantly from the Münir Nurettin version. As we have seen, these transformations involve a process of rhythmic and metrical regulation in which the supple ambiguities of the Münir Nurettin original are ironed out. It also involves various processes of fragmentation, musically speaking. The literary text is broken up as a literary object. The units of vocal interpretation are not so much lines, sentences, and paragraphs but morphemes and syllables, located and embellished by the singer in the context of the sound space of the music rather than in the literary effect of the poem. And the voice itself is split through the basic studio process of multitracking. Three contrasting "call to prayer" voices are heard either simultaneously or in quick succession: an emotion-laden and highly eroticized solo voice (Bülent the transsexual *arabesk* star), the solo voice of the "call to prayer" (Bülent as muezzin), and the collective and reflective voice of women (the female chorus). These two processes—rhythmic and metrical regulation and vocal fragmentation—might be considered as two facets of a general processes of "arabeskization."

## "Aziz İstanbul": Timur Selçuk's Version on *Babamın Şarkıları*

Timur Selçuk, Münir Nurettin's son, was born in 1946. He moved to Paris in 1964, where he attended the École Normal de Musique. After his graduation he immersed himself in the French world of professional pop music making.[42] In 1972 he returned to Turkey,[43] set up bands and orchestras,[44] and

---

42. Towards the end of Ersoy's stay in Paris, though, he was rekindling his connections with Turkish professional music worlds. An article in *Hey* 9 February 1972, p. 18, reports on his first recording in Turkey, "Kara sevda"/"Duyar mısın"—a piece evidently in a rock/pop idiom with many Turkish folk and classical music additions to the standard rock/pop band (including saz, *ney*, and *kemençe*). This must have been some months before his "official" return. After graduation he was working in Paris as composer, vocalist, and arranger for Barclay, Pathé-Marconi and Philips. Interview 12 September 2008.

43. Ahmet Kılıç reported on his return in *Hey* (Kılıç 1972a). Timur Selçuk rowed out onto the Sea of Marmara from Caddebostan and surveyed the scene in poetic terms. "*Ey gözünü sevdiğin memleket. Bu zevk-ü şefa nerde var?*" (O beloved homeland. Where (else) is this beauteous repose to be found?)

44. According to Kılıç (1972b), the lineup of his first band was: Hayati Sünnetçiler on drums, Yaz Baltacıgil on bass, Mehmet Duru on guitar, Saim Gökyılmaz on organ and Selim Selçuk, his brother, on percussion.

established a reputation as a conductor and arranger—a process that was to culminate in his conspicuous involvement in the Eurovision song contest later in the 1970s.[45] In 1977 he founded the Istanbul Chamber Orchestra and the Contemporary Music Center in Cihangir, close to Taksim Square in Istanbul. He also began to make a name for himself in Turkey as a composer and singer of his own settings of republican-era poetry by Orhan Veli, Nazım Hikmet, and Mustafa Faruk Çamlıbel. He composed film music and released albums throughout the 1980s.

After his return, Timur Selçuk turned slowly but decisively to the modernization of the Turkish art music tradition. His father had not gone out of his way to teach him.[46] He observed his father's music-making quietly from a distance, he told me.[47] He taught himself Turkish art music theory while studying at Paris, having persuaded his conservatory professor to allow him to write on that subject to satisfy a curriculum requirement. Timur's relationship with Turkish art music has always had this somewhat distanced quality. His embrace of his father's repertory on *Babamın şarkıları* in 2003 marked perhaps his most conspicuous and intense engagement with that musical heritage. It was a major project. *Babamın şarkıları* was performed in New York in the spring of 2006,[48] and a few months later in the Açıkhava Tiyatrosu in Istanbul. Emel Sayın, a well-known art music vocalist who had herself performed with Münir Nurettin as a member of his chorus, was the soloist.[49]

Timur Selçuk's assumption of the role of protector, defender, and promoter of his father's music coincided with his political transformation from young socialist to religious-nationalist, albeit of a complex and idiosyncratic kind. In 1976, shortly after his return to Turkey, he announced that he had

---

45. Timur Selçuk conducted the 1975 Turkish entry in the Eurovision competition. His rising stock in the world of conducting and arranging can be sensed in the claim that in the TRT's "Light Music" competition earlier that year, of the bill of one million Turkish liras footed by the TRT for the entire competition, Timur Selçuk was reputed to have been paid 20,000 Turkish liras (see note in *Hey* 29 January 1975, p. 3).

46. His father's birthday celebrations were held in the Fitaş cinema in Istanbul in January 1974, according to a brief note in *Hey* 16 January 1974, p. 15. One of his first engagements upon his return was to join his father, together with his brother Selim, at the Moda Deniz Klübü (Kılıç 1972a). But the father's cultivation of his son's musical career does not seem to have been particularly consistent or devoid of complication. In conversation, this struck me as being a difficult topic for Timur Selçuk.

47. Interview 12 September 2008.

48. Timur Selçuk put on a concert based on *Babamın şarkıları* at the Kaufman Center in New York City on 16 April 2006.

49. I went to this very well-attended concert on 28 August 2006. It marked the twenty-fifth anniversary of Münir Nurettin's death.

decided to embrace "his worker, his villager, the soil" (*isçime, köylüme, toprağa*), revolutionary struggle, and the radical poetry of Nazım Hikmet and Ahmet Arif.[50] In 2006 he announced to a large crowd at the Açıkhava Tiyatrosu (and to significant applause) that "we [Turks] are to treasure our two sources [*kaynak*-s]: our worldly [*dünyevi*] Mustafa [Kemal Atatürk] and our spiritual [*ilahi*] Mustafa [i.e., the prophet Mohammad]." The more Timur Selçuk was attacked by the leftist intelligentsia, the more vociferously he insisted on the compatibility of his nationalism, his religion, and his socialism.[51] This, then, constitutes the broader context of *Babamın Şarkıları* and his version of "Aziz İstanbul."

The language with which Timur introduces the song in the accompanying CD booklet is striking, and worth quoting in full:

> Lower voices smelling of earth, sky-blue upper voices, a broad acoustic space, the flavor of a hymn (*ilahi*) decorated by the *bendir* (large frame drum) and the chorus, the mixture of lullaby and call to prayer. . . . "Aziz İstanbul," in other words. Low down the strings, fertile soil; up on top the woodwinds, the nurturing sun; the brass in the middle and traditional instruments constituting the backbone of the ensemble. At the end, like a strong call to prayer from a minaret, an utterance of praise (*hamdediş*) on the *Tizneva* (top D) axis. Then, to Istanbul, to him who created it, a *Tizacem* (top F) and a *Tizhüseynî* (top E). I don't know. Do I really need to say more about this piece, which I have tried to sing with a voice that has seen a bit of life [*yaşamış bir sesle*]? (Selçuk 2003, p. 14)

For the recording, Timur Selçuk imagines the acoustic space of the song in spatial terms and puts rich orchestral textures at the service of the poetry. The orchestra is quite large, using the resources of the Istanbul Chamber Orchestra and a traditional art music ensemble—bass *kemençe* (short-necked bowed bass lute), *kemençe* (short-necked bowed lute), oud, *kanun, ney*, and *tanbur*—drawn from Istanbul conservatory circles. But Timur uses it sparingly. The art music ensemble plays the melody and is clearly audible

---

50. See Türk 1976b, an interview with Selçuk in Izmir printed in *Hey* 5 July 1976, p. 26.

51. I am grateful to Cihangir Gündoğdu for alerting me to a short article in *Ekşi Sözlük* (an online subcultural encyclopedia) that details an exchange with singer Gökhan Tepe on late-night television around the year 2000. Timur Selçuk had just declared his utter contempt for Tepe's version of one of his father's songs, "Dönülmez bir akşamın ufkundayım." Tepe recalls Selçuk expressing his objections in an angry phone call that was broadcast live. True or not, the anecdote says something about the rather negative ways in which Timur Selçuk's nettled response to "unauthorized" versions of his father's songs was being registered by some sections of the Turkish intelligentsia. See also note 59 below.

throughout, accompanying the voice in a more or less traditional heterophonic style. The orchestration is sparse and in the background. It holds drones, hints occasionally at harmonic movement, and colors individual lines. So at the line, "Has lived, I say, in the sweetest and longest of dreams," the strings and brass suddenly melt away. Pointed woodwinds, flutes to the fore, color the line. To employ his own metaphors, the poet has suddenly left the "ground" constituted by the strings, and seems to be floating in air and sunlight.

The lack of drums or percussion permits Timur the kind of rhythmic flexibility and metrical ambiguity that characterized his father's recorded version. The pauses are rendered in a similar way, as is the extensive rubato of the dream sequence. Instruments follow the voice closely. Vocally, Timur Selçuk follows in his father's footsteps, observing the phrasing and microtonal inflections of the version rereleased in 1989, and seeming to bear out his own advice to those who would sing his father's songs: that if they wish to be faithful to his legacy, they should listen closely to the recordings rather than relying on memory and notation. In the *meyan* (middle section), though, a different voice sounds momentarily. Timur Selçuk doesn't possess his father's effortless high register and relies instead on a burst of energy to make the upper octave, necessitating gulps of breath between the words. The father's bel canto style gives way momentarily to the son's pop vocal aesthetic, and to a sense of words being reached for rather than caressed. The generational shift is briefly registered.

The introduction of a harmonic and contrapuntal language constitutes the major departure in Timur Selçuk's version. Münir Nurettin's career had spanned decades of intense argument about the application of Western harmonic and contrapuntal technique to Turkish music. Were these techniques to be applied to art music or folk music? Were musicians to prefer quartal harmony (held by some to be in tune with "natural principles" of indigenous performance practice) or triads? Were these techniques to be developed with Turkish or Western instruments in mind? Were they to be rejected in their totality or embraced in their totality?[52] Münir Nurettin had ducked and woven his way through these polemics, only occasionally introducing contrapuntal elements. Otherwise had he asserted his musical modernism relatively unobtrusively. He had chosen literary poetry, sung in concert halls, and avoided nightclubs; he had inhabited the rationalized and systematized *makam* world of the Turkish radio ensembles at that time. The music he recorded throughout his life had been conceived predominantly in

---

52. See Stokes 1992, chapter 2, for a discussion of these debates.

a monophonic idiom. Timur Selçuk's version of "Aziz İstanbul" is, by contrast, resolutely polyphonic and harmonic. In the first two notes he seems to have Bülent Ersoy's version in mind, as though intent on erasing it from the public memory. Ersoy renders the opening descending fourth as an unambiguous movement from tonic to dominant; the following passage reverts to a monophonic texture devoid of harmony. Timur Selçuk does exactly the opposite, leaving the descending fourth harmonically unassigned as a bare unison; the passage that follows is harmonized.

Timur Selçuk's harmonic language in this song is subtle and ambiguous. Strong A pedal notes alternate with a pedal G, as though at random and out of step with the obvious harmonic implications of the tune. In the inner voices, ii–IV movements are emphasized at the expense of dominants and tonics, resisting closure and the harmonic chunking of phrases (common when harmony is added to much Turkish popular music by background keyboards and bass). Simple triads with thirds and fifths are avoided systematically. As Timur put it to me in interview, he extends and anticipates the *karar, güçlü,* and *yeden* of the *makam* (the "tonic," "dominant," and "leading note," to make a crude comparison with Western tonal practice) as pedal notes, often adding fourths and fifths above and below them. These constitute a "safety net" (*güvence*)—a matter, as he put it, of knowing where "home" is, modally speaking. But at the same time, one must avoid "extreme nationalism" (*aşırı milliyetçilik*)—in other words, emphatic and overly obvious use of these pedal notes at phrase endings.[53] Timur's harmonic techniques might be seen as an extension into the harmonic process of the metrical ambiguities of his father's version of the song. At the same time, these techniques exert a gravitational force on the melodic line: the altered A major chords that tend to cluster around the "tonic" of the *makam* are both points of repose and potentially dominants implying movement toward a tonic D which rarely materializes, least of all at the conclusion. Traditions of harmonizing *makam* in the Mediterranean area are well established, internalized, and widespread, as Manuel showed some time ago (Manuel 1989)—but they are also ambiguous, putting contradictory gravitational fields into play. Harmonization

---

53. It is worth mentioning here Timur's comments to me in interview (12 September 2008) about his compositional process. He said he composed first in the head and then, with pencil and manuscript paper, whose smell he found comforting and productive. Next he would write up a version of the piece for two pianos, at which stage he would add corrections and make changes (he is a very proficient pianist). Then he would write it up in Finale on the computer, hearing it first with piano sound. Then came the orchestration. This process would seem to allow for the prioritization of modal form, melodic line, and memory of his father's original version—and would also allow him to work outwards, with harmonization, as an abstract process, followed by orchestration.

significantly complicates the way one hears *makam* phrases, and the harmonization of "Aziz İstanbul" relocates it in a musical universe that in some ways is as alien to the original as was Bülent Ersoy's *arabesk* version.

Timur Selçuk himself had much to say on the topic. In the essay mentioned above (Selçuk 2003), in conversation with me, and in the talk that accompanies his concert performances, he argues for a "dervish-like" attitude towards musical modernization—one that puts aside arrogant convictions regarding methods and techniques.[54] Instead, he says, the musical progressive needs to commit himself or herself to the traditional moral virtues of art music practice: respect for tradition and the intimate social bonds (the *usta-çırak*, master-apprentice relationships) that animate it. He declares that he is a modernizer and a modernist, and that one needs to render a monophonic tradition in a contemporary polyphonic idiom. And yet "national heritage," here meaning art music instruments and the *makam* tradition, must be preserved "as long as this nation exists." He prefers to think of polyphonic techniques as "a carpet," something "upon which one can walk around," rather than as a set of tools that will inexorably destroy the key virtues of *makam*-based music. He concludes his advocacy of a less doctrinaire modernism, sensitive to the moral virtues of the tradition, with some thoughts about his father. He says that his father's heritage has caused him suffering; irresponsible singers have traduced Münir Nurettin's songs "in a *meyhane* style" (i.e., in a style suited to bars and nightclubs) even while outwardly respecting the notated versions and sometimes even claiming his personal authority. Memory, says Timur, is a false friend. He relies therefore on his father's *recordings*, rather than the notations, which could be full of mistakes. And as a secondary source he uses his father's own markings on these manuscripts, in which nuances of *makam* modulation were noted.

Timur Selçuk's version of "Aziz İstanbul" has two aims. One is to reclaim and extend his father's populist modernism, which is based on *makam*, the republican literary heritage, and popular song practice. Harmony and counterpoint are thus to be added, but with sensitivity to the modal properties of *makam*, and only as an accompaniment to the voice and the poetry. The other aim is to erase from his father's recordings the grubby and distorting marks of the market and *meyhane* culture as well as the modern processes of transmission (particularly notation). Bülent Ersoy may or may not have

---

54. As he put it to me in interview (12 September 2008), unlike Western art music (where Beethoven, for instance, is a "*kule*"—a "tower"), Turkish art music is "a small house, with a garden, some trees, a cat and a dog. . . ." At all stages the monumentalization associated with Western art music is to be rejected, and appropriately scaled—one might say "intimate"—alternatives sought instead. Interview, 12 September 2008.

been on Timur's mind, but the project is explicitly a corrective move and a counterproposition.

In this chapter so far, I have tried to lay out the ways in which the recordings of "Aziz İstanbul" by Bülent Ersoy and Timur Selçuk might be understood as being "in conversation" with the original Münir Nurettin recording and with one another. In the absence of a developed musicological language for talking about differences between recordings and performances,[55] and with the added complication of describing a musical and poetic tradition that may not be familiar to all readers, the previous section may have been slow going. I have tried, though, to contextualize them very briefly and stick to observable and audible differences as they would be experienced and understood by a musically literate listener in Turkey. To summarize, the differences in question involve rhythm and meter (ambiguous or nonambiguous); vocal style (literary or musical); forms of harmony and counterpoint (triadic or modal); derivation from sources (notated, recorded, oral tradition); "liveness" versus studio production; and embodiment versus fragmentation of voice, orchestration, and instrumental accompaniment.

## Conversation and Circulation

I have described these different versions as being "in conversation." I should qualify this metaphor immediately since the conversation in question, if that is indeed the right term, is an acrimonious one. As we saw in the case of Zeki Müren, prominent professional musicians would sometimes make a point of avoiding one another's repertoire and scaring others off their own. But classics have in fact been recorded and rerecorded since the Turkish recording industry began. The metaphor of conversation is entirely appropriate here, with different vocalists presenting their takes on a given piece, responding to each other's versions, and contributing to an ongoing dialogue. In the circulation of a single song various performance traditions, chains of stylistic authority, recordings, and notations merge and separate. Within Turkish art music communities the process takes place unobtrusively for the most part, without much verbal commentary. In the case of the versions of the Münir Nurettin classic being discussed here, however, the process is quite different: the "conversation" seems to be not only between generations but across genres, and thus between competing and antagonistic conceptions of music.

---

55. Cook's work (1998, 1999) in bringing performance theory to bear on musicology is already changing this situation.

Bülent Ersoy's version of "Aziz İstanbul" caused a minor flurry of public anxiety when it was released. I would often hear that the cassette had caused outrage amongst Islamists for its overly explicit reference to the call to prayer and for its gender-problematic eroticization. I never actually heard any direct evidence of this alleged outrage. Islamist anger is no longer aimed at figures such as Ersoy; it goes much deeper than anything her modestly selling cassette was capable of evoking.[56] If there was outrage over Ersoy, my impression was that it was located more on the secular left than on the Islamist right. For those on the left, Ersoy and all she represented were perhaps entirely beyond redemption, but her recording of "Aziz İstanbul" did confirm the deeply held conviction on the part of many that *arabesk*'s proletarian consumer culture was linked at some level with the Islamist takeover of the city. The checks, balances, and redistributive mechanisms of the nation-state were being dismantled in the name of a liberal and populist Islam. Complex and unstable desires were being unleashed. Ersoy's "Aziz İstanbul" illustrated the problem exactly.

Timur Selçuk's version of "Aziz İstanbul" also generated angry polemic, but Timur seems to have initiated most of it himself. A current of frustration, even rage, was in evidence in the "social postscript" (*sosyal hamis*) included in the CD booklet. Timur described "*sıkıntılı günler*" (tough days) of political apathy and ignorance, American domination, a consumer economy neglecting production, an irreversible split between secularists and Islamists, and conflict in the Kurdish southeast of the country. He called for a new nationalist movement to echo the first *Kuvay-ı Milli* (the name given to Atatürk's national struggle). At the time Timur was writing this piece (24 February 2003), the Bush administration's proposal to stage an assault on Iraq from Turkish territory was being vehemently rejected by both left and right in Turkey. Yet even this brief moment of national unity gave him few grounds for optimism. The first *Kuvay-ı Milli* was a moment of genuine national crisis, he suggested—one that hardly compared with today's "tragicomedy."

These angry thoughts in the "social postscript" eventually led in a musical direction. For Timur Selçuk, the first steps in becoming a modern, "civilized" (*uygar*), and democratic intellectual were to support freedoms of thought, expression, belief, and association. The last step of the journey was

---

56. The opening "call to prayer" figure of the Bülent Ersoy version was sampled, after all, by the radical Islamist rappers Sert Müslümanlar (Tough Muslims) in "Allahu ekber bizlere güç ver" ("God is great; give us strength") on *Ay yıldız yıkılmıyacak* (The star and crescent will never be destroyed), released in 2000 (Solomon 2006). The sampling does not seem to have been intended as ironic. I am grateful to Tom Solomon for pointing this out to me.

to understand music, without which the process of becoming modern, civilized, and democratic would always be incomplete. He called for an effective education system that would pass Turkish folk and classical music to the next generation. He called for commissions for opera and symphonic composers. He asked for music festivals to be reoriented towards the needs of young Turkish musicians, not simply to provide a stage for foreign stars. He stated that corporations should fund orchestras and make sure good editions of the modern classics of the early republican era circulated.[57] Music modernized in this way would secure the national virtues of the nation (*ulus*) and guide it towards "the universal" (*evrensel*). Without this firm moral handrail, the nation would be led "inexorably" to Hiroshima and Nagasaki.

The language was hyperbolic and emotional. The precariousness of Timur's self-fashioning as a "Muslim socialist" may well have induced anxiety, especially in the light of the public criticism he was receiving from the intelligentsia, his former fan base.[58] Unauthorized versions of his father's songs also may have been causing him more and more frustration.[59] Timur had reached a point in life at which musicians become concerned about posterity. Even with these considerations in mind, the language of the "social postcript" was excessive. The processes by which "Aziz İstanbul" circulated amongst musicians were not unobtrusive or taken for granted, as had been the case with the circulation of songs in an earlier generation. They were, by contrast, accompanied by polemic and public anxiety.

This might in part be understood as a case of schizophonic mimesis—the turbulent process in which copies generate copies (Feld 1996). Intricate social protocols and mechanisms of circulation established earlier in the cen-

---

57. Scores of the music of Adnan Saygun, Ferit Alnar, Cemal Reşit Rey, and many other Turkish composers in the Western art-music tradition from the early to mid-twentieth century—the people Timur Selçuk has in mind here—are generally impossible to find outside the country and very hard to find within it.

58. Note, for instance, Dilmener's comment, in his *Eleştirmenin günlüğü* (Critic's journal): "I wrote the Timur Selçuk article I had long wanted to write earlier and always postponed thinking I would have difficulty holding myself back [*çenemi tutamam diye*], [but] I was frightened by what might spring to mind, that I might say too much. The words he said to Emel Armutçu—'I have said my daily prayers since middle school, but back then I never felt the need to say so'—wounded me deeply [*beni derinden yaraladı*]. I felt he had been deceiving me. Had he said this back then, I found myself thinking, I wouldn't have involved myself so intensely with most Timur Selçuk songs, I wouldn't have based entire moments of my life on the things he said, I wouldn't have gone to a single concert. . . ." (Dilmener 2006, pp. 9–10). Dilmener, whose general outlook is secularist, finds his nostalgia for Selçuk's songs deeply compromised by Selçuk's later statements about his religious belief.

59. Gökhan Tepe was the singer whose performance of Münir Nurettin's "Dönülmez bir akşamın ufkundayım" caused the enraged response quoted in the *Ekşi sözlük* above. See footnote 51.

tury had been disrupted not by the recording industry per se,[60] but by the recording industry in its post-1980s cassette-culture form. Cover versions proliferated across previously inviolable stylistic and generic boundaries, and seemed to have lost their moorings in the increasingly shadowy notion of "originals." Who could now say what was *arabesk,* art music, folk music, rock, or pop? How were the new processes of musical circulation evidenced by "Aziz İstanbul" to be understood? There were no easy answers to these questions. Instead, a discourse about copying, versions, and appropriations seemed to grapple with the idea of fragmentation and competing claims to musical authenticity.

But I would suggest that there was also another dynamic at play concerning the subject of this particular song, the melancholic wanderer lost in poetic contemplation of a view of the city. I will argue that a significant but until recently rather inchoate struggle has been taking place over this figure since 1996. The terms of this struggle are constituted by questions about who this wanderer is, what relations of intimacy and desire are implied in his or her gaze, and what exactly he or she is looking at. It has involved rather deliberate efforts by the city's new managers to co-opt this figure and secure its meanings within the new regime of intimacy and urban civility accompanying neoliberal transformation. It has also involved complex forms of accommodation or resistance on the part of both popular classes and the intelligentsia. The turbulent circulation of "Aziz İstanbul" in recent decades has intersected and interacted with these processes in particular ways.

### Music as a Way of Seeing: The Views from Çamlıca

First, who in the 1990s is doing the viewing, what is the viewpoint, and what is being viewed? Most people I know firmly associate the viewpoint of "Aziz İstanbul" with Çamlıca, which has been a park since 1867—a place of fresh air and wonderful views of the city. In late Ottoman times Çamlıca was a place where palace and administrative society maintained villas and artistic circles. The beautiful view, the elegant houses, the sounds of nature, and the famous fountain had long been celebrated by the Ottoman literati.[61] Many

---

60. But see chapter 4 on Zeki Müren, recordings, and the disruption of chains of stylistic authority transmitted by *meşk.*

61. The fountain broke in 1837. Its literary celebrants include Namık Kemal, Sezai Bey, and others. See Giz 1969, who also mentions that the area was predominantly inhabited by Armenians and was the site of an important Bektaşi *tekke* (lodge). Belge discusses parks (including Çamlıca) in popular culture as public transport made movement about and beyond the city a possibility for the new middle classes of the late nineteenth century (Belge 1983a).

**Figure 5c.** Enjoying the view from Çamlıca. Photograph by the author.

consider the "golden years" of Çamlıca to have been the middle years of the nineteenth century, before it was opened as a public park (see, for instance, Giz 1969). It was the building and then the asphalt surfacing of Alemdağı Street (which takes one from the quay at Üsküdar to the foot of the hill) soon after the park was established that really opened it up to the public, finally bringing it within reach of ordinary city dwellers. Çamlıca became famous for its *incesaz* (small art music) orchestras and its open-air theaters. Today it remains a site of popular rather than elite pleasures, easily accessible by public transport, and a place to stroll, eat ice creams, enjoy the gardens, and visit the Turkish Automobile Association's restoration of the elegant Ottoman *köşk* in the grounds of the public park.[62]

For many, though, the character of this park, its view, and the viewers had begun to change in the mid-1990s. I'll start with a personal anecdote. In the summer of 1996 I was teaching at Boğaziçi. My wife, Lucy, and our children, then very young, met up at Çamlıca with İbrahim, a long-standing friend, and his wife, Gülşen, who was then expecting their second child. I

---

62. On the association of the Automobile and Touring Association and the Metropolitan Municipality in restoring Ottoman monuments in public parks, see the official website (http://www.turing.org.tr/tr/tarihcemiz.asp.

had often been to Çamlıca but never with İbrahim. It was a beautiful day and we were eating ice cream, admiring the view, and enjoying a Yahya Kemal–esque moment of peace, quiet, and reflection on the routes that had bought us all here. İbrahim pointed out to me all the places he had lived, and told me that he would often come up here to think about his life, tracing his progress from one neighborhood to another in the city he could see spread out below him like a map.

As the afternoon progressed, the park seemed to fill up with people, most of whom were local folk. Gülşen seemed to be the only person not wearing the Islamist regalia for women fashionable at the time, a fact rendered all the more conspicuous by her advanced state of pregnancy. In recent years Çamlıca had become an Islamist stronghold. Disapproving glances were exchanged. A mood of irritability descended on Gülşen and İbrahim. What was happening to this city? Where had these people come from? Why were they so sure of themselves and their moral superiority? Was this really what our faith required of us? Why were we being made to feel so uncomfortable and unwelcome? Did our faith really endorse this kind of ostentation and belittling of others? A shadow had fallen over the scene. As we later made our way back to their car, my friends suddenly became dispirited and uncommunicative. For İbrahim and Gülşen, what was on display was the future, not the past—the one their children were to grow up into and inhabit. An orderly love affair with the past, and indeed with the city itself, seemed increasingly less possible to couples like them. The view had changed. How had things ended up this way? And where could they possibly go from here?

In step with such middle-class, secular-left anxieties, literati and intellectuals began a project of reimagining the view of the city. If the Islamists were now bent on rendering the city as an Ottoman cosmopolis, as a silhouette to be viewed from a safe distance, a different kind of new Istanbul was beginning to emerge in highbrow literary and Western-inspired popular culture. Writer Orhan Pamuk, for instance, imagined the "day the Bosphorus dried up"—perhaps one of the most celebrated passages in his 1995 novel *Kara kitab* (The black book), in which the shifting of tectonic plates drains the Black Sea and the Mediterranean and the city's historical and material subconscious, the unwanted detritus of millennia, is exposed for all to see at the bottom of the Bosphorus. Pamuk's Istanbul is dark, baroque, and multilayered. The protagonists of his novels are haunted by the fear of surveillance and are constantly on the run. His recent collection of memoirs and essays on the city, *İstanbul: Memories and the City* (Pamuk 2005) describes his obsessive, sexually charged, and invariably unsuccessful efforts to *paint* the city, to recapture the visual omnipotence that European artists of the colonial era seemed to claim.⁶³

For the secular left, calm visual contemplation of the city—the project of the city's Islamists—was now out of the question. These radical reimaginings were based on a nostalgic sense of disappointment, on the idea of a once-beautiful view now ruined. But they were also based on a sense of struggle with Islamists and the Metropolitan Municipality, over the very idea of Istanbul as an object of visual cathexis. If the Islamists and the Metropolitan Municipality imagined the new urbanite as the infantilized cartoon character of the *Istanbul Bülteni* mentioned above, Orhan Pamuk's melancholic wanderer either struggles and fails to objectify the city in his gaze (as in Pamuk's Istanbul memoir) or imagines views which expose everything that has been repressed in the dominant public history of the city (lying hidden at the bottom of the Bosphorus).

These concerns were shared by popular nostalgists. Sadun Aksüt introduces his transcription of "Aziz İstanbul" in a book of songs of the city with these words: "Just have our master Yahya Kemal look at the Golden Horn from the Galata Tower today.... I wonder if he would be able to see this vision of blue. Would he be able to see clean water like this? No way [*Nerdeee*].... Loving the Golden Horn now? Worth a whole life? How can one love the poor old Golden Horn now? If you want to lose yourself in your daydreams on top of the Galata Tower, you have to look out into the distance, to the open Marmara Sea...." (Aksüt 1994, p. 34).

The kind of love for the city described by Yahya Kemal seems to be out of the question these days, at least for Aksüt. The best one can do, he suggests, is to avert one's eyes and exercise one's imagination, thinking of the old songs. And these words were written many years after the initiation of Bedrettin Dalan's Golden Horn restoration project. At that point one could have been forgiven for thinking of the project as an enormously expensive

---

63. Possibly with Yahya Kemal's uxorious gaze in mind, Pamuk describes the difficulties. "Painting allowed me to enter the scene on the canvas. This was a new way into the second world of my imagination, and when I had penetrated the most "beautiful" part of that world—when the painting was all but done—a strange ecstasy would overtake me.... The joy I felt upon finishing a painting was so great that I wanted to touch it, pick out some detail to embrace, even take it into my mouth, bite it, eat it. If something got in the way of this fantasy, if I did not quite lose myself in my painting, if (as happened more and more often) the first world intruded to ruin my childish game, I'd be overcome by an urge to masturbate" (Pamuk 2004, p. 267). As in "Aziz İstanbul," the gazed-upon city is heavily cathected and sexualized, though here the process of gazing is imagined, in postcolonial hindsight, as problematic.

mistake only benefiting contractors and a corrupt municipality.[64] Cynicism about Islamist ambitions to reimagine the city's visual impact was running deep. It would seem that the more one looked at the city in the mid-1990s, the more one just saw a filthy mess.

For critics on the left and popular nostalgists alike, viewing the city now seemed to involve complex and unaccountable pleasures and currents of desire. The melancholy wanderer of the Yahya Kemal poem was a figure of privilege. He had leisure, time to spare and an education to locate and appreciate what he was looking at. He was able to avoid the crowds and enjoy his solitude. And he was male. His viewing of the city was imagined in gendered and sexualized terms, securely embedded in an orderly and modern heterosexual narrative. This scenario seemed remote from Çamlıca in the mid-1990s when the place was full of people, most of them poor and relatively uneducated. Without a proper understanding of Turkish history, people like İbrahim and Gülşen would have wondered what pleasures these people could really derive from the view. And what pleasures, in relation to this view or indeed anything else, could people who so emphatically rejected Turkish republican ideals of modern companionate marriage possibly entertain? My friends were clearly surrounded by people enjoying themselves that afternoon—people just like us, wandering around, taking in the view, chatting, eating ice creams, and enjoying the fresh air. But for İbrahim and Gülşen the pleasures on display amongst these headscarfed and conservatively dressed people were different, rooted in other (problematic) ways of viewing, other (problematic) ways of thinking about love and intimacy, and other (problematic) ways of thinking of themselves as Turks and citizens.

It was in these contexts then—contexts of a newly problematized sense of the city as viewed object, and of a new sensitivity to the circuits of desire in which this act of viewing was embedded—that "Aziz İstanbul" came to constitute a site of struggle and contest. This, I have suggested, was a contest over ways of imagining the city as visual object, of constituting desire in the act of viewing the city, and of constituting urbanity and civility in the act of viewing the city. Though Yahya Kemal's poem and Münir Nurettin

---

64. Bedrettin Dalan, Istanbul's rightist-Islamist mayor during the Özal years, initiated many of the efforts to clean up the city and render it as the object of visual attention described in this chapter. He boasted that he would make the (then appallingly polluted) waters of the Golden Horn "as blue as my eyes." The claim seemed improbable at the time, and it became a cynical byword for managerial hubris. Though it is still too early to assess the costs, social and otherwise, involved, the Metropolitan Municipality's efforts to clean up Istanbul's seashores and waterways have surely been a success. Fish and marine wildlife have returned to the city. The parks that line the shores are now full of people fishing, and the fish are edible. In the mid-1980s there were simply no fish to catch, and the Golden Horn smelled like an open sewer.

Selçuk's version of it have complex histories of circulation and reception in the 1950s, a new kind of struggle over them began in the 1990s. These were years which saw the aggressive neoliberalism of the Özal years produce a succession of Islamist governments, a military coup, an economic collapse, endemic public cynicism, and—by the end of the period in question—a chastened Islamist government espousing an aggressively nationalist politics that had succeeded, in certain areas of debate and discussion, in uniting right and left. Bülent Ersoy's 1995 version captures the twin tug of a nostalgia for Ottoman culture and a turbulent consumerist libertarianism: the dominant cultural script of the neoliberal moment. Timur Selçuk's 2003 version speaks of a moment of anxious retrenchment and a reassertion of national priorities and developmentalist modernism. While Ersoy's version speaks of turbulent currents of desire in a chaotic and sprawling urban environment, Timur's version speaks of a legible love for the city that is once more—but for how long, who can know?—in the service of the nation and modernity.

The complex of melancholy, nostalgia, urban imagining, and struggle for a national modernity described in these pages is hardly unique to Turkey. And yet the broader phenomenon is one that has resisted characterization in historical and social scientific terms. "Sentimentalism" still has a bad name. Efforts to engage the questions raised by emotions in modernity have generally been Western-focused, concerned primarily with literature, and characterized by well-known anxieties about their implication with political authoritarianism. Reflecting on the last four chapters of this book, the last chapter will propose a different perspective.

# 6

## Conclusion

Roland Barthes saw the possibilities of a new kind of social critique taking shape in the effort to "write love." But this "unwarranted discourse" is a lonely and precarious project: "The lover's discourse is today *of an extreme solitude*" (Barthes 1979, p. 1, emphasis in the original). Driven into this social backwater, "it has no recourse but to become a site, however exiguous, of an *affirmation*. That *affirmation* is, in short, the subject of the book which begins here" (Barthes 1979, p. 1). Barthes acknowledges with these words both the possibility and the fragility of a critical engagement with society in such terms. The point with which he begins his book serves well at the conclusion of mine. The *Republic of Love* is intended, first and foremost, as just such an affirmation.

But the terms of this affirmation are somewhat different. Where Barthes sees solitude, I see sociability and collective culture-making. And where Barthes is concerned with reading and writing, I am interested in the play of feeling across a broader social and aesthetic field. I noted in chapter 1 that the key questions surrounding sentimentalism are questions, ultimately, about *distribution* in an economy of affect. For "right feeling" is a zero-sum game; those who have it have it only at the expense of others. So who derides whom for their sentimentalism and wrong feeling? Who draws the lines, across what kinds of spaces, and how? Under what circumstances? When they are tied to other forms of privilege and exploitation, as is so often the case, how are they contested? For what stakes? These are social, historical, and political questions. Neoliberal politics, which displaces issues of social justice and welfare with insistent appeals to right feeling, has ensured that such questions are now globally pressing.[1]

As I have tried to show in this book, such questions gain a sharp focus in a discussion of popular music, where "right" and "wrong" feeling are often sharply distinguished. But there are problems. Since I have been talking about a musical culture that may be unfamiliar to some readers of this book, questions arise about the projection of Euro-American notions of normativity and transgression onto other cultures (where the lines separating "warranted" from "unwarranted" discourse may be hard to determine, and complicated in the postcolonial gaze). In formulating the kinds of questions that shape this book, then, I have had to range widely, drawing on the anthropology of emotion; on a broad critical literature concerning cultural intimacy, the senses, and the public sphere; and on an ethnomusicology engaged with globalization, the voice, and modernity.

My immediate aim in this book has been to find a way of talking about the singular contributions of Zeki Müren, Orhan Gencebay, Sezen Aksu, and those connected with the "Aziz İstanbul" case study to Turkish culture. It is not that they have been neglected by officialdom, scholarship, or popular culture. But the attention paid to these figures has, I have argued, often sanitized them. Müren's homosexuality and his turn to *arabesk* later in life have often been filtered out of contemporary discussion. Gencebay's "Batsın bu dünya" came to stand for a moment of progressive subcultural politics, from which later work has appeared as a kind of retreat. Aksu's diva persona, celebrated in Fatih Akın's film *Crossing the Bridge*, obscures the rather more complex figure she projected in the 1970s and in the aftermath of the 1980 coup. A "debased" "Aziz İstanbul" shores up the aura of Münir Nurettin Selçuk's original—an original that may yet be reclaimed for an authentic Turkish modernism by his son, Timur.

Thus I have not been trying simply to address neglect, fill in gaps, bring cultural figures in from the margins, or make a plea that Müren, Gencebay, and Aksu might finally be taken seriously. Rather, I have attempted to understand these musicians as complex wholes, however elusive their traces in Turkish culture. In particular, I have attempted to take account of the embarrassment they so often induce—an embarrassment that quickly gets

---

1. As many have remarked. I have drawn extensively in this book on Berlant 1998, Berlant 2008, Ellison 1999, Giddens 1992, Herzfeld 1997, Özyürek 2006, and others.

written out of what one might call the "official picture." As Herzfeld has suggested, shared embarrassment affords "rueful self-recognition" (Herzfeld 1997, p. 6) and "an assurance of common sociality" (Herzfeld 1997, p. 3) in societies in which official representations of identity dominate the discursive environment. This book has been an attempt to understand these figures from the theoretical perspective of cultural intimacy. This perspective, I have argued, sheds some light on their ambivalent politics and their complex roles as "ideal citizens."

It has also been an attempt to understand them from the perspective of music. I believe their music making certainly has been neglected and sometimes vilified, even as their broader importance to Turkish culture is being asserted. Müren, as we have seen, is still held directly responsible for the pollution of classical tradition by the *piyasa*, the "market." In Gencebay's case, a progressive politics was sought in lyrics and films, particularly those of the late 1960s and early 1970s; but with few exceptions his evolving sound world after 1980 has been ignored or disparaged. Aksu's diva status and mass-media ubiquity seem to have prohibited serious engagement with her music. For all these artists, the music they make has been central to their complex social effects. I have tried to show in each chapter how their music has engaged and transformed the Turkish sense of nation, citizenship, and place in the world.

At a more general level this book contributes to a growing interest in what Lauren Berlant describes as "sentimentalism's unfinished business" (Berlant 2008).[2] Discredited by romanticism and modernism, the Western culture of sentiment either disappeared from view or was pushed to the ideological margins. But it has persisted as popular culture, where its dissonant registers of affective recognition constitute powerful, if politically ambivalent, claims about intimacy in the public sphere. As is well known, the "fantasy of a common emotional world marked by the historical burden of being harshly treated" (Berlant 2008, p. 10) has been ruthlessly manipulated by the right in recent decades. But this fantasy also quietly maintains a critical everyday sense of social reciprocity, decency, and fairness with which all must reckon. To borrow Berlant's phrase, in this book "the work of critical distance in the context of the reproduction of life focuses on scenes of ordinary survival,

---

2. On sentimentalism I have drawn on Bell 2000, Boltanski 1999, Berlant 2008, Chapman and Hendler 1999, Clark 1991, Giddens 1992, Griswold 1999, Marcus 2002, Mullan 1988, and Noble 2000 in particular. In musicology, thinking about sentimentalism from these kinds of critical angles has been relatively sparse (to the best of my knowledge), though Castelvecchi 1996 and Frith 1996 have been particularly important to me.

not transgression, on disappointment, not refusal, to derive a register of critique" (Berlant 2008, p. 24–25).

Describing Müren, Gencebay, and Aksu as sentimentalists raises some obvious questions. Is Turkish sentimentalism to be understood as an exported (and thus derivative and debased) product of Western modernity? Are cultural differences not at play? Does one risk distorting a Turkish culture of love, affection, and tearfulness by describing it as "sentimentalism?" Conversely, is the idea of sentimentalism weakened when one applies it willy-nilly to any form of dissident public emotionality, in any part of the world, that is deemed somehow at odds with the business of modernity?

This book acknowledges these questions but it also, I hope, resists the easy answers. There is a complex and multidirectional traffic in cultures of love, which are forged in common and coterminous encounters with modernity, as Andrews and Kalpaklı's comparison of early modern Ottoman and English poetry shows (Andrews and Kalpaklı 2005). Despite the historical power and significance of Western cultural forms—a product of the colonial and quasi-colonial relations that have generally pertained between Europe and the Middle East—it would be a mistake to see only one-way traffic. It is certainly important to understand localized understandings of such cultures of love, particularly when they are framed by claims about the nation-state, but it is also important to be able to see them in the context of a regional traffic in emotions, tropes, genres, and styles.

The challenge continues to be one of understanding the historical connections and broader processes of circulation that connect sentimental musical practices in well-studied genres such as tango, banda, conjunto, *kroncong*, country music, *arabesk*, *musica sertaneja,* rembetika, enka, rai, and many others.[3] These genres have been habitually treated as isolates, as specifically national ways of doing emotion. But many are connected, either regionally or by broader flows of technology, migration, and so forth. Joining the dots and attempting this bigger picture might prove worthwhile. We may prove to have more in common than we think, to paraphrase Marshall Berman.[4]

---

3. I refer here in particular to the work of Savigliano (1995), Simonett (2001), Kornhauser (1978), Fox (2004), Rasmussen (1996), Tragaki (2007), Yano (2002), and Schade-Poulsen (1999)—detailed, engaging, and theoretically provocative case studies that seem to move in the direction of a more general account of sentimentalism, though they rarely use that term.

4. The full quote is as follows: "If our years of study have taught us anything, we should be able to reach out further, to look and listen more closely, to see and feel beneath surfaces, to make comparisons over a wider range of space and time, to grasp hidden patterns and forces and connections, in order to show people who look and speak and think and feel differently from each other—who are oblivious to each other, or fearful of each other—that they have more in common than they think. We can contribute visions and ideas that will give people a shock of recognition, recogni-

And, like Berman, we might consider the implications of some of these moves outside our bookish circles. The pleasures and emotional drives of the other (in our midst or just beyond our borders) so often serves as a focus for the rage of social groups that feel their core identities are under threat. "We" may not know exactly what it is that so disturbs us about "them," but the popular cultural signs of their pleasures in life (the smell of their cooking, the exuberance of their football or cricket fans, "that awful wailing they consider music," and so forth) can be relied on by anti-immigrationists and petty nationalists across the world to provoke the most violent and visceral reactions. As technology and migration bring cultures into ever-increasing proximity, the claim that "we have more in common than we think" might become more difficult to make, and the stakes of such assertions may rise.

Gencebay once described *arabesk* as "a shared musical culture . . . a sense of freedom, of autonomy . . . a recognition of everyday life . . . of such ways of knowing the world" (see chapter 3). This might almost work as a general definition of sentimentalism, understood in the lively and non-pejorative sense that I intend here. Gencebay's words point to sentimentalism as a kind of civic project, a way of imagining affable relations of dependence upon strangers in modern society. The shrunken public spaces of late twentieth- and early twenty-first-century city life often appear to offer little room for such thoughts, or make them seem merely compensatory or reactionary. In the nation-states of the Middle East and the fringes of Europe, where the public sphere has often been imagined by techno-political elites exclusively as a space for instruction and discipline (Mitchell 2002), and by neo-orientalists as simply absent, the issue is particularly poignant. But this is not the whole story. At least this is my claim for Turkey since 1950. *The Republic of Love* points to a sustained and consequential imagination of public life in affectionate terms, and to popular music as the vehicle of this imagination.

---

tion of themselves and each other, that will bring their lives together. That is what we can do for solidarity and class consciousness. But we can't do it . . . if we lose contact with what those lives are like. Unless we know how to recognize people as they look and feel and experience the world, we'll never be able to help them recognize themselves or change the world. Reading *Capital* won't help us if we don't also know how to read the signs on the street" (Berman 1999, p. 169).

# Sources

### Bibliography

Abacı, Tahir. 2000. *Yahya Kemal ve Ahmet Hamdi Tanpınar'da müzik.* Istanbul: Pan.
Abbate, Carolyn. 2001. *In Search of Opera.* Princeton, NJ: Princeton University Press.
Abu Lughod, Lila. 2005. *Dramas of Nationhood: The Politics of Television in Egypt.* Chicago: University of Chicago Press.
Adlı, Ayşe. 2005. "Devletin sırtı hâlâ Türk müziğine dönük." *Aksiyon* 572 (http://www.aksiyon.com.tr/detay.php?id=22882, accessed 1 February 2008)
Adorno, Theodor, with the assistance of George Simpson. 2002. "On Popular Music." In *Essays on Music,* selected, with introduction, commentary, and notes, by Richard Leppert. Berkeley: University of California Press.
Ahıska, Meltem, and Zafer Yenal. 2006. *Aradığınız kişiye şu an ulaşılmıyor.* Istanbul: Osmanlı Bankası Arşiv ve Araştırma Merkezi.
Ahmad, Feroz. 1977. *The Turkish Experiment in Democracy, 1950–1975.* Boulder: Westview Press.
———. 1993. *The Making of Modern Turkey.* New York: Routledge.
Akgün, Fehmi. 1993. *Yıllar boyunca tango, 1865–1993.* Istanbul: Pan.
Akın, A. Vedat. 1951. "Zeki Müren sorulan sualleri cevaplandırıyor." *Resimli radyo dünyası* 35:22–26.
Akın, Erkan, and Ömer Karasapan. 1988. "The Rabıta Affair." *Middle East Report* 153:15.

Aksoy, Bülent. 2002. *Zeki Müren: 1955–63 Kayıtları/Recordings* (CD booklet). Kalan: Istanbul.
Aksoy, Ozan. 2006. "The Politicization of Kurdish Folk Songs in Turkey in the 1990s." *Music and Anthropology* 11. http://levi.provincia.venezia.it/ma/index/ma_ind.htm
Aksu, Sezen. 1996. "O Annelerin yerindeyim." *Aktüel* 262(96): 26–29.
Aksüt, Sadun. 1994. *Şarkılarda İstanbul*. Istanbul: Altın Kitaplar.
Aktürk, Sener. 2007. "Incompatible Visions of Supra-Nationalism: National Identity in Turkey and the European Union." *European Journal of Sociology* 48(2): 347–72.
Akyıldız, Erhan. 1974. "Orhan Gencebay İzmir Fuarında." *Hey* 4(9): 12–15.
———. 1977. "Bir rakı şişesinde Orhan Gencebay." *Hey* 7(21): 18–19.
Alkan, Türker. 2006. "'Bizler' ve 'Sizler.'" *Radikal*, 2 August. http://www.radikal.com.tr/haber.php?haberno=194576
Allen, Ray, and Lois Wilken, eds. 1998. *Island Sounds in the Global City: Popular Music and Identity in New York*. New York: New York Folklore Society.
Altan, Mehmet. 1996. "12 numeralı mikrofon." *Sabah Gazetesi*, 26 September. http://www.sanatgunesi.com/bir_cift_soz_basin02.htm
Altınay, Rüştem Ertuğ. 2008. "Reconstructing the Transgendered Self as a Muslim, Nationalist, Upper-Class Woman: The Case Of Bulent Ersoy." *Women's Studies Quarterly* 36(3–4): 210–29.
Anderson, Benedict. 1983. *Imagined Communities: Reflections on the Origin and Spread of Nationalism*. London: Verso.
Andrews, Walter. 1984. *Poetry's Voice, Society's Song: Ottoman Lyric Poetry*. Seattle: University of Washington Press.
Andrews, Walter, and Mehmet Kalpaklı. 2005. *The Age of Beloveds: Love and the Beloved in Early Modern Ottoman and European Culture and Society*. Durham, NC: Duke University Press.
Arel, Hüseyin Sadettin. 1969. *Türk Musikisi kimindir?* Istanbul: Milli Eğitim Basımevi.
———. 1992. *Prozodi dersleri*. Istanbul: Pan.
Arıkan, Mümtaz. 1979. "Zeki Müren efsanesi." *Hey* 9(38): 10–11.
Armbrust, Walter. 1996. *Mass Culture and Modernism in Egypt*. Cambridge: Cambridge University Press.
———. 2000. "Introduction: Anxieties of Scale." In *Mass Mediations: New Approaches to Popular Culture in the Middle East and Beyond*, edited by Walter Armbrust; 1–31. Berkeley: University of California Press.
Aşan, Emine. 2003. *Rakipsiz sanatkâr Zeki Müren*. Istanbul: Boyut.
Ateş, Amir. 2008. "Bir ilahi musikidir kainat." *Vizyon Dergisi* 10 (August):51–53.
Auslander, Philip. 1999. *Liveness: Performance in a Mediatized Culture*. New York: Routledge.
Aya, Gökhan. 1996. *Bir Cem Karaca kitabı*. Istanbul: Ada.
Balakrishnan, Gopal. 2003. "Algorhythms of War." *New Left Review* 23:5–33.
Baron, Beth. 2005. *Egypt as a Woman: Nationalism, Gender, and Politics*. Berkeley: University of California Press.

Barthes, Roland. 1977. "The Grain of the Voice." In *Image, Music, Text*, edited and translated by Stephen Heath, 179–89. London: Fontana.

———. 1979. *A Lover's Discourse*. London: Jonathan Cape.

Bartok, Bela. 1976. *Turkish Folk Music from Asia Minor*, edited by Benjamin Suchoff. Princeton, NJ: Princeton University Press.

Bartu, Ayfer. 1999. "Who Owns the Old Quarters? Rewriting Histories in a Global Era." In *Istanbul: Between the Global and the Local*, edited by Çağlar Keyder, 31–45. Lanham: Rowman and Littlefield.

Başbakanlık Devlet İstatistik Enstitü (Prime Ministerial State Statistics Institute). 1988. *Türkiye istatistik cep yıllığı*. Ankara: Devlet İstatistik Enstitüsü.

Behar, Cem. 1992. *Zaman, mekân, müzik: Klâsik Türk musıkisinde eğitim* (Meşk), *icra ve aktarım*. Istanbul: Afa.

Beken, Münir. 2003. "Aesthetics and Artistic Criticism at the Turkish Gazino." *Music and Anthropology* 8. http://www.muspe.unibo.it/period/ma/index/number8/ma_ind8.htm.

Bel, Nur Gülmez. 2006. "Popo mu ses mi karar vereceksin." *Vatan Magazin* (30 August): 2.

Belge, Murat. 1983a. "Türkiye'de günlük hayat." In *Cumhuriyet dönemi Türkiye ansiklopedisi*: 836–76. Istanbul: Iletisim.

———. 1983b. *Tarihten güncelliğe*. Istanbul: Alan.

———. 1990. "Toplumsal değişme ve arabesk." *Birikim* 17:16–23.

Bell, Michael. 2000. *Sentimentalism, Ethics and the Culture of Feeling*. Houndmills: Palgrave.

Berkes, Niyazi. 1964. *The Development of Secularism in Turkey*. Montreal: McGill University Press.

Berlant, Lauren, and Michael Warner. 1998. "Sex in Public." *Critical Inquiry* 24(2): 547–66.

Berlant, Lauren. 1997. *The Queen of America Goes to Washington City: Essays on Sex and Citizenship*. Durham, NC: Duke University Press.

———. 1998. "Intimacy: A Special Issue." *Critical Inquiry* 24(2): 281–88.

———. 2008. *The Female Complaint: The Unfinished Business of Sentimentality in American Culture*. Durham, NC: Duke University Press.

Berman, Marshall. 1999. *Adventures in Marxism*. London: Verso.

Beyatlı, Yahya Kemal. 1964. *Aziz İstanbul*. Istanbul: Milli Eğitim Basımevi.

Bhabha, Homi. 2004. *The Location of Culture*. London: Routledge.

Bildirici, Faruk. 2002. "Istanbul kaltağını benim için öp." *Tempo Online*. www.tempodergisi.com.tr/kose/faruk_bildirici/00296.

Bohlman, Philip V. 1998. "The Schechinah, or the Feminine Sacred in the Musics of the Jewish Mediterranean." *Music and Anthropology* 3. http://www.provincia.venezia.it/Levi/ma/index/number3/bohlman/bohl_0.htm.

———. 1999. "Ontologies of Music." In *Rethinking Music*, edited by Nicholas Cook and Mark Everist, 17–34. Oxford: Oxford University Press.

———. 2002. "World Music at the End of History." *Ethnomusicology* 46(1): 1–32.

Boltanski, Luc. 1999. *Distant Suffering: Morality, Media and Politics*. Cambridge: Cambridge University Press.

Boran, Orhan. 1975. "Dünün karton plakları şimdi altın oldu." *Hey* 6(2): 10–13.

Born, Georgina. 1998. Anthropology, Kleinian Analysis, and the Subject in Culture. *American Anthropologist* 100(2): 373–86.

———. 2005. "On Musical Mediation: Ontology, Technology and Creativity." *Twentieth-Century Music* 2(1): 7–36.

Boym, Svetlana. 2001. *The Future of Nostalgia*. New York: Basic Books.

Bozdağ, İsmet. 1998. "Bir ses ustası: Münir Nurettin Selçuk." *Musiki Mecmuası* 51(462): 8–13.

Buchanan, Donna. 2006. *Performing Democracy: Bulgarian Music and Musicians in Transition*. Chicago: University of Chicago Press.

Büker, Seçil 2002. "The Film Does Not End With An Ecstatic Kiss." In *Fragments of Culture: The Everyday of Modern Turkey*, edited by Deniz Kandiyoti and Ayşe Saktanber, 147–70.

Bulaç, Ali. 1992. "Modern ve mahrem." *Birikim* 33:74–80.

Calhoun, Craig. 1992. "Introduction: Habermas and the Public Sphere." In *Habermas and the Public Sphere*, edited by Craig Calhoun, 1–50. Cambridge, MA: MIT Press.

Cambazoğlu, Cumhur. 1995. "Işık ikitellide yükseldi." *Cumhuriyet*, 29 July: 14.

———. 1996. "Sezenciklerin parçaları yaz albümü." *Cumhuriyet*, 20 June: 14.

Castelvecchi, Stefano. 1996. "From Nina to Nina: Psychodrama, Absorption, and Sentiment in the 1980s." *Cambridge Opera Journal* 8(2): 91–112.

Çayır, Kenan. 2006. "Islamic Novels: A Path to New Muslim Subjectivities." In *Islam in Public: Turkey, Iran, and Europe*, edited by. Nilüfer Göle and Ludwig Ammann, 191–225. Istanbul: Bilgi University Press.

Çelik, Zeynep. 1986. *The Remaking of Istanbul: Portrait of an Ottoman City in the Nineteenth Century*. Seattle: University of Washington Press.

Chakrabarty, Dipesh. 2000. *Provincializing Europe: Postcolonial Thought and Historical Difference*. Berkeley: University of California Press.

Chapman, Mary, and Glenn Hendler. 1999. "Introduction." In *Sentimental Men: Masculinity and the Politics of Affect in American Culture*, edited by Mary Chapman and Glenn Hendler, 1–16. Berkeley: University of California Press.

Chion, Michel. 1999. *The Voice in Cinema*, translated by Claudia Gorbman. New York: Columbia University Press.

Çınar, Alev. 2005. *Modernity, Islam, and Secularism in Turkey: Bodies, Places, and Time*. Minneapolis: University of Minnesota Press.

Clark, Suzanne. 1991. *Sentimental Modernism: Women Writers and the Revolution of the Word*. Bloomington: Indiana University Press.

Clarke, David. 2007. "Elvis and Darmstadt, or: Twentieth-Century Music and the Politics of Cultural Pluralism." *Twentieth-Century Music* 4(1): 3–45.

Clarke, Eric. 2007. "The Impact of Recording on Listening." *Twentieth-Century Music* 41): 47–70.

Cleto, Fabio. 1999. "Introduction: Queering the Camp." In *Camp: Queer Aesthet-

*ics and The Performing Subject: A Reader,* edited by Fabio Cleto, 1–43. Ann Arbor: University of Michigan Press.

Cook, Nicholas. 1998. *Analysing Musical Multimedia.* Oxford: Clarendon.

———. 1999. "Analysing Performance, Performing Analysis." In *Rethinking Music,* edited by. Nicholas Cook and Mark Everist, 239–61. Oxford: Oxford University Press.

Costello-Branco, Salwa al-Shawan. 2002. "Western Music, Colonialism, Cosmopolitanism, and Modernity in Egypt." In *The Garland Encyclopedia of World Music: Middle East,* edited by Virginia Danielson, Scott Marcus, and Dwight Reynolds, 607–13. New York: Garland.

Currid, Brian. 2000. "'A Song Goes Round the World': The German Schlager, as an Organ of Experience." *Popular Music* 19(2): 147–80.

Danielson, Virginia. 1997. *The Voice of Egypt: Umm Kulthum, Arabic Song, and Egyptian Society in the Twentieth Century.* Chicago: University of Chicago Press.

Delaney, Carol. 1991. *The Seed and the Soil: Gender and Cosmology in Turkish Village Society.* Berkeley: University of California Press.

Dikici, Radi. 2005. *Cumhuriyet'in divası Müzeyyen Senar.* Istanbul: Remzi.

Dilmener, Naim. 2003. *Bak bir varmış, bir yokmuş: Hafif Türk pop tarihi.* Istanbul: İletişim.

———. 2006. *Eleştirmenin günlüğü.* Istanbul: Everest.

Dolar, Mladen. 1996. "The Object Voice." In *Gaze and Voice as Love Objects,* edited by Renata Salecl and Slavoj Zizek, 7–31. Durham, NC: Duke University Press.

Dorsay, Attila. 2003. *Ne şürüp-şeker şarkılardı onlar: Kişisel bir 20. yüzyıl pop müzik tarihi.* Istanbul: Remzi Kitabevi.

Douglas, Mary. 1997. *Natural Symbols: Explorations in Cosmology.* London: Routledge.

Duben, Alan, and Cem Behar. 1991. *Istanbul Households: Marriage, Family, and Fertility, 1880–1940.* Cambridge: Cambridge University Press.

Dueck, Byron. 2007. "Public and Intimate Sociability in First Nations and Métis Fiddling." *Ethnomusicology* 51(2): 30–63.

Eğribel, Ertan. 1984. *Niçin arabesk değil?* Istanbul: Süreç.

Eickelman, Dale. 1989. *The Middle East and Central Asia: An Anthropological Approach.* Upper Saddle River, NJ: Prentice Hall.

Ellingsen, Anne. 1997. "Ibrahim Tatlıses and the Popular Music Genre Arabesk in Turkey." *Studia Musica Norvegica* 23:65–74.

Ellison, Julie. 1999. *Cato's Tears and the Making of Anglo-American Emotion.* Chicago: University of Chicago Press.

Erdener, Yıldıray. 1995. *The Song Contests of Turkish Minstrels: Improvised Poetry Sung to Traditional Music.* New York: Garland.

Erlmann, Viet. 1999. *Music, Modernity and the Global Imagination: South Africa and the West.* Oxford: Oxford University Press.

Estukyan, Pakrat. 2003. "İstanbul'da Ermeni müziği." *Istanbul* 45:83–85.

Feld, Steven. 1996. "Pygmy Pop: A Genealogy of Schizophonic Mimesis." *Yearbook for Traditional Music* 28:1–35.

Feld, Steven, Aaron A. Fox, Thomas Porcello, and David Samuels. 2004. "Vocal

Anthropology: From the Music of Language to the Language of Song." In *A Companion to Linguistic Anthropology*, edited by Alessandro Duranti, 321–45. Oxford: Blackwell.

Feldman, Walter. 1996. *Music of the Ottoman Court*. Berlin: Verlag für Wissenschaft und Bildung.

———. 2002. *Music of the Sultans, Sufis and Seraglio Volume 2: Music of the Dancing Boys*, liner notes. New York: Traditional Crossroads CD 4302.

Fox, Aaron A. 2004. *Real Country: Music and Language in Working-Class Culture*. Durham, NC: Duke University Press.

Frishkopf, Michael. 2003. "Some Meanings of the Spanish Tinge in Contemporary Egyptian Music." In *Mediterranean Mosaic: Popular Music and Global Sounds*, edited by Goffredo Plastino, 199–220. New York: Routledge.

Frith, Simon. 1996. *Performing Rites: On the Value of Popular Music*. Cambridge, MA: Harvard University Press.

Fuller, Mia. 2007. *Moderns Abroad: Architecture, Cities and Italian Imperialism*. New York: Routledge.

Gell, Alfred. 1998. *Art and Agency: An Anthropological Theory*. Oxford: Clarendon.

Gellner, Ernest. 1981. *Muslim Society*. Cambridge: Cambridge University Press.

Giddens, Anthony. 1992. *The Transformation of Intimacy: Sexuality, Love and Eroticism in Modern Societies*. Stanford, CA: Stanford University Press.

Gilsenan, Michael. 1982. *Recognizing Islam: Religion and Society in the Modern Arab World*. New York: Pantheon.

———. 1990. "Very Like a Camel: The Appearance of an Anthropologist's Middle East." In *Localizing Strategies: Regional Traditions in Ethnographic Writing*, edited by Richard Fardon, 222–39. Washington, DC: Smithsonian Institute Press.

Giz, Adnan. 1969. "Çamlıca: İstanbul'un mutena semtlerinden." *Hayat Tarih Mecmuası* 5(10): 27–31.

Gökalp, Ziya. 1923. *Türkçülüğün esasları*. Ankara: Milli İçtimiyat Kitabhanesi.

Göle, Nilufer. 1996. *The Forbidden Modern: Civilization and Veiling*. Ann Arbor: University of Michigan Press.

———. 2000. "Snapshots of Islamic Modernities." *Daedalus* 129(1): 91–117.

Gordon, Joel. 2002. *Revolutionary Melodrama: Popular Film and Civic Identity in Nasser's Egypt*. Chicago: Middle Eastern Documentation Center.

Grainge, Paul. 2002. *Monochrome Memories: Nostalgia and Style in 1990s America*. Westport, CT: Praeger.

Griswold, Charles. 1999. *Adam Smith and the Virtues of Enlightenment*. Cambridge: Cambridge University Press.

Güç, Ceyhan. 1996. *Şimdi uzaklardaysın*. Istanbul: Ad.

Güneyli, Deniz. 1996. "Yılın pop balonları." *Müzük* 1:8.

Güngör, Nazife. 1990. *Sosyokültürel açıdan arabesk müziği*. Ankara: Bilgi.

Habermas, Jürgen. 1984. *A Theory of Communicative Action*. Boston: Beacon Press.

———. 1991. *The Structural Transformation of the Public Sphere: An Inquiry into a Category of Bourgeois Society*. Cambridge, MA: MIT Press.

Hansen, Miriam. 1994. *Babel and Babylon: Spectatorship in American Silent Film*. Cambridge, MA: Harvard University Press.
Hasgül, Necati. 1996. "Türkiye'de pop müzik tarihinde 'anadolu pop' akımının yeri." *Dans müzik kültür: Folklora doğru* 62:51–74.
Herzfeld, Michael. 1985. *The Poetics of Manhood: Contest and Identity in a Cretan Mountain Village*. Princeton, NJ: Princeton University Press.
———. 1997. *Cultural Intimacy: Social Poetics in the Nation-State*. New York: Routledge.
Hiçyılmaz, Ergün. 1997. *Dargınım sana hayat: Zeki Müren için bir demet yasemin*. Istanbul: Kamer.
Hirschkind, Charles. 2006. *The Ethical Soundscape: Cassette Sermons and Islamic Counterpublics*. New York: Columbia University Press.
Hisar, Abdülhak Sinasi. 1978. *Boğaziçi mehtapları*. Istanbul: Ötüken.
Holbrook, Victoria. 1994. *The Unreadable Shores of Love: Turkish Modernity and Mystic Romance*. Austin: University of Texas Press.
Houston, Christopher. 2008. *Kurdistan: Crafting of National Selves*. New York: Berg.
İnal, İbnülemin Mahmut Kemal. 1958. *Hoş sadâ: Son asır Türk musiksinaşları*. Istanbul: Maarif.
Isık, Caner and Nuran Erol. 2002. *Arabeskin anlam dünyası: Müslüm Gürses örneği*. Istanbul: Bağlam.
Işık, Sadettin. 1951. "Güzel sanatlar akademisi talebesi Zeki Müren." *Resimli müzik dünyası* 74: 9-12.
Jones, Andrew. 2001. *'Like A Knife': Ideology and Genre in Contemporary Chinese Popular Music*. Ithaca, NY: Cornell University Press.
Kandiyoti, Deniz. 1991. Introduction to *Women, Islam, and the State*, edited by Deniz Kandiyoti. Philadelphia: Temple University Press.
———. 1994. "The Paradoxes of Masculinity: Some Thoughts on Segregated Societies." In *Dislocating Masculinities: Comparative Ethnographies*, edited by Andrea Cornwall and Nancy Lindisfarne: 197–213. New York: Routledge.
———. 2002. "Introduction: Reading the Fragments." In *Fragments of Culture: The Everyday of Modern Turkey*, edited Deniz Kandiyoti and Ayse Saktanber: 1–21. London: I. B. Tauris.
Kaplan, Mehmet. 1954. *Şiir tahlilleri 1: Tanzimat'tan cumhuriyet'e*. Istanbul: Dergâh.
———. 1963. *Tanpınar'ın şiir dünyası*. Istanbul: Baha.
Karakayalı, Nedim. 1995. "Doğarken ölen: Hafif müzik ortamında ciddi bir proje olarak Orhan Gencebay." *Toplum ve bilim* 67:135–56.
Karpat, Kemal. 1963. "The People's Houses in Turkey: Establishment and Growth." *Middle East Journal* 17:55–67.
Katırcıkara, Ayhan. 1996. "Fantezi ve kulis." *Türkiye gazetesi,* 26 September (http://www.sanatgunesi.com/0bir_cift_soz.htm) (accessed 3/10/07).
Kayhan, Aslı. 2003. "Bu barlarda ne söyleniyor? Türkülerin yeni mekânı: Türkü bar." *Istanbul* 45:125–27.

Keyder, Çağlar. 1987. *State and Class in Turkey: A Study in Capitalist Development.* London: Verso.

———. 1999. "The Setting." In *Istanbul: Between the Global and the Local*, edited by Çağlar Keyder, 3–28. Lanham, MD: Rowman and Littlefield.

———. 2004. "The Turkish Bell Jar." *New Left Review* 28:65–84.

Kılıç, Ahmet. 1972a. "Türkiye'ye dönen Timur Selçuk." *Hey* 2(35): 3–4.

———. 1972b. "Timur Selçuk orkestra kurdu." *Hey* 2(40): 3.

Kingsbury, Paul. 2007. "The Extimacy of Space." *Social and Cultural Geography* 8(2): 235–58.

Kocabaşoğlu, Uygur. 1980. *Şirket telsizinden devlet radyosuna: TRT öncesi dönemde radyonun tarihsel gelişimi ve Türk siyasal hayatı içindeki yer*. Ankara : S. B. F. Basın ve Yayın Yüksek Okulu Basımevi.

Koçu, Reşat Ekrem. 1969. "İstanbul'da ezan musikisi." *Hayat tarih mecmuası* 5(11): 18–20.

Kornhauser, Bronia. 1978. "In Defence of Kroncong." In *Studies in Indonesian Music*, edited by Margaret Kartomi. Clayton: Center for Southeast Asian Studies, Monash University: 104–83.

Krebs, Harold. 1987. "Some Extensions of the Concepts of Metrical Consonance and Dissonance." *Journal of Music Theory* 31:99–120.

Kulin, Ayse. 1996. *Bir tatlı huzur: Fotoğraflarla Münir Nurettin Selçuk'un yaşam öyküsü*. Istanbul: Sel.

Lewis, Bernard. 1961. *The Emergence of Modern Turkey*. Oxford: Oxford University Press.

Lewis, Geoffrey. 1955. *Turkey*. London: Benn.

Manuel, Peter. 1986. "Modal Harmony in Andalusian, Eastern European, and Turkish Syncretic Musics." *Yearbook for Traditional Music* 21:70–94.

———. 1993. *Cassette Culture: Popular Music and Technology in North India*. Chicago: University of Chicago Press.

Marcus, George. 2002. *The Sentimental Citizen: Emotion in Democratic Politics*. University Park: Pennsylvania State University Press.

Mardin, Şerif. 1989. *Religion and Social Change in Modern Turkey: The Case of Bediüzzaman Said Nursi*. Albany, NY: State University of New York Press.

Markoff, Irene. 1986. "The Role of Expressive Culture in the Demystification of a Secret Sect of Islam." *World of Music* 28(3): 42–56.

———. 1990/91. "The Ideology of Musical Practice and the Professional Turkish Musician: Tempering the Creative Impulse." *Asian Music* 22(1): 129–45.

McCracken, Allison. 2001. "Real Men Don't Sing Ballads: The Radio Crooner in Hollywood, 1929–1933." In *Soundtrack Available: Essays on Film and Popular Music*, edited by Pamela Wojcik and Arthur Knight, 105–33. Durham, NC: Duke University Press.

Meeker, Michael. 1991. "The New Muslim Intellectuals in the Republic of Turkey." In *Islam in Modern Turkey: Religion, Politics and Literature in a Secular State*, edited by Richard Tapper, 189–219. London: I. B. Tauris.

Meriç, Murat. 1996. "Türkiye'de pop müziğin öyküsü." *Müzük* 1:50–2.

———. 1999a. "Türkiye'de caz: Bir uzun serüven." In *Cumhuriyet'in sesleri*, edited by Gönül Paçacı, 132–41. Istanbul: Tarih Vakfı.
———. 1999b. "Türkiye'de popüler batı müziği'nin 75 yıllık seyrine bir bakış." In *Cumhuriyet'in sesleri*, edited by Gönül Paçacı, 132–41. Istanbul: Tarih Vakfı.
Middleton, Richard. 1990. *Studying Popular Music*. Milton Keynes: Open University Press.
———. 2006. *Voicing the Popular: On the Subjects of Popular Music*. New York: Routledge.
Miller, Jacques-Alain. 2005. "A and a in Clinical Structures." In *The Symptom: Online Journal for Lacan.com* (http://www.lacan.com/symptom6_articles/miller.html).
Mitchell, Timothy. 1988. *Colonising Egypt*. Cambridge: Cambridge University Press.
———. 2002. *Rule of Experts: Egypt, Techno-politics, Modernity*. Berkeley: University of California Press.
Moore, Allan. 1993. *Rock, the Primary Text: Developing a Musicology of Rock*. Buckingham, UK: Open University Press.
Motooka, Wendy. 1998. *The Age of Reasons: Quixotism, Sentimentalism, and Political Economy in Eighteenth-Century Britain*. New York: Routledge.
Mullan, John. 1988. *Sentiment and Sociability: The Language of Feeling in the Eighteenth Century*. Oxford, UK: Clarendon.
Müren, Zeki. 1995. *Bildircin yağmuru*. Istanbul: Istanbul Matbaası.
———. 1996. "Kendi sözleriyle Zeki Müren." From TRT *Batmayan güneş* documentary, 10–12 September. http://www.sanatgunesi.com/0bir_cift_soz.htm.
Murray, Stephen, and Will Roscoe. 1997. *Islamic Homosexualities*. New York: New York University Press.
Najmabadi, Afsaneh. 2005. *Women with Mustaches and Men without Beards: Gender and Sexual Anxieties of Iranian Modernity*. Berkeley: University of California Press.
Navaro-Yashin, Yael. 2002. *Faces of the State: Secularism and Public Life in Turkey*. Princeton, NJ: Princeton University Press.
Nettl, Bruno, ed. 1978. *Eight Urban Musical Cultures: Tradition and Change*. Champaign-Urbana: University of Illinois Press.
Nettl, Bruno, and Roland Riddle. 1998. "Taqsim Nahawand Revisited: The Musicianship of Jihad Racy." In *In the Course of Performance: Studies in the World of Musical Improvisation*, edited by Bruno Nettl with Melinda Russell, 363–94. Chicago: University of Chicago Press.
Noble, Marianne. 2000. *The Masochistic Pleasures of Sentimental Literature*. Princeton, NJ: Princeton University Press.
Ochoa Gaultier, Ana Maria. 2003. *Músicas locales in tiempo de globalización*. Buenos Aires: Norma.
O'Connell, John Morgan. 2002. "From Empire to Republic: Vocal Style in Twentieth-Century Turkey." In *The Garland Encyclopedia of World Music: Middle East*, edited by Virginia Danielson, Scott Marcus, and Dwight Reynolds, 781–87. New York: Garland Publishing.
———. 2003. "Song Cycle: The Life and Death of the Turkish Gazel." *Ethnomusicology* 47(3): 399–414.

———. 2005a. "Sound Sense: Mediterranean Music from a Turkish Perspective." In *The Mediterranean in Music: Critical Perspectives, Common Concerns, Cultural Differences*, edited by David Cooper and Kevin Dawe, 3–25. Lanham, MD: Scarecrow Press.

———. 2005b. "In the Time of Alaturka: Identifying Difference in Musical Discourse." *Ethnomusicology* 49(2): 177–205.

———. 2006. The Mermaid of the Meyhane: The Legend of a Greek Singer in a Turkish Tavern. In *Music and the Sirens*, edited by Linda Austern and Inna Naroditskaya, 273–93. Bloomington: Indiana University Press.

Oğuztan, Ümit. 1975. "Yedi yönlü sanatçı." *Ses* 52:16–17.

Ok, Akın. 1994. *'68 Çığlıkları: Müziğimizde büyük stılım dönemi*. Istanbul: Broy.

———. 1997. *İstanbul'un kalbini alan dansözleri ve eğlence dünyası'nın saklı şiddeti*. Istanbul: Broy.

Ok, Sema. 1996. "Bazıları farklıdır." http://www.sanatgunesi.com/0bir_cift_soz.htm.

Ömürlü, Yusuf. 1999. *Yahya Kemal'in bestelenmiş şiirleri*. Istanbul: Istanbul Fetih Cemiyeti.

Öncü, Ayse. 1999. "Istanbulites and Others: The Cultural Cosmology of Being Middle Class in the Era of Globalization." In *Istanbul: Between the Global and the Local*, edited by Çaglar Keyder, 95–119. Lanham, MD: Rowman and Littlefield.

Oransay, Gültekin. 1985. *Atatürk ile küğ: Belgeler ve veriler*. İzmir: Küğ Yayını.

Ossman, Susan. 2002. *Three Faces of Beauty: Casablanca, Paris, Cairo*. Durham, NC: Duke University Press.

Özbek, Meral. 1991. *Popüler kültür ve Orhan Gencebay arabeski*. Istanbul: İletişim.

Özer, Yetkin. 2003. "Crossing the Boundaries: The Akdeniz Scene and Mediterraneanness." In *Mediterranean Mosaic: Popular Music and Global Sounds*, edited by Goffredo Plastino, 199–220. New York: Routledge.

Özışık, Edip. 1963. *Musıki sanatı*. Istanbul: Nurgök.

Öztuna, Yılmaz. 1987. *Türk musikisi: Teknik ve tarih*. Istanbul: Lâle Mecmuası.

Öztürkmen, Arzu. 2005. "Folklore on Trial: Pertev Naili Boratav and the Denationalization of Turkish Folklore." *Journal of Folklore Research* 42(2): 185–216.

Özyürek, Esra. 2006. *Nostalgia for the Modern: State Secularism and Everyday Politics in Turkey*. Durham, NC: Duke University Press.

Paçacı, Gönül. 1999. "Cumhuriyet'in sesli serüveni." In *Cumhuriyet'in sesleri*, edited by Gönül Paçacı, 10–29. Istanbul: Tarih Vakfı.

Pamuk, Orhan. 2005. *Istanbul: Memories and the City*, translated by Maureen Freely. New York: Vintage.

———. 2008. *Masumiyet müzesi*. Istanbul: İletişim.

Perna, Vincenzo. 2005. *Timba: The Sound of the Cuban Crisis*. London: Ashgate.

Petkov, Steven. 1995. "Ol' Blue Eyes and the Golden Age of the American Song." In *The Sinatra Reader*, edited by Steven Petkov and Leonard Mustazza, 74–84. Oxford: Oxford University Press.

Picken, Laurence. 1975. *Folk Musical Instruments of Turkey*. Oxford: Oxford University Press.

Poizat, Michel. 1992. *The Angel's Cry: Beyond the Pleasure Principle in Opera.* Ithaca, NY: Cornell University Press.

Potuoğlu-Cook, Öykü. 2007. "Sweat, Power and Art: Situating Belly Dancers and Musicians in Contemporary Istanbul." *Music and Anthropology* 11. http://research.umbc.edu/eol/MA/index/number11/potuoğlu/pot_0.htm.

Racy, Ali Jihad. 2003. *Making Music in the Arab World: The Culture and Artistry of Tarab.* Cambridge: Cambridge University Press.

Rassmussen, Ljerka Vidic. "The Southern Wind of Change: Style and the Politics of Identity in Prewar Yugoslavia." In *Retuning Culture: Musical Changes in Central and Eastern Europe*, edited by Mark Slobin, 99–116. Durham, NC: Duke University Press.

Regev, Motti. 2006. "Cultural Uniqueness and Aesthetic Cosmopolitanism." *European Journal of Social Theory* 9(4): 563–78.

Regev, Motti, and Edwin Seroussi. 2004. *Popular Music and National Culture in Israel.* Berkeley: University of California Press.

Rice, Timothy. 1996. *May It Fill Your Soul: Experiencing Bulgarian Music.* Chicago: University of Chicago Press.

Robins, Kevin, and Asu Aksoy. 1995. "Istanbul Rising: Returning the Repressed to Urban Culture." *European and Regional Studies* 2(3): 223–35.

Robins, Kevin, and David Morley. 1996. "Almancı, Yabancı." *Cultural Studies* 10(2): 248–54.

Rona, Mustafa. 1970. *Yirminci yüzyıl Türk musıkisi.* Istanbul: Türkiye.

Rowson, Everett. 1991. "The Categorization of Gender and Sexual Irregularity in Medieval Arab Vice Lists." In *Body Guards: The Cultural Politics of Gender Ambiguity,* edited by Julia Epstein and Kristina Straub, 50–79. New York: Routledge.

Şafak, Elif. 2006. "Türkiye'de aşk yasak mi?" *Zaman,* 19 December 2006 (http://www.zaman.com.tr/webapp-tr/yazar.do?yazino=473993)

Sarhon, Karen Gerson. 2003. "Türk müziği ve Los Pasaros Sefaradis grubu." *Istanbul* 45:78–79.

Sassen, Saskia. 1998. *Globalization and Its Discontents.* New York: New Press.

———. 2006. *Territory, Authority, Rights: From Medieval to Global Assemblages.* Princeton, NJ: Princeton University Press.

Savigliano, Marta. 1995. *Tango and the Political Economy of Passion.* Boulder, CO: Westview Press.

Saymaz, İsmail. 2008. "28. yılında 12 eylül'ü protesto." *Radikal,* 11 September, 9.

Schade-Poulsen, Marc. 1999. *Men and Popular Music in Algeria: The Social Significance of Rai.* Austin: University of Texas Press.

Scognamillo, Giovanni. 1979. "Minik Serçe." *Hey* 9(15): 38.

———. 1997/8. "Être levantin à Istanbul." *Mediterraneans* 10:93–100.

Seeman, Sonya. 2006. "Presenting Gypsy, Re-Presenting Roman: Towards an Archeology of Aesthetic Production and Social Identity." *Music and Anthropology* 11. http://www.provincia.venezia.it/Levi/ma/index/number11/seeman/see_0.htm.

Selçuk, Timur, 2003. "Sosyal hamiş," in CD liner notes to *Babamın şarkıları,* 20–23. Istanbul: Balet Plak.

Sennett, Richard. 1976. *The Fall of Public Man*. London: Faber.
Seroussi, Edwin. 1989. *Mizimrat Qedem: The Life and Music of R. Isaac Algazi from Turkey*. Jerusalem: Renanot, the Institute for Jewish Music.
Seufert, Günter, and Petra Weyland. 1994. "National Events and the Struggle for the Fixing of Meaning: A Comparison of the Symbolic Dimensions of the Funeral Services for Atatürk and Özal." *New Perspectives on Turkey* 11:71–98.
Shafak, Elif. 2004. "Transgender Bolero." *Middle East Report* 230:26–29, 47.
Shankland, David. 2006. *The Alevis in Turkey: The Emergence of a Secular Islamic Tradition*. London: Routledge.
Shannon, Jonathan. 2006. *Among the Jasmine Trees: Music and Modernity and the Aesthetics of Authenticity in Contemporary Syria*. Middletown, CT: Wesleyan University Press.
Shaw, Arnold. 1995. "Sinatrauma: The Proclamation of a New Era." In *The Sinatra Reader*, edited by Steven Petkov and Leonard Mustazza, 18–30. Oxford: Oxford University Press.
Shissler, Holly. 2003. *Between Two Empires: Ahmet Ağaoğlu and the New Turkey*. London: I. B. Tauris.
———. 2004. "Beauty is Nothing to Be Ashamed Of: Beauty Contests as Tools of Women's Liberation in Early Republican Turkey." *Comparative Studies of South Asia, Africa and the Middle East* 24(1): 107–22.
Signell, Karl. 1977. *Makam: Modal Practice in Turkish Art Music*. Washington, DC: Asian Music Publications.
Silverman, Kaja. 1988. *The Acoustic Mirror: The Female Voice in Psychoanalysis and Cinema*. Bloomington: Indiana University Press.
———. 1992. *Male Subjectivity at the Margins*. New York: Routledge.
Silverstein, Michael, and Greg Urban. 1996. "The Natural History of Discourse." In *Natural Histories of Discourse*, edited by Michael Silverstein and Greg Urban, 1–18. Chicago: University of Chicago Press.
Simonett, Helena. 2001. *Banda: Mexican Musical Life across Borders*. Middletown, CT: Wesleyan University Press.
Sirman, Nükhet. 2000. "Writing the Usual Love Story: The Fashioning of Conjugal and National Subjects in Turkey." In *Gender, Agency, and Change: Anthropological Perspective*, edited by Victoria Ana Godard, 250–72. Routledge: London.
Solomon, Thomas. 2005a. "Living Underground is Tough: Authenticity and Locality in the Hip-Hop Community in Istanbul, Turkey." *Popular Music* 24(1): 1–20.
———. 2005b. "'Listening to Istanbul': Imagining Place in Turkish Rap Music." *Studia Musicologica Norvegica* 31:46–67.
———. 2006. "Hardcore Muslims: Islamic Themes in Turkish Rap in Diaspora and in the Homeland." *Yearbook for Traditional Music* 38:59–78.
Somay, Bülent. 1997/8. "Istanbul's Traffic Nightmare." *Mediterraneans* 10:165–70.
Sönmez, Mustafa. 1996. *İstanbul'un iki yüzü: 1980'den 2000'e değişim*. Ankara: Arkadaş.
Stewart, Kathleen. 1996. *A Space on the Side of the Road: Cultural Poetics in an "Other" America*. Princeton, NJ: Princeton University Press.

Stokes, Martin. 1992a. *The Arabesk Debate: Music and Musicians in Modern Turkey*. Oxford: Clarendon.

———. 1992b. "The Media and Reform: The Saz and Elektrosaz in Turkish Popular Music." *British Forum for Ethnomusicology* 1:89–102.

———. 1998. "Imagining the South: Hybridity, Heterotopias and Arabesk on the Turkish-Syrian Border." In *Border Identities: Nation and State at International Frontiers*, edited by Thomas Wilson and Hastings Donnan, 263–88. Cambridge: Cambridge University Press.

———. 2002a. "Turkish Rock and Pop." In *The Garland Encyclopedia of World Music: Middle East*, edited by Virginia Danielson, Scott Marcus, and Dwight Reynolds, 247–53. New York: Garland Publishing.

———. 2002b. "Afterword: Recognizing the Everyday." In *Fragments of Culture: The Everyday of Modern Turkey*, edited by Deniz Kandiyoti and Ayşe Saktanber, 322–38. London: I. B. Tauris.

———. 2004. "The Tearful Public Sphere: Turkey's Sun of Art, Zeki Müren." In *Music and Gender: Perspectives from the Mediterranean*, edited by T. Magrini, 307–28. Chicago: University of Chicago Press.

———. 2007a. "Adam Smith and the Dark Nightingale: On Twentieth Century Sentimentalism." *Twentieth-Century Music*.

———. 2007b. "Shedding Light on the Balkans: Sezen Aksu's Anatolian Pop." In *Balkan Popular Culture and the Ottoman Ecumeme*, edited by Donna Buchanan. Lanham, MD: Scarecrow.

———. 2008. "Listening to Abd al-Halim Hafiz." In *Global Soundtracks: Worlds of Film Music*, edited by Mark Slobin, 309–33. Middletown, CT: Wesleyan University Press.

Süreya, Cemal. 1989. *99 Yüz: İzdüzümler/söz senaryosu*. Istanbul: Kaynak.

Swedenburg, Ted. 2000. "Sa'ida Sultan/Danna International: Transgender Pop and the Polysemiotics of Sex, Nation, and Ethnicity on the Israeli-Egyptian Border." In *Mass Mediations: New Approaches to Popular Culture in the Middle East and Beyond*, edited by Walter Armbrust, 88–119. Berkeley: University of California Press.

Tagg, Philip. 2003. *Ten Little Title Tunes: Towards a Musicology of the Mass Media*. New York: Mass Media Music Scholar's Press.

Tanpınar, Ahmet Hamdi. 2003. *Beş şehir*. Istanbul: Dergâh.

Tanrıkorur, Cinuçen. 2003. *Osmanlı dönemi Türk mûsikîsi*. Istanbul: Dergâh.

Taussig, Michael. 1993. *Mimesis and Alterity: A Particular History of the Senses*. New York: Routledge.

Tekerek, Tuğba. 2007. "Fethullah Gülen, Hande Yener'i, Gülben'i solladı." *Milliyet*, 17 December. http://www.milliyet.com.tr/2006/12/17/ekonomi/axeko01.html.

Théberge, Paul. 2003. "Microphone." In *The Continuum Encyclopedia of Popular Music of the World: Performance and Production*, edited by John Shepherd, David Horn, Dave Laing, Paul Oliver, and Peter Wicke, 245–47. London: Continuum.

Tragaki, Dafni. 2007. *Rebetiko Worlds: Ethnomusicology and Ethnography of the City*. Newcastle, UK: Cambridge Scholars Publishing.

Tuna, Banu. 1999. "Gelenek el değiştiriyor." *Hürriyet* 17 June. http://arsiv.hurriye tim.com.tr/istanbul/turk/99/06/17/isthab/06ist.htm.
Tunca, Hulusi. 1976. "Ajda Pekkan ile Zeki Müren on-iki yıl sonra buluştular." *Hey* 6(43): 10–11.
Tura, Yalçın. N.d. *Geçmişten günümüze Türk müziği*. Istanbul: Boyut.
Turino, Thomas. 1999. "Signs of Imagination, Identity, and Experience: A Piercian Semiotic Theory for Music." *Ethnomusicology* 43(2): 221–55.
———. 2000. *Nationalists, Cosmopolitans, and Popular Music in Zimbabwe*. Chicago: University of Chicago Press.
Türk, Bektaş. 1976a. "Hatalarımı vurabilirim." *Hey* 7(5): 24–25.
———. 1976b. Timur Selçuk İzmir'de açıkladı." *Hey* 6(36): 24–26.
Ünsü, Ibrahim.1984. "Ve Sezen Bebek'te park etti! . . ." *Hey* 1(5): 26–27.
Ünver, Yasemin. 1977. "Sezen Aksu Fuar'da çıkacak." *Hey* 7(12): 10–11.
Varzi, Roxanne. 2006. *Warring Souls: Youth, Media and Martyrdom in Post-Revolutionary Iran*. Durham, NC: Duke University Press.
Warner, Michael. 2002. *Publics and Counterpublics*. London: Zone Books.
Waxer, Lise. 2002. *The City of Music Memory: Salsa, Record Grooves, and Popular Culture in Cali, Colombia*. Middletown, CT: Wesleyan University Press.
Wedeen, Lisa. 1999. *Ambiguities of Domination: Politics, Rhetoric, and Symbols in Contemporary Syria*. Chicago: University of Chicago Press.
White, Jenny. 2002. *Islamist Mobilization in Turkey: A Study in Vernacular Politics*. Seattle: University of Washington Press.
Wikan, Unni. 1977. "Man Becomes Woman: Transsexualism in Oman as a Key to Gender Roles." *Man* 12:304–19.
Wright, Owen. 2000. *Demetrius Cantemir: The Collection of Notations. Volume 2: Commentary*. Aldershot, UK: Ashgate.
Yalçın, Emre. 1997/8. "Les belles maisons et leurs curieux habitants." *Mediterraneans* 10:340–51.
Yang, Mayfair Mei-Hui. 2002. "Mass Media and Transnational Subjectivity in Shanghai: Notes on (Re)Cosmopolitanism in a Chinese Metropolis." In *The Anthropology of Globalization: A Reader*, edited by Jonathan Xavier Inda and Renato Rosaldo, 325–49. Oxford, UK: Blackwell.
Yano, Christine. 2002. *Tears of Longing: Nostalgia and the Nation in Japanese Popular Song*. New York: Harvard University Press.
Yavuz, Hakan, and John Esposito, eds. 2003. *Turkish Islam and the Secular State: The Gülen Movement*. Syracuse, NY: Syracuse University Press.
Yerasimos, Stefanos. 1997/8. "Espoirs et utopies pour une cité à la dérive." *Mediterraneans* 10:53–62.
Yılmaz, Zeki. 1977. *Türk musikisi dersleri*. Istanbul: Ismet Sedele.
Žižek, Slavoj. 1996. "There Is No Sexual Relationship." In *Gaze and Voice as Love Objects*, edited by Renata Salecl and Slavoj Zizek, 208–49. Durham, NC: Duke University Press.

## Archival Resources

*Ses, Müzik Magazin, Boom, Hey, Resimli Radyo Dünyası, Müzük* during all years of publication.

## Select Discography

Note: Dates printed on CDs and cassettes do not always reliably indicate the dates at which they first appeared. For the purposes of this discography I have used my own collection and the World Wide Web in an attempt to identify the earliest dates of recordings. However, there may well be mistakes.

*Artık Sevmeyeceğim.* 2006. Kalan CD 379. Film music songs from the 1960s and 1970s, with a booklet including notes by Naim Dilmener.

Aksu, Sezen. 1975. *Haydi şansım / Gel bana*, 45 rpm single. Melodi Plak 75 004.

———. 1978. *Kaybollan yıllar / Neye yarar*. LP. Kent Plak 1108.

———. 1978. *Serçe*. Kent LP 137.

———. 1982. *Firuze*. Kervan Plak LP 66 / CD 25.

———. 1984. *Sen Ağlama*. Sembol LP 114 / CD 001.

———. 1986. *Git*. LP. Fono.

———. 1988. *Sezen Aksu '88*. Cassette. Foneks. K.T.B. Ü34.88.582.

———. 1993. *Deli Kızın Türküsü*. Tempa/Foneks CD 014. 93.34.Ü814.014.

———. 1995. *Işık doğudan yükselir / Ex Oriente Lux*. Seyhan 12 (2005)/ KB.95.34.Ü.814.054.

———. 1997. *Düğün ve cenaze*. CD. Raks 97.34.Ü.918.

———. 2005. *Bahane*. DMC Müzik CD 20174.

———. 2006. *Allahaısmarladik + 45' lıkler, 1976–1979*. CD, SN Müsik Yapim 01.

Ersoy, Bülent. 1995. *Alaturka 95*. Cassette, Raks/S-Müzik KB.95.34.Ü.918.003. Includes Ersoy's version of "Aziz Istanbul."

Gencebay, Orhan. 1969. "Başa gelen çekilirmiş" / "Sensiz bahar geçmiyor." 45 rpm single. Istanbul Plak 9134.

———. 1970. "Sevenler mesut olmaz" / "Benide Allah yarattı." 45 rpm single., Istanbul Plak 9150.

———. 1971. "Bir teselli ver" / "Yorgun gözler." 45 rpm single. Istanbul Plak 9175.

———. 1975. *Batsın bu dünya*. Kervan Plak LP 19.

———. 1976. *Hatasız kul olmaz*. Kervan Plak 109.

———. 1976. *Sarhoşun biri / Kader diye diye*. Kervan Plak LP 24.

———. 1980. *Aşkı ben yaratmadım*. Kervan Plak LP 52.

———. 1985. *Beni biraz anlasaydın*. Cassette. Kervan Plak LP 78.

———. 1986. *Cennet gözlüm*. Cassette. Kervan Plak LP 84.

———. 1992. *Sen de haklısın*. Cassette. Kervan Plak CD 011/MC-232.

———. 1994. *Yalnız değilsin*. Kervan Plak CD 026/KB.94.34.Ü.036.020.

———. 1998/2001. *Orhan Gencebay klasikler 1 ve 2*. CD. Kervan Plakçılık. KB.98.34.Ü.036.041.

———. 2004. *Yürekten olsun.* CD. Kervan Plak.
*Haydar Haydar: Masters of Turkish Music.* 2003. CD. Rounder 821.611.140-2. Includes classics from the early to mid-twentieth century, with booklet.
*İsak Algazi Efendi: Osmanlı-Türk ve Osmanlı-Yahudi musıkisinin büyük sesi.* 2004. CD. Kalan 333. Ottoman Turkish/Jewish music from the early decades of the republic, with booklet.
*Kani Karaca: Dinî musıki (arşiv serisi).* CD. Kalan 01.34.Ü.852.202. Archival recordings of Karaca's religious music.
Müren, Zeki. 1981. *Kahır mektubu.* CD. Türküola LP-341.
———. 1986. *Helal olsun.* Cassette. Lider Plak KTB 87.34.Ü.083.03, 1987.
———. 1987. *Aşk kurbanı.* CD. Türküola. KTB.90.34.Ü.083, 1990.
———. 1994. *Bir tatlı tebessüm.* CD. Coşkun Plak KB.94.34.U.044.008, 1994. HMV/Sahibin Sesi recordings from the 1950s.
———. *Türk sanat müziği konseri.* 1993. CD. Coşkun Plak 93.34. Ü.044.005, 1993. HMV/Sahibin Sesi recording, circa 1960.
———. *1955–63 Kayıtları / recordings (arşiv serisi).* CD. Kalan KB.2002.34.Ü. 852. Early radio recordings, with detailed liner notes by Bülent Aksoy.
———. c. 2005. *Zeki Müren Selahattin Pınar şarkıları.* Kalan CD 352. Early recordings of music by composer Selahattin Pınar.
———. c. 2005. *Zeki Müren Saadettin Kaynak şarkıları.* Kalan CD 353. Early recordings of music by composer Saadettin Kaynak.
———. 2006. *Zeki Müren ile başbaşa,* 1-3. Artvizyon 0710822, 0740822, and 073822. Three CDs containing archival material, including spoken voice, from Müren's Saturday-evening Band Reklam broadcasts from the 1960s and early 1970s.
———. 2006. *Zeki Müren anısına (Originals of 26 Zeki Müren Hits).* CD. Yavuz & Burç Plakçılık. Arabesk-style hits, mainly from the 1980s.
*Operetler, Kantolar, Fanteziler.* 1996. CD. Yapı Kredi YK.96.43.1. Popular operetta, *kanto*-s and *fantezi*-s from the late Ottoman and early republican period.
Safiye Ayla. 2004. *Safiye Ayla, arşiv serisi.* CD. Kalan 313-314.
Selçuk, Münir Nurettin. 1989. *Kalamış.* CD. Coşkun Plak. HMV/Sahibin Sesi recordings. mainly from the late 1940s and early 1950s. Includes Selçuk's version of "Aziz İstanbul."
Selçuk, Timur. 2003. *Babamın Şarkıları.* CD. Balet Plak. KB 2003. Includes Timur's version of "Aziz Istanbul."
———. 2003. *Abdülhamid düşerken.* Balet Plak. Film music.
———. 2004. *Bedreddin.* CD. Balet Plak. Music theater pieces, some recorded originally in 1980.
———. N. d. *İstanbul Oda Orkestrası / The Istanbul Chamber Orchestra.* CD. Balet Plak. Recordings of Ottoman art music arranged for chamber orchestra by Selçuk.
———. N. d. *Timur Selçuk seçkiler.* CD. Balet Plak. Early popular songs, including "İspanyol Meyhanesi."

## Select Filmography

Akın, Fatih, director. *Crossing the Bridge: The Sound of Istanbul*. Strand Releasing, 2005.

Ceylan, Nuri Bilge, director. *Uzak*. 2002.

Alyanak, Arşavir, director. *Son Beste*. 2004.

## Interviews

Aksu, Sezen (by the author and Anne Ellingsen). Levent, 12 July 1996.

Gencebay, Orhan. Levent, 4 August 1995.

Karaca, Cem (by the author and Anne Ellingsen). Beyoğlu, July 1996.

Özpınar, Muzaffer (by the author and Anne Ellingsen). Levent, August 1996.

Selçuk, Timur. Cihangir, 12 September 2008.

Yurdatapan, Şanar. Üsküdar, 11 September 2008.

# Index

*Page numbers followed by f denote figures.*

Abd al-Halim Hafiz. *See* Hafiz, Abd al-Halim
Abd al-Wahhab, Mohammed, 19, 47n40, 58, 97n36
Abu Lughod, Lila, 4n7, 16n35
Adalet ve Kalkınma Partisi (AK, Justice and Development Party), 133n66
Aksu, Sezen, 5, 23, 115n26, 115n30; and Aegean, 141–45; and Ajda Pekkan, 119n41; and *arabesk*, 114; and critics, 114, 129; and *Crossing the Bridge*, 144–45; and Eurovision, 122, 127; and feminism, 128–29; and folksong, 135; and gender, 119, 124, 128–29, 140; impersonations of, 63n65; *Işık doğudan yükselir / Ex Oriente lux*, 5; and love, 144; and melancholy, 109–11, 113n17, 121, 125, 126, 144; and neoliberal citizenship, 105, 107–47; and 1980 coup, 112, 121–22; recording industry and, 11n7, 112n13, 115n27; transnational popularity of, 14; and TRT, 112, 117, 132; and *Türk halk müziği*, 131–40; and *Türk sanat müziği*, 112, 117, 132; voice of, 112, 113n17, 114n22, 124–25, 134, 137, 140, 143, 144. *See also* "Ne Ağlarsın"
*alaturka*, 14n30, 132, 150, 168–69, 168n35

Alevi culture in Turkey, 21–22n55, 101, 101n
Alexiou, Haris, 137–38, 138n74, 139, 143
Altındağ, Perihan, 22n55, 37, 41, 44n31
*Anadolu* rock, 14, 19n44, 116–17
Anatolian rock. *See Anadolu* rock
"Anatolianism," 127n58
Anavatan Partisi (ANAP; Motherland Party), 93, 93n31
Andrews, Walter, 28–30, 32, 49, 158n19, 169n37, 192
androgyny, 63, 64, 66
Ar, Müjde, 81, 81n22, 119n42
*arabesk*, 5, 14, 15, 125, 182; and Aksu, 114; and Arab music, 19, 74n4, 97n36, 97–98n36; and the "*arabesk* debate," 73, 74n3, 74n4; and cassette piracy, 126; and Ersoy, 149, 168–73, 180; and Gencebay, 25, 73–105, 193; and Islam, 22n57, 23; and Müren, 47, 47n41, 58–59, 190; and Özal, 93; and sentimental culture, 192; and TRT, 121; and Turkish popular music 19
*aranjman*, 14, 113, 113n16, 118n36
Arel, Hüseyin Sadettin, 17, 36, 163n25, 164n27, 171n

Armbrust, Walter, 4n6, 16n35
Armenian Church, 123, 135
Armenian musicians, 20, 20n50
Armenian song, 134n69, 135, 135n69
Arslan, Fahrettin, 25
art music. See *Türk sanat müziği* (Turkish art music)
*aşık*, music of, 28, 100n44, 107n3, 108n, 109n4, 128
Aşık Daimi, 108n, 108 music example 4a, 109, 128
*aşk*, 26, 26n, 27n66, 96, 101. See also love; *sevgi*
Atatürk, Mustafa Kemal, 8, 9, 69, 93, 175; and the Kuvay-ı Milli, 180; and Münir Nurettin, 162; in official history, 16; representations of, 13, 71, 162; on Turkish music, 16n36
"Aziz İstanbul," 5, 149–82, 185n, 186, 190; and Ersoy, 149n6, 149–51, 168–73, 187; and Münir Nurettin, 149n4, 149n5, 149–51, 162–68, 170, 171–73, 179, 186–87, 190; and Timur Selçuk, 149, 149n4, 150, 173–82, 190; and Yahya Kemal, 149, 154, 155–62

Bacanos, Yorgo, 43
*bağlama*. See saz
Barthes, Roland, 7, 31, 124, 189
"Batsın bu dünya," 5, 79–92, 94, 95–96, 104, 190; critiques of, 83–84. See also Gencebay, Orhan
Behar, Cem, 15n31, 17n37, 21n52, 60, 110n9, 157, 158, 171n41
Belge, Murat, 94, 94n34, 182n61
belly dancing. See *Oriyental* (belly dancing)
Berlant, Lauren, 2–3, 4n9, 32, 32n778, 111, 190n, 191–92
Berman, Marshall, 192–93, 192n4
Beyatlı, Yahya Kemal, 5, 147n2, 149, 155–62, 185, 186; "Bir bir çalan saatler," 61; and Münir Nurettin Selçuk, 162–72; and Pamuk, 185n; and Parnassians, 164; and time, 159–62. See also "Aziz İstanbul"
Beyoğlu, viii, 24n60, 65n70, 117n34; *gazino*-s in, 24n62, 44n30; gentrification of, 12; and Müren, 2n2, 67
Beyoğlu Halkevi, 160
Bhabha, Homi, 74, 96, 103

"Bir bir çalan saatler." *See under* Beyatlı, Yahya Kemal
Born, Georgina, 6n10, 7n
Bosphorus, 144–47 passim, 152, 154, 158; *alem* parties, 157, 157n18; bridge, 149n6; nightclubs on, 44n30; and Pamuk, 184, 185; and Yahya Kemal, 161, 163n25
*bozlak*, 88, 90
Bregovic, Goran, 137–39, 137n73, 143
Bursa, 36–37, 37n6, 41n22, 60–61n59, 65, 123n50, 168n35

cadential patterns, 39n13, 51, 57, 87, 87n27, 88, 172
call to prayer, 9n17; in "Aziz İstanbul," 165–68, 166n32, 172–73, 175, 180n56; and *makam*, 52, 167
Çamlıca, 60n58, 182–84, 186
camp, 35, 36n2, 44–47 passim
cassette piracy, 116, 126
cassette production in Turkey, 126, 126n55, 135, 168
CD (compact disc) production in Turkey, 126–27
Cemil, Mesut, 17
cinema: Egyptian, 19, 97n36; Hindi, 44n34; Turkish, 42n25, 69, 81, 81n21, 97n36, 119n41
citizenship: and Aksu, 107–45; and Ersoy, 68n77; and identity politics, 70; and intimacy, 32; and Müren, 35, 68–69; neoliberal, 105; 1980 coup and, 73n1
Clarke, David, 8n13
cosmopolitanism: and Aksu, 136–40; "from below," 20; and Gencebay, 77, 99, 99n38, 101; and Müren, 47; and nationalism, 20n51; and Pekkan, 119; in Turkish art music, 17; in Turkish popular music, 18, 117
counterpublics, 4
coup d'état, 9, 13n, 187; and Aksu, 120–22, 129, 190; and Gencebay, 102; and hyper-liberalism, 105; "postmodern," 9, 9n18, 10; of 12 March 1971, 118; of 12 September 1980, 13n28, 18, 19, 22, 68, 71, 73, 73n1, 76, 112, 114n, 121n47
cultural intimacy, 2, 8, 32–33, 190–93; and cultures of love, 32; and gaze, 151, 182; Istanbul as site of, 145, 147, 151; and

Müren, 35; in Turkey, 150; and voice, 15, 125
Cumhuriyet Halk Partisi (CHP; Republican People's Party), 110
cynicism, 3, 13, 27, 36, 70–71, 186–87

Dalan, Bedrettin, 93, 151, 185, 186n
Darü'l-Elhan, 17n37
"deep state," 121n
Demokrat Parti (DP; Democratic Party), 9, 93n31
*Denetim Kurulu.* See Turkish Radio and Television
*deyiş*, 107, 107n3, 128n59, 138
diction, 39, 59, 63–64, 64n68. *See also* voice
Dilmener, Naim, 121, 122, 126, 181n58
Dink, Hrant, 9–10, 69–70n79
*Dün, Bugün, Yarın*, 114, 114n23

*elektrosaz*, 80n17, 80n18, 85, 86, 91–92
emotion: and lyric poetry, 28; and modernity, 187, 192; and national identity, 4n7, 73, 134, 144; and politics, 102, 104; and religion, 22; and neoliberalism, 111, 191; and voice, 57, 85, 122, 124, 173
entextualization, 6n11
Erener, Sertab, 127
Ersoy, Bülent: and *arabesk*, 168–69, 171, 178; and "Aziz Istanbul," 149n6, 149–51, 168–73, 187; biography of, 168n35, 173n42; at Gülhane Park, 75; and Islamist movement, 180, 180n56; at Izmir Fair, 46; on *Popstar*, 9; rivalry with Müren, 68, 169n36; and Timur Selçuk, 177, 178–79; and transnational transgendered communities, 68n77; voice of, 61n59, 171–73, 179
ethnicity, 14, 133, 138
European Union, 10n19, 70n81, 135, 138
Eurovision Song Contest, 18, 18n43, 116, 118n36, 119, 119n40; and Aksu, 122, 127; and Eastern and Central Europe, 138n76; and Erener, 139; and Timur Selçuk, 174
*ezan.* *See* call to prayer

*fantezi*, 18n40, 48, 49, 55, 80, 80n20
*fasıl*, 2n2, 14, 15, 24, 132

Fatih, 151
Fecr-i Ati, 155–56, 156n13, 161
feminism, 11n22, 27, 110, 111, 127n58, 128–30, 137
Fersan, Refik, 37, 38n9
folk music. *See Türk halk müziği* (Turkish folk music)

*gazel*, 21n53, 21n54, 28, 51, 56–58, 163n. *See also* lyric poetry
*gazino*, 2n63, 75; and Arslan, 25; Bebek Park, 123n50; and belly dancing, 19n48; and Ersoy and, 168; and Gencebay, 25, 76n8; history of, 24–25; Küçük Çiftlik Parkı, 44, 46–47n39; Maksim, 44, 44n33, 46–47n39; and Müren, 40, 43–47, 57, 57n56; and musical style, 15, 17n37; and Pekkan, 118; Tepebaşı, 62
*gecekondu*, 9n17, 74nn3–4, 75, 101, 152
Gencebay, Orhan, 73–105; and *arabesk*, 25, 74n3, 75–76; biography of, 75; "Bir Teselli Ver," 75, 76n7, 80n18; and citizenly virtue, 71; and *gazino* culture, 25, 76n8; and Kervan, 76n8, 77n11; and love, 95–96, 97, 100n, 101–3; and *makam*, 81n20, 85, 87–90; and melancholy, 94; and musicology, 14; nostalgia for, 92, 94; *Orhan Gencebay klasikleri*, 76n7; and political violence, 5; *poz*, 78; and TRT, 75, 98, 101, 105; and *Türk halk müziği*, 99n38–39; voice of, 15, 74, 77n11, 80n19, 81, 83, 84, 84n25, 88, 103. *See also* "Batsın bu dünya"
gender: ambiguity, 169, 169n37; and Aksu, 119, 124, 128–29, 140; and citizenship, 105; and Ersoy, 168n35, 169n36, 180; and gaze, 151, 167, 167n34, 186; and Islam, 11n22, 169, 180; and modernity, 110, 142n81; and Müren, 45, 66n72; and national identity, 105, 110, 131, 142; and representation, 66; and transgendered communities, 66n77; in the Turkish republic, 68
globalization, 10, 11–12, 33, 105, 190
Gökalp, Ziya, 16, 16n36, 155, 155n12, 162
Golden Horn, 152, 152nn8–9, 185, 186n
Göle, Nilüfer, 10n21, 11n22, 27–28n68, 94
Gülen, Fethullah, 22, 23n59
Güler, Ara, 145n84

Gülhane Park, 75, 75n6, 77
Gürel, Aysel, 113n17, 114n21, 122, 124, 125

Hafiz, Abd al-Halim, 42n26, 69n78
Herzfeld, Michael, 2, 32–33, 190n, 191
Hey Dergisi, 45n35, 47n41, 76n7, 83, 83–84n24, 102, 116; and campaigns against TRT, 118, 118n36, 118n37; charts, 113n20, 116, 125; "Oskars," 117n33
hip-hop, 19, 19n45, 80, 115
Hirschkind, Charles, 4n7, 4n8, 4n9, 22
Holbrook, Victoria, 28n69, 29n71
Hume, David, 30
*Hüsn ü aşk* (Şeyh Galip), 29n71
*hüzün*, 54, 54n22, 113n17, 124, 125

identity: civic, 5; and cultural intimacy, 33, 191; and ethnic difference, 10n19, 69n79, 70, 98, 131, 133, 137–38; national, 8–9, 20, 26n64, 66, 134, 138; sexual, 68–69, 70
identity politics, 105
Işılay, Sadi, 37, 42, 42n24, 48n42
Islam, 8–11, 15n34, 16, 180; and culture of love, 28, 69n79, 93; and mysticism, 25, 99, 100n44, 136, 152, 154; and popular music, 20–23; and public sphere, 100, 134n68; and sexuality, 169, 169n37
Islamist movement in Turkey, 10, 133, 133n, 151–54, 161; and gendered identities, 169, 169n37; and Istanbul, 151–54. *See also* Refah Partisi (RP; Welfare Party); Adalet ve Kalkınma Partisi (AK; Justice and Development Party)
Istanbul: and Islamist movement, 151–54; book-benches in, 147–48, 147n2, 148f; city planning in, 152n9; conquest of, 155, 160, 161; as global city, 10, 11–12; Metropolitan Municipality, 10, 147–49, 147–48n3, 152, 154, 185, 186, 186n; in national imaginary, 151–52; as Ottoman cosmopolis, 184; parks in, 148n, 152, 152n9, 154, 182n61, 183n62, 186n64; views of, 147, 148, 152–54, 152n9, 154n10, 157, 182–83. *See also* Beyoğlu; Bosphorus; Çamlıca; Fatih; *gecekondu*; Golden Horn; Unkapanı
Istanbul State Conservatory, ix, 17, 18n39, 24n60

Izmir, 1, 120, 135; and Aksu, 112–15, 120
Izmir Fair, 46n38, 80n19, 115, 120

Kalan, viii, 20n, 21n53, 21n54, 39n13, 55n54, 60n
Kalpaklı, Mehmet, 28–30, 32, 158n19, 169n37, 192
Kandiyoti, Deniz, 11n, 30n74, 36n2, 111n11, 169n37
*kanto*, 18, 18n40
Kardeş Türküler, 135n69, 135n70
Kaya, Ahmet, 97n35, 135, 135n71
Kaynak, Sadettin, xiv, 21n53, 21n54, 39n14, 48, 97n36
Keyder, Çağlar, 3, 11–12, 12nn25–26, 111n11, 121n, 151
Kurdish diaspora, 3n4
Kurdish language, 70, 131, 131n62, 141
Kurdish music, 70, 108, 121, 134, 134n69, 135
Kurds: and Alevis in Turkey, 101n45; and identity in Turkey, 3, 3n4, 28, 33, 69, 131, 134, 135n71; and Kurdish insurgency in Turkey, 71, 180; and Partiya Karkerên Kurdistan (PKK; Kurdistan Worker's Party), 3n4, 107n1, 107, 111
Kusturica, Emir, 137

Lewis, Bernard, 8n15, 11n23
liberalism, 18, 31, 67–68, 126; and Islam, 180; and media, 135; and multiparty democracy, 3, 10n20; in Turkey, 3, 3n4, 33–34, 47, 63, 69, 112, 132, 136, 151
love: and Aksu, 144; culture of, 28–30, 33, 192; and citizenship, 69–70; and the city, 151, 157–62, 185; and discourse, 31, 189–90; divine, 29; and Gencebay, 95–96, 97, 100n, 101–3; and modernity, 31–33; and nuclear family, 32, 110, 157; and the nation, 36; romantic, 110; and time, 159. *See also aşk*; *sevgi*
lyric poetry, 28–29, 149, 157. *See also gazel*

Macias, Enrico, 117n33, 119, 119n39
*maganda*, 76–77n10
*makam*, 15n; and call to prayer, 167, 167n33; choice of, in performance, 38, 38n8, 54; combinatory, 87; complexity of, 39n13;

Gencebay's renditions of, 81n20, 85, 87–90; *hicaz makamı*, 164, 167, history of, 39n14, 53n50; and meaning, 52–54, 167; modulation, 48, 55, 59, 178; *muhayyerkürdi makamı*, 86n27, 87–90; Müren's renditions of, 39, 53, 59; *nihavent makamı*, 51–54, 56f, 59; in pop music, 123, 123n51; and *raga*, 99n41; theory, 53n51, 87, 164, 176; and tonality, 51–54, 90, 177–78; transposition, 53, 60n58; *uşşak makamı*, 87, 163n25. See also *seyir*

Markoff, Irene, 22n55, 108n, 109, 128n

mass media, 4, 4n6, 4n8; in Turkey, 22, 60. See also Turkish Radio; Turkish Radio and Television

*maya*, 38, 38n11, 39, 51, 56–58

Mediterranean music, 18, 19

Mediterranean tonality, 88, 170, 177

Mediterraneanism, 18n43, 134, 134n68, 155n

melancholy: and Aksu, 109, 110–11, 113n17, 121, 125, 126, 144; and Gencebay, 94; and *makam*, 39n13, 54–55; and Müren, 49, 52, 58; and national identity, 187; and Yahya Kemal, 149, 186. See also *hüzün*

Menderes, Adnan, 9, 9n17

"Menekşelendi sular," 5, 48–58. See also Müren, Zeki

MESAM (Musiki Eseri Sahipleri Meslek Birliği), 83, 112n13, 126n56

*meşk*, 60–61, 182n60

meter in Turkish music. See *usûl*

metrical dissonance, 172

Mevlevi order, 21, 21n52, 21n54, 100n54, 132

Mevlid-i Şerif, 21, 21n53–54

*meyan*, 59–60, 60n58, 82–83, 87n27, 89

microphone: and "Bir teselli ver," 80n18; and crooning, 61, 61n62; and *Işık doğudan yükselir*, 123, 124; Müren's, 1–2, 25, 48, 61

Mitchell, Timothy, 2, 152n9, 193

Milliyetçi Hareket Partisi (MHP; Nationalist Action Party), 131

mode in Turkish music. See *makam*

modulation. See *makam*

mosaic, Turkey as, 130–36, 138–39, 144

Mukadder, Mualla, 44n31, 45, 120n45

Münir Nurettin. See Selçuk, Münir Nurettin

Müren, Zeki, 1–3, 25; and *arabesk*, 47n41, 59, 97n36; and Bodrum, 47–48, 62f, 67; and clothing, 45n35; costumery, 45, 45n35; death of, 1–3; diction, 59, 63–64, 64n68; and *gazino* culture, 40, 43–47, 57, 57n56; impersonations of, 63n65; and Liberace, 45, 45n36; microphone, 1–2, 61; and musical film, 42–43, 81; nostalgia for, 70–71; obituaries, 35, 35n1, 58; and queer culture in Turkey, 2, 5, 35–36, 65–67, 69; and sexuality, 64–69, 169; and sound recording, 41; and TRT, 40n17; and *Türk sanat müziği*, 44, 48–64; and Turkish Radio, 37–38, 40n17, 60n58; vocal style, 38, 41, 58–64

music reforms, 16–17, 89f, 164, 165, 165n31, 171, 172, 176

Navaro-Yashin, Yael, 3, 13, 13n27, 70–71

"Ne ağlarsın," 5, 107–12, 132. See also Aksu, Sezen

neoliberalism, 2n3, 5, 12, 182, 190; critique of, 10; and intimacy, 13, 111, 151; and Islam, 105, 187; and modernization theory, 10n20; and public sphere, 31–32; in Turkey, 93, 111, 151. See also liberalism

*nezaket*, 58, 64n67

nostalgia, 3–4, 3n5, 5, 104, 104n48, 150, 187; charts, 126; for Gencebay, 92, 94; for Kemalism, 13; market for, 170n39; for Müren, 70–71; for 1950s and 1960s, 145, 149; for 1970s, 104; for Ottomans, 157, 187; for Timur Selçuk, 181

O'Connell, John, 14n30, 15nn33–34, 16n36, 19n46, 20n50, 149n5, 150, 155n12, 162nn24–25

operetta in Turkey, 18, 18n40, 24

orientalism, 8n15, 43, 74, 131n60, 193

*Oriyental* (belly dancing), 19, 99n38

Özal, Turgut, 3n4, 9n18, 74, 93n1, 112, 121n47, 187; and *arabesk*, 93, 95, 102n46; funeral of, 151; and mass media, 135

Özbek, Meral, 16n35, 74n5, 80n18, 86, 87n27, 126n55, 162n23; and Gencebay, 94–96, 99n39, 110n44, 102

Özdemiroğlu, Atilla, 114n22, 125

Özışık, Edip, 62–63, 74n4
Özpınar, Muzaffer, 47n40, 169–70, 169n38
Özyürek, Esra, 13–14, 30n75, 31, 71n82, 190

Pamuk, Orhan, viii, 26n64, 54n52, 145n84, 147n1, 184–85, 185n63
Pekkan, Ajda, 116, 117n33, 118–19, 118n38, 119n41
Pınar, Salahattin, 38n10, 39n14, 43n29
poetics: Ottoman, 49; social, 32
postcolonial theory, 2, 30n74, 96
Prost, Henri, 152n9
public sphere, 2–5, 27; and gender, 11n2, 142; and Islam, 9–11, 15n34, 22, 93, 100, 190–93; and neoliberalism, 31–32; public space, 126, 147n3

queer culture: and queer identities, 70; in Turkey, 36n2, 64n68; and Zeki Müren, 2, 5, 35–36, 65–67, 69
Qur'an, 21, 21n54, 23n58, 39n15, 46n38, 110n6

Radio Ankara, 41, 41n22
Radio Istanbul, 41, 41n22, 43n28
Raks, 126n55, 169
rap music, 19, 19n45, 180n56
recording industry in Turkey, 15, 17n37, 19, 24, 42n24, 117, 179, 182
Refah Partisi (RP; Welfare Party), 10, 133, 133n66, 154
Regev, Motti, 2, 111, 138n77
rhythmic mode. See *usûl*
Roma, 19, 19n49, 21n53, 24
Rumelihisarı, 109, 109–10n6, 157n18, 158
rural-urban migration, 9, 9n17, 28, 43, 74, 100

Şafak, Elif, 26–28, 33, 36
Sağ, Arif, 22n55, 108, 110, 110n8, 128n59
Samsun, 76, 99n39, 120n46
Sarısözen, Muzaffer, 17
*şarkı*, 21, 24, 48n44, 51, 59, 80n20, 164
"Saturday Mothers," 127n58, 129
Sayın, Emel, 174
Sayın, Suat, 97, 97n36
saz, 15, 75, 79n14, 80nn17–18, 88, 108. See also *elektrosaz*; *şelpe*
secularism, 8–13, 20–23; and the city, 180, 185; and religious reaction, 46, 47, 93, 180; and time, 159, 162
Selçuk, Münir Nurettin: anniversary of death, 174n49; and Atatürk, 162; and "Aziz İstanbul," 149n4, 149n5, 149–51, 162–68, 170–73, 179, 186–87, 190; "Dönülmez akşamın ufkundayım," 175n51, 181n59; and Egypt, 19; films, 97n36; and *gazel*, 163n25; and popularity beyond Turkey, 14n29; recordings of, 170n39; and Timur Selçuk, 173–74, 174n46, 175n51, 176, 178, 190; and Turkish radio, 176; voice of, 61n59, 167; and Yahya Kemal, 149n5, 156, 162–64, 163n25, 163n26, 166n32
Selçuk, Timur, 5; and "Aziz Istanbul," 149, 149n4, 150, 173–82, 187; and critics, 181n58; and "Dönülmez akşamın ufkundayım," 175n51, 181n59; and Emel Sayın, 174; and Ersoy, 179; and Eurovision, 174n45; harmonic language of, 177, 177n53; and Islam, 175, 181; orchestration, 175–76; return from France, 173; and Turkish art music, 174; and Münir Nurettin, 173, 174, 174n46, 175n51, 176, 178, 190; voice of, 175–76, 179
*şelpe*, 108f, 110
Senar, Müzeyyen, 57n56, 60, 61n59
Sennet, Richard, 2, 4, 5n7
sentimentalism, 2, 30–32, 47n41, 58, 187, 189–93; and *arabesk*, 93; and film, 69, 81n21, 119; and voice, 62–63, 122. See also sympathy
Seroussi, Edwin, 2, 21, 64n66
Servet-i Fünun, 155–56, 156n13, 161
*Ses*, 76, 80n18, 84
*sevgi*, 26n65. See also *aşk*; love
*seyir*, 53, 163n25
sitar, 99, 99–100n41
"sly civility," 74, 103
Smith, Adam, 30, 30n73, 32n77
squatter town. See *gecekondu*
Sufi lodges, 17n37, 20, 22, 28. See also Mevlevi order
Sufism in Turkey, 36, 132. See also Mevlevi order; Islam
supplement, 92
Susurluk incident, 13, 13n27, 70–71
sympathy, 30, 62, 67. See also sentimentalism

Taksim (area of Istanbul), 24, 24n62, 43, 75n6, 129, 174
*taksim* (instrumental improvisation), 24, 38, 53, 54, 159, 169
Taksim Belediye Gazinosu, 43n28
Tanburi Cemil Bey, 42n24, 48n42, 156, 159
tango in Turkey, 18, 18n41, 20, 116n31, 192
Tanrıkorur, Çinuçen, 163n25, 164n27
*tarab*, 41n21, 57, 57n56, 58n57
*tasavvuf*, 99. *See also* Islam: and mysticism
Tatlıses, İbrahim, 75, 84n26, 94, 108n, 112n13, 121
Tatlıyay, Haydar, 19n47, 97n36
*tavır*, 67, 80n17
TRT. *See* Turkish Radio and Television
Tunar, Şükrü, 38, 38n9, 40, 40n16, 40n18
Tunç, Onno, 122–24, 122n48, 122n49, 123n50, 125, 135n69; and *Işık doğudan yükselir*, 127, 132n65; Onno Tunç Orchestra, 123n51
*Türk halk müziği* (Turkish folk music), 21–22n55, 44, 59; Aksu and, 131–40; Gencebay and, 99n38, 99n39; instrumental style in, 80n17; modes in, 38n8, 88; and reform, 14–18, 150, 176
*Türk sanat müziği* (Turkish art music), 1, 14–15, 14n30, 35–71, 98n37, 99n39, 147–87; and Aksu, 112, 117, 132; and *arabesk*, 25, 80n17; and Müren, 44, 48–64; reform of, 17–18; and Sufism, 20–21; theory of, 15n31, 52, 82, 86–88; and Turkish Radio, 37n7. *See also fasıl*
Turkish Radio, 17, 18, 121; and art music, 17, 37n7, 43; and Karaca, 21n54; and Münir Nurettin Selçuk, 176; and Müren, 37–38, 40n17, 60n58
Turkish Radio and Television, 16, 18, 121, 126; and Aksu, 107, 111, 113, 121, 132–33, 136, 139; and Alevi music, 22; and *arabesk*, 93; boycott by popular musicians of, 118n37; *Denetim Kurulu* in, 118, 118n36; and Gencebay, 75, 98, 101, 105; and Müren, 40n17; performance style of, 107n2; and state conservatory, 18n39, 24n60; and Timur Selçuk, 174n45

Umm Kulthum, 19, 41, 41nn20–21, 47, 47n40
Unkapanı, 76, 112n13, 170n39
*usûl*, 51, 74n4, 164n27, 164–65, 172
*uyum*, 59. *See also* diction; voice

*vakıf*, 13, 13n28, 35
*vezin*, 156, 156n14, 164
voice: of Aksu, 112, 113n17, 114n22, 124–25, 134, 137, 140, 143, 144; in *arabesk*, 84n26, 85, 171; of Ersoy, 61n59, 171–73, 179; of Gencebay, 74, 77n11, 80n19, 81, 83, 84, 84n25, 88, 103; and gender, 166–67, 171–73; metaphysics of, 58; of Müren, 2, 38n12, 39–41, 47, 58–64; and psychoanalytic theory, 6–7, 7n12, 150; as "timbral sociality," 7; of Timur Selçuk, 175–76, 179. *See also* diction; *uyum*

"world beat," 137. *See also* "world music"
"world music," 11, 136–40 passim. *See also* "world beat"

Yahya Kemal. *See* Beyatlı, Yahya Kemal
Yahya Kemal Institute, 149n5
Yurdatapan, Şanar, 114, 144nn22–23, 118n37

Zeki Müren museum in Bodrum, 48, 62f
*zemin*, 82–83, 89f, 164

www.ingramcontent.com/pod-product-compliance
Lightning Source LLC
Chambersburg PA
CBHW032149010526
44111CB00035B/1362